D0119476

# RONALD J. SEIDLE

# Air Time

## HOLBROOK PRESS, INC.
## BOSTON

Illustrations by David B. Leach

## Photo Credits

Courtesy Quick-Set, Inc., p. 5

Courtesy International Video Corp., pp. 7, 76

Photos of lighting instruments provided courtesy
of Mole-Richardson Co. of Hollywood,
pp. 22, 23, 25

Photos of lighting instruments courtesy of
Strand Century, Inc., pp. 24, 26

Courtesy the Grass Valley Group, Inc., p. 62

Courtesy WBUR, Boston University Radio, p. 112

Courtesy Broadcast Electronics (Spotmaster),
pp. 132, 151

Courtesy Pickering and Company, Inc., p. 145

Courtesy the Revox Corporation, p. 147

Courtesy Capitol Records, Inc., p. 152

Courtesy Columbia Broadcasting System, p. 194

Printed in the United States of America.

**Library of Congress Cataloging in Publication Data**

Seidle, Ronald J
    Air time.

    Bibliography: p.
    Includes index.
    1. Broadcasting.    I.  Title.
PN1990.8.S4        384.54        76–26699
ISBN 0–205–05602–4

# CONTENTS

Preface    *v*

Introduction    *vii*

**Part 1**    *STUDIO TIME*

**1 · THE TELEVISION STUDIO**    *3*

*Cameras Lights Sets Graphics Floor Managing Video Switching The Audio Console Projection Videotape Scripts TV Logs Directing*

**2 · THE RADIO STUDIO**    *113*

*The Radio Board Microphones Turntables Tape Recorders Patch Panel Radio Scripts The Radio Log The Radio Producer*

**3 · BROADCASTING ELECTRONICS**    *169*

*Television Cameras Master Control and Television Transmitting Television Receivers AM Radio FM Radio Radio Transmission Radio Reception*

**Part 2**    *STATION TIME*

**4 · BROADCASTING'S PAST**    *195*

*The Theories and Their Early Use Television Arrives, Radio Grows Television Advances Postwar Broadcasting After the Freeze Changes: Formats, Audiences, Equipment*

**5** · **STATION ORGANIZATION**  *211*

*Rating Services  Station People—The General Manager  Station People—The Program Director  Station People—The Sales Manager  Station People—The Promotion Director  Station People—The News Director  Station People—The Editorial Board  Station People—Engineering  Station People—Accounting  Station People—On-Air Talent*

**6** · **STATION AFFILIATION AND REGULATION**  *251*

*Television: Network Affiliates  Radio Affiliation  Station Regulation*

**Part 3**  *CHANGING TIME*

**7** · **NEITHER STATION NOR STUDIO**  *275*

*CATV  Industrial and Educational  Home, and the Day after Tomorrow*

Bibliography  *285*

Glossary  *287*

Index  *293*

# PREFACE

I think broadcasting is fun. I enjoy playing around in a studio and getting all the equipment to produce something that conveys the meaning I had in mind. I like dealing with the people who work at a station because their interests and mine are similar and because I find them more creative and more diversified than most people in most other businesses. A lot of people will find they enjoy broadcasting as much as I do. But they have to start somewhere.

That's what this book is about. It's a start in learning about studios and station offices. I'll admit nothing matches the experience of actually working with the equipment or actually sitting in those offices dealing with people in broadcasting. But I've found that no one gets everything down pat the first time s/he walks into those studios or offices. No one's memory is that good, and no one takes notes that thoroughly. No matter how good the presentation in the studio, the time is short and I have found it helps to have something to refresh your memory once you walk out the door. And that "refresher" should give you information about color equipment in television, as black and white is going the way of the dinosaurs. Hence I talk of beam splitting and chroma-key. In radio, stereo has to be a consideration, so I've included some discussion of stereo boards. And in all cases, I've tried to talk in terms of situations rather than of theories. That's what you hit first in a studio anyway.

But studios aren't the whole of broadcasting. Stations, their management, affiliations, ownership, and regulation are equally important. Most people start out fascinated by the machines of broadcasting, but they must deal with the people behind them as well. So I've tried to indicate who's responsible for what, who makes what decisions, and even what sort of training and background you should have for most positions. I've talked of the deals stations have made with networks, of the organization by group owners, and of the arrangements of the totally independent stations. I've talked of formats and their varieties and the search for the right fragment of the audience. These are "people" not "machine" decisions. These decisions have to make sense to the new broadcaster too.

This broadcaster is who I'm writing for. Up till now, that new broadcaster has had to get a dozen different books to find out what happens in studios and offices. That kind of disregard for those just starting out is what I've tried to avoid. And since I don't find broadcasting a very formal business, I've tried to be casual as well. I hope this scope and this approach are what you're looking for.

# Introduction

All of us already know something about broadcasting. We have grown up hearing radio programs and watching television shows. That's never been true before in the history of the world. Broadcasting is an aspect of our culture that is totally without precedent in the preceding several thousand years of recorded history. But we accept it casually enough to have no sense of awe or wonder about it. Broadcasting is just a part of our lives, and a part we often complain about or criticize.

So we already know something about a field no one else before us even imagined. That's not enough, though. We can imagine purposes for cameras or microphones which will be useful, informative, or just plain fun. So we want to learn how to get the machines working right and how to join the people behind the machines so as to accomplish these purposes. In other words, we want to know what buttons to push and which people to go to. The programs we have listened to or watched come from microphones and cameras, out of the stations. How does the equipment work? What is the organization of the stations?

We start with knowledge of what programs are like. Let's go deeper and find out about the equipment and about the stations.

# PART 1

# Studio Time

# 1

# THE
# TELEVISION
# STUDIO

## CAMERAS

When you first walk into a television studio, you are confronted by an array of gadgets and wires and jumbles that seem complex and unmanageable. You know, of course, that's not true but until you know where to start, the equipment remains useless to you. So let's take one thing at a time and go over all of its aspects. Probably the camera is the most obvious place to start. You know what it does (take pictures) so all you now need to know is what the parts are and what to do with them.

Let's start at the front of a camera and see what it's composed of. That round part sticking out the front is a *zoom lens*, and it has a cap over the front of it. The cap prevents dust from accumulating on the glass inside but, most importantly of all, it protects the pick-up tubes inside the camera from being hit by light strong enough to cause damage. Next, somewhere near the lens tube is a light, generally red, which goes on when that camera goes on the air. This is the *tally light*, and it lets the talent know which camera is active.

The tally light is on the body of the camera, which looks like a big box. It is. But inside are all the electronic gadgets, gremlins, and gizmos which produce the picture. Leave that stuff to a qualified engineer to play with because if you don't know what you're doing, you'll either damage the camera, yourself, or maybe both. Now, this box is mounted on a *head* of some sort. A

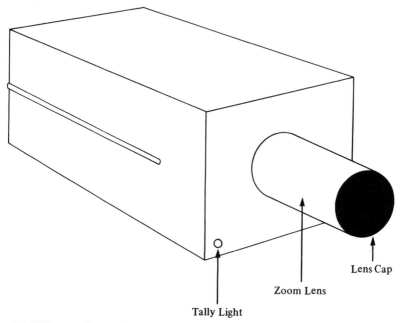

*FIGURE 1.1*   Front of a camera

head is a support device that allows you to move the box around in different directions—left, right, up, down, and so on. But you don't want the whole thing moving around all the time. When you walk away from it, you want it to stay steady instead of suddenly swinging around and hitting something. So the head has *locks* on it. They will be on one side or the other, and there are two of them.

One, when it is tightened down, will stop movement right and left. The other, obviously, stops up-and-down movement. Generally, on the other side of the head are *tension knobs*, although these may be integrated with the locks. Their function is to exert a bit of drag on the left-and-right or up-and-down movement. The locks will prevent any movement, but these controls just make the movements easy or hard to make. You'll want a bit of resistance to free movement or you'll find the camera swings farther than you intend and responds so readily the picture you get won't be steady. With a bit of drag, you can get a steady, nonbouncing picture yet can move smoothly to another picture. So set these tension knobs to the drag that suits you best.

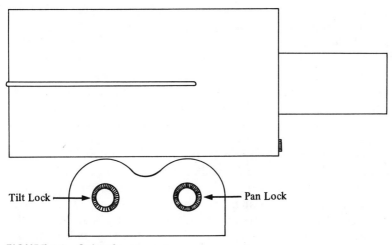

*FIGURE 1.2*    Side of a camera

This head, with its locks and tension knobs, rests on some-thing tall enough to keep it up off the floor, and that's referred to as the *mount*. It will be either a *tripod mount* or a *pedestal mount*.

On most tripod mounts, there is a crank to turn to raise and lower the camera. But this movement is jerky and generally to

*FIGURE 1.3*    A pedestal mount and a tripod mount

be avoided on the air. Most tripod mounts have locks for the three wheels too, so before you run a camera, be sure the wheels are unlocked.

Now, on the pedestal mount, you can raise and lower the camera just by pulling or pushing on the *steering ring*. The movement is smooth and even and looks good on the air, so you may want to do that for a special result sometimes. Take a good look at that steering ring. Notice it has an arrow or dot or some such indicator on two on the four spokes.

The mount will only go in the direction those two spokes point; you *cannot* pull it off to the side. To change the direction the mount will move, you have to move the steering ring around. And you easily can just by turning it. So when you work with a pedestal mount, keep one hand on the ring just beside the marked spoke so you can quickly turn the ring and go in the proper direction.

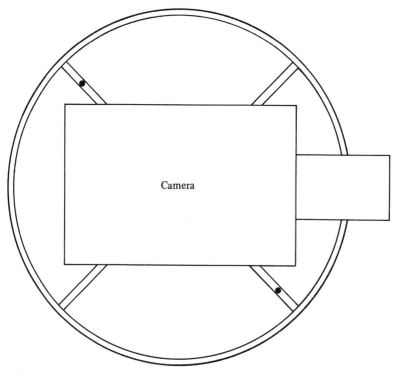

*FIGURE 1.4*   Looking down on the steering ring

Now, let's go back to the camera. The next part we encounter is the *viewfinder* on the back of the camera. It shows
what the camera sees and is just like the television sets you
are used to watching. It has controls beside it for brightness,
contrast, maybe even vertical and horizontal hold, and buttons
to activate a particular gun inside, or maybe all three guns. If
you push the button for the green gun, the viewfinder will show
you the scene as the green pick-up tube by itself sees it. This,
by the way, gives you the best view of what a black-and-white
receiver will show of your picture. Any other buttons or knobs
around the viewfinder should generally be left alone, as they
belong to the engineering staff. But while you are a camera-

*FIGURE 1.5* Rear of a color camera

person, your view of the world should be confined to that viewfinder only. Somewhere near that viewfinder will be a tally light
so you, just like the talent, will know when your camera is on
the air.

Fastened to the camera somewhere near the viewfinder will
be a long cord, and at the end of that will be the *headset*. This
has an earpiece (maybe two) with which you can hear the conversation of the other crew members, and a mouthpiece with
which you can join in on the conversation. You have to com-
municate with the rest of the crew, and that's the method you
use.

Your eyes, ears, and mouth now can be connected to the
camera, but how about your hands? That's the function of the
*pan handle*, that long rod coming out the back of the camera.
Hold on to it and move it, and the camera moves also. You can,
therefore, move the camera in the direction you want.

But we have overlooked a couple things. One is fastened to
the end of the pan handle and one is on the camera box at the
rear side and on the side opposite to the pan handle. These are
extensions of the zoom lens. The one on the camera itself is a
crank that changes the picture you see by magnifying or re-
ducing portions of the scene. Cranked as far as it goes one way,
the picture in the viewfinder will show everything in the scene.
Cranked the other way, a portion of the scene will fill the viewfinder. This crank moves pieces of glass in the lens to achieve
these changes. Sometimes this crank is replaced by a button
which electrically moves the glass; this button can be put almost anywhere the cameraperson can reach. Sometimes it's
at the back of the camera, sometimes it's on a separate pan
handle, and sometimes it's on the single pan handle. But still,
the glass in the lens moves and provides a continuously changing size of shot. But what does that other extension do?

It's a *focus control.* Sometimes the picture will look blurred.
That's when you turn the knob or press the button (it too
comes both ways) until the picture comes into focus. Later on
I'll tell you about the only proper time to set your focus.

The last part of our front-to-back movement over the camera
and mount is the *cable* which connects the camera to the rest
of the television system. This cable comes out of the camera
at the rear and from underneath. It's long enough to let you
move all over the studio, and it carries your picture back to
various monitors, control devices, and so on. Your major prob-

lem with this cable will be to keep it out of your way. You don't want to run over it when you move the camera, and you don't want to be too restricted by it. So you'll probably end up kicking it around with your feet. Just try to do it quietly.

These are the elements of the camera. Now, how do you deal with them?

The first thing you do when you walk up to that camera is to put on the headset. Then you unlock it, and finally you uncap it. That's the process, but what, exactly, does it mean?

The headset, first of all, is a way for you to hear and talk to the other members of the production who are working behind the scenes. Through the earpiece, you will hear the director's orders and the comments of the various other crew members. Through the mouthpiece, you will be able to talk to the director and the other crew members. You don't want to say anything that isn't absolutely essential because it makes noise in the studio which the microphones might pick up, and besides, the director needs to say so much and think about so much that s/he needs as few distractions on the headset as possible. But when you first put on the headset, you have to let people know you are there and can now be communicated with. Hence you tell them with a phrase like "Camera 2 on headsets." Use your own good judgment here; if no one else is on the headsets and you know it, there's no point in saying anything. Later, however, if you hear the director just announce "Director on headsets," you'll want to respond with "Camera 2 on headsets" just so s/he knows who else is on.

Remember those locks on the side of the head that I mentioned earlier? They get your attention next. Loosen them and you can now move the camera up and down and from side to side. Always unlock the camera before you make the next move, which is to uncap. There's a good reason for this. When you remove the lens cap from the camera's one sensitive spot—the lens—you must instantly become careful of the camera's insides. The single most damaging thing which can happen to a camera is to have a light shine into the lens and onto the pick-up tubes inside. It's very similar to shining a very bright light in someone's eyes. If the light is sufficiently bright, the eyes can be injured. The pick-up tubes too can be injured by a light, and by one not bright enough to injure your eyes much at all. So if you should remove the lens cap while the camera is still locked tight, and a light happens to be shining in the lens, you can't easily and rapidly move the camera out of the beam. But if the locks are loosened before you uncap, and a light is shining in, you can easily swing the camera away. It's smart to check where the lights are before you uncap, but play it doubly safe and unlock before you uncap.

Then find a safe place on the camera or mount on which to put the lens cap. Don't put it in your pocket, as you might walk off with it. Don't put it in a place where a sudden move of the camera will throw it off on the floor, as the mikes will pick up that clatter very clearly. Some spot near the base of the mount is generally good as there is less chance of its falling off.

When you leave a camera, the process is just the reverse. First cap the camera, then tighten the locks with the camera level, then announce something like "Camera 2 leaving headsets," and finally take the headsets off. Of course you'll put the camera back in the spot where it belongs, generally at the back of a studio or out of the way in a corner, and you'll arrange its cable in whatever pattern your engineering staff prefers but that's a matter of striking the studio rather than running the camera. All that is the cameraperson's responsibility, but it is supplementary to the major duty of running the camera.

The major duty is everything done between the first uncapping and the final recapping of the camera. That's when the cameraperson can give the director what s/he needs. And everything the cameraperson does is a composite of some basic, simple moves.

First, the cameraperson holds on to the pan handle. By moving it, remember, s/he moves the camera but not the mount. There are two moves s/he can make with the camera alone—a *pan* and a *tilt*. A pan is a movement from side to side. So you can pan left or pan right. If you need to see more to the left, you pan left. If part of the scene if off to the right, you need to pan right. Now let me introduce a confusing note, but hopefully one I can straighten out for you. When you pan right, you move the pan handle left. Look at Figure 1.6 and I think you'll see why. It's because the camera is fastened down in the middle. To be safe then, go strictly by your viewfinder. If you can't see enough of what's happening to the right, move the camera so you see more to the right. That's a pan right, even though you move the pan handle to the left.

The next movement is a tilt and you can guess that's a movement up or down. If you need to see more below the

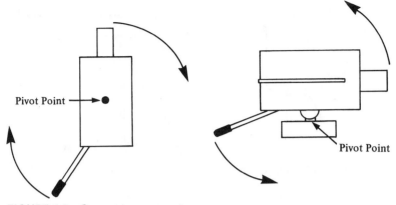

*FIGURE 1.6*  Camera movements

scene, you tilt down and if the action is above where you are, you tilt up. Also, the movements of the pan handle are reversed for these moves, just like they are for a pan. Check Figure 1.6 again to see why. As before, play it safe and look in your view-finder. If you need more space up above, tilt *up* and don't worry about the fact that you push *down* on the pan handle.

Now, there are a couple moves you can make with the mount and the camera together. If the camera is mounted on a tripod, you grab one of the legs and push to get everything moving. Then you can generally keep it moving, or stop it, by pushing or pulling on the pan handle. If you are running a pedestal mount, you grab the steering ring at the marked spot and push, steering it in the direction you want to go. Obviously, with either mount you can go right or left, and you can go in or out. The right or left movement is called a *truck*, and the in or out movement is called a *dolly*. So you can move the whole mount and camera left when the director says "Truck left," and you can move everything in when s/he says "Dolly in." Generally, these moves must be made rapidly while another camera is on the air. So you will be grabbing for the tripod leg or the steering ring in a hurry. If you are wearing any rings, they will hit the metal and the resounding click will be picked up by the mikes. So before you start to run camera, be sure to take your rings off and put them in a pocket. If you have a ring you can't or won't remove, then bring in some adhesive tape and put several layers over it as it's impossible to be careful enough not to hit anything at least once during a production.

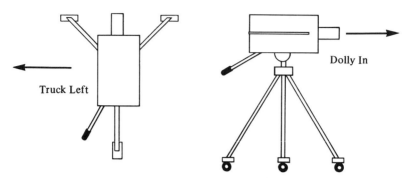

*FIGURE 1.7*   Camera movements

There are a couple of tricky moves that involve the mount and the camera, one tricky by virtue of the type of mount, and the other because the move is just hard to do. First, a dolly on a tripod has to be finished off in a certain way because the wheels on a tripod turn so freely. If you dolly in, the wheels are pointed in, as shown in Figure 1.8. If you have to dolly out while you're still on the air, you might think the wheels would stay in position and just let you go back. That's very rarely the case. The wheels will turn around, making a little circle, and settle into pointing outward. The result is a wobble as you start back. That bounces your picture. To avoid that, when you come to the end of your dolly in, move slightly to one side or the other and start back out. It's a "fishhook" movement, as Figure 1.9 shows. Make it a brief movement, as brief as possible, and it's unnoticeable on the air. But it sets your wheels in the correct direction, and you can then start back smoothly when the time comes for you to do so.

The other movement is generally done with someone else's help. It's really a combination of trucking and dollying, so

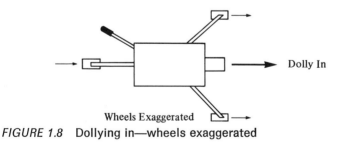

*FIGURE 1.8*   Dollying in—wheels exaggerated

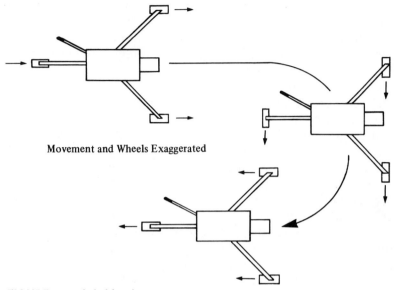

Movement and Wheels Exaggerated

*FIGURE 1.9*    A fishhook movement

what you get is a curved movement usually called an *arc.* The problem is in not letting your picture bounce as you go. If you have to prevent the bounce and move the mount at the same time and without help, you simply have to practice a lot. It's easier, but still not easy, to have someone else pulling the mount in the arc pattern while you concentrate on keeping a smooth, flowing picture. The effect on the screen can be very impressive, especially if you are circling a solo performer or

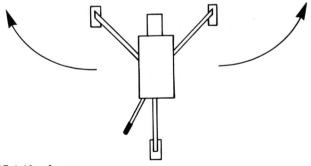

*FIGURE 1.10*    An arc

two people in an embrace or some similar single point of interest.

There's one other thing you can do with a camera that can almost be called a movement, but that really only involves the lens. That's a *zoom.* Remember I said the zoom lens magnifies a portion of the picture as you turn the zoom crank or press the zoom button. On the viewfinder, it looks like you are moving in toward the object. If the director calls for a tighter shot, you can either dolly in or zoom in. Generally you will zoom in because it's so much faster and doesn't upset your focus. That's the critical problem with a zoom lens. To set your focus, you zoom in to the tightest picture you can get. Then you turn the focus control till you have the sharpest picture possible. Then zoom out to the sort of picture your director calls for. Now you are in focus for the widest down to the narrowest shot. If, however, either you or your subject moves, you'll need to get another focus setting. Setting the focus is only good for one distance—that between you and the object. But once your focus is set, you can zoom in to give your director the tighter shot s/he calls for, and do it generally faster than with a dolly. It will, however, look different from a dolly so you may sometimes want to dolly instead. A zoom will merely magnify a portion of the picture, but a dolly changes the perspective on various objects in the shot and gives a much greater sensation of going past an obstacle or person or portion of the scene.

Twice now we have talked about the quality of the picture you get and not just how you get it. The dolly-zoom difference is one, and the arc around a single point of interest is the second. The mark of a really good cameraperson is not in how well s/he makes the mechanical moves but in how good-looking the shots are. Of course s/he must be able to get those shots through a mastery of the techniques, so being a good cameraperson does depend on being able to dolly smoothly while adjusting focus, while panning diagonally upward, while . . . . But if s/he has no eye for composition of if s/he isn't alive to the aesthetic difference between a dolly and a zoom, s/he'll be only a competent technician.

I'm assuming you want to be good, not just competent. Running camera smoothly and well is a personal satisfaction which can make you feel just plain good inside. So what are some of the basic elements to be aware of for good composition?

FIGURE 1.11   A wide shot

Let's start with the widest shot you can get. This will show everything relevant within the scene. As you move in, either by zooming or dollying, you come to a medium shot, and that shows a portion of the scene which you want to emphasize. Here is your first opportunity to compose the picture. On the wide shot, you must simply show everything and about your only possible worry is whether or not the elements are balanced left and right and up and down. But with a medium shot, you show only a portion of the scene. Do you want the elements you're showing to be balanced as before? Or do you want them off to the right of the shot?

That sort of unbalancing tends to draw attention to the left of the picture, and can lead the viewer to see something over there s/he would not have noticed otherwise. Then as you move closer in, you concentrate attention on one object. If it's

FIGURE 1.12   Portion of a scene

*FIGURE 1.13* Directing attention

an object, it may be the major clue to the murder that everyone else is overlooking. If it's a person, you may be moving in on the interior thoughts or the real motives. Move in on the butler's eyes, and he becomes the murderer.

Suppose you do want to draw attention to the butler, while showing the other people as well. Think of a pyramid. It's a balanced, stable figure, but it still emphasizes the topmost point. Shoot your scene like a pyramid and you'll have good composition plus attention to the butler because he's up there at the top. Turn the pyramid over and you'll have an unstable picture that's going to break up into action. The cops enter behind the butler and, as the pyramid must fall over, the butler must run. Later, at headquarters, the detective will question the butler and try to trap him with words. We want to see only the faces as they fight it out, so we use close-ups and cut back and forth between them.

*FIGURE 1.14* The guilty party

*FIGURE 1.15*   Dominant point

*FIGURE 1.16*   An unbalanced picture

*FIGURE 1.17*   Leading faces

The space above the heads is called *headspace.* That's logical. Don't leave much space, but don't have their heads bouncing into the top of the picture. Be balanced. But notice we leave more room in front of the faces than behind them.

That subconsciously establishes where the other person is in relation to the face we see. If we go in for a full-face close-up on the butler as he realizes he's doomed, we lose some of the top of his head in order to get in the features of his face. This should always be your approach—mouth and jaw and chin are more important than hair, so cut off the top of a head rather than the bottom.

One further point in showing faces. Imagine a line running through a person's ears and inside the head. The longer the line appears, the better your shot. As the line gets shorter and shorter (as the person's head turns so the side is toward you), you finally see nothing but a dot (a full profile), and the worse your shot is.

As the show ends and the butler is led away to death row, you will probably have to get a shot of a card with printing on it. This will be the title of the show, the director's name, "The End," or some other such graphic. If you aren't directly in front of the card, the printing will look big at one end and small at the other.

This is called *keystoning*. The remedy is to move over directly in front of the card or to have the card turned till it faces you squarely. Most often, the titling won't look as obvious as in Figure 1.19. It will merely look like it isn't level, like it runs downhill. The remedy is the same—move the camera or move the card. Generally, the camera needs to move in an "uphill" direction to level the titling.

Obviously, this covers only a small portion of the shots you can get or will be faced with. But it gives you some idea

*FIGURE 1.18*   A tight face shot

*FIGURE 1.19* Keystoning

of what to look for and what to avoid. Something else must be added, though, before the camera is of any use at all to you—that's light. With no light at all, your eyes see nothing. A television camera is the same way, but in general, it needs more light by which to "see" than you do. So we'll have to arrange those lights hanging all over the studio ceiling.

## LIGHTS

Look at a person standing in the sunshine. There's a shadow on the ground, a shadow on the face from the nose, shadows from the eyebrow ridges, a bit of shadow from the lips, and so on. That's one of the ways we detect roundness and three dimensions. Without shadows, the world would begin to look as flat as a comic strip. So one of the purposes of lighting is to give shadows. What a viewer at home sees is flat—as flat as the face of the television screen. So it's up to you to fool viewers into seeing three dimensions, and one of the ways you will do that is by lighting to create shadows.

Let's go back outside in the sun. That light comes from one direction. The shadows all flow away from it. Back inside, in the studio, we want to recreate that one-sided effect. So we put a light at one side of the person we are lighting. That becomes our "sun" in the studio and is the key point of light on which all our other lighting will depend. So that light gets called the *key light.* Put it out in front of the person you're lighting, about 45 degrees off to one side and about 45 degrees up from the face.

Now look at the subject and you will see those same shadows beneath the eyebrows, out from the nose, and so on. But the television cameras won't respond well to that lighting. There's too much contrast between the black shadows and the light skin. The pick-up tubes aren't as sensitive as your eyes, so those shadows can end up looking almost like holes. So we have to fill those shadows with light—not enough to get rid of them altogether but enough to soften them and make them less dark. Since we are filling them up with light, we call the light that does it a *fill light*. It goes on the opposite side from the key light, but also 45 degrees off to one side and 45 degrees up from the face. There's another difference between these two lights, and that has to do with the kind of instruments they are, but I'll talk about that later.

Now we have to put in one more light that's totally artificial, and doesn't occur anywhere outdoors. Directly be-

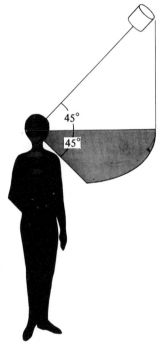

*FIGURE 1.20*   Angles of lights

hind the person and shining down at about 60 degrees or so, we put a light to shine on his back. So it's called a *back light.* Aim it so it hits the part of the head where a man often starts going bald—that round spot at the back. When you look at him from the front now, you'll see a rim of light on his shoulders and on his hair. Speaking of baldness, if he is bald, lower the light so it hits the back of his neck or you'll get some wild glare off the top of his head. The purpose of this rim of light is again three-dimensional. Without a backlight, people tend to look smashed up against the background. Turn on the backlight and they suddenly seem separated from what's behind them. Look at the anchor newspeople on the network news and you'll notice a halo of light around them. It's not their saintliness, it's their backlights.

That's the basic three-point lighting set-up. It makes a person look three-dimensional and separates him from the background. There are other ways to light which give certain effects which are not three-dimensional but you will find these ways useful at certain times. We'll come back to those times later.

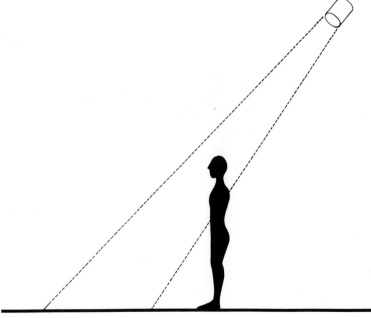

*FIGURE 1.21*   A backlight

Right now, though, let's take a look at the instruments you have used to get this three-point lighting. The back and key lights should be *spotlights*. That is, they are generally round and rather like a tube. Their beam of light can be concentrated in a large or a small spot by turning a knob on the back of the instrument. As the spot gets larger, the intensity of the light hitting a subject will go down. As it gets smaller, the intensity obviously will go up. Spotlights give hard light, causing sharp-edged shadows. They are directional lights, going exactly where you aim them.

The fill light, on the other hand, is a soft light causing no hard-edged shadows and generally spilling out all over the area in which you point it. You can't adjust its beam at all. It looks significantly different from the spotlights. Most generally, these fill lights are called *broads* and are shaped like rectangles rather than circles. The container itself is more like a box than a tube. It's a very open sort of light.

These instruments are all quartz-halogen lights. The name comes from the type of bulb inside that gives the light. It's a long tube bulb, nothing like the round bulbs you use at home. It burns very hot and very bright and should never be touched.

*FIGURE 1.22* A spotlight

*FIGURE 1.23*  A broad

First of all, you might burn yourself, and second, the oil from your fingers messes up the quartz and causes the bulb to burn out faster. The great advantage of these bulbs is they don't get dimmer as they get older. They keep on giving out the same kind of white light till they quit altogether. The bulbs like the ones you have at home are incandescent tungsten, and they get dimmer and dimmer as they age. So their light gets yellower and yellower. In color television, that's bad news. So most stations have gone to the quartz-halogen lights. But the tungsten lights still have some uses, so you can still find them around. They are good lights, but you can't let them get old.

If you are working with tungsten lights, you'll still have spots. But the broads will be called *scoops* because they are housed in a big conical shell as shown in Figure 1.24. A scoop can be quartz halogen as well as tungsten, but you never find broads that are tungsten.

You'll also have a specific spot called a *Fresnel* (pronounced freh-NEL) as it is named after the Frenchman who designed the

*FIGURE 1.24*    A scoop on a pantograph

lens in it. That glass with concentric rings cut in it concentrates the light into the spot pattern and does it very accurately. Then there's the ellipsoidal spot which has sliding panels to cover part of the beam to make any shape you want. You can get a triangular beam of light, or a tilted rectangle, or almost anything. These two types of lights can be either tungsten or quartz halogen.

If you work with first one type, then the other, you will notice you need far more tungsten lights to get the same light level as you need of the quartz type. The tungsten lights just don't give out as much light as the quartz. That's another reason why most places have quartz lights.

Suppose, though, you have too much light on your subject. How can you reduce it? The easiest way is to turn the knobs on the back of the key lights so the beam spreads out and the intensity drops. Another way is to move the light back farther

FIGURE 1.25    A fresnel spotlight

away from the subject. A third is to put something of neutral color in front of the light. This could be a thin piece of asbestos cloth, which won't catch on fire and will still cut down the amount of light hitting the subject. One thing you should not do is put the light on a dimmer to bring down the intensity.

This is why. A dimmer is a way to reduce the amount of electricity reaching an instrument. It's generally a lever swinging through an arc—something you can stop at any point between full on and full off and thus get exact control of the flow of electricity. You can use a dimmer for a lot of things in television. You can start out with all the light on the background and none on the subject. That gives you a silhouette. Then you can bring up the dimmers on the subject and take down the ones on the background. That gives you a nice lighting effect. You can dim the light down to nothing on one object and bring it up full on another, and thus shift your viewer's point of interest. That's all legitimate. But if you use a dimmer to lower intensity, you make the bulb burn with a yellowish light instead of a white one, and the colors won't come out true on the screen.

*FIGURE 1.26* An ellipsoidal spotlight

The cameras will sometimes react before your eye will, so don't take the chance of sending out an unbalanced picture. Keep the lights on full except for special effects.

Those are the instruments you work with. Now let's go back to the subject you're using them on.

Generally, your subject is reasonably close to the background, and some light from the key and fill lights spills onto that background. That way you can see what's there. But suppose you pull your subject away from the background. Replace the broad you are using for fill with a spot and move the key light and the new fill light farther around toward the sides of your subject.

Now you will have the subject lit up in a pool of light and all around will be darkness. To further this set-up, there are devices called *barn doors*, which fit on the spotlights. They are just pieces of metal which can be swung in front of the light so as to block off part or all of the beam. Bring the barn doors

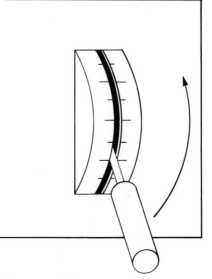

*FIGURE 1.27*    A dimmer switch

in till the beam hits nothing but the subject. Now you don't have any extra light hitting the floor or the background. This is called *cameo lighting*, and it is very dramatic. It's also rough on the engineers who are trying to adjust the cameras to give a good picture because there is such a contrast between the black background and the light foreground. So sometimes you need just a bit of light on the background to ease the contrast. Try to work it out with the engineers so all of you are reasonably satisfied.

Do the exact reverse (put light on the background and none on the subject) and you have *silhouette lighting.* This tends to look like black-and-white TV and so is of limited use in color television, but it can be effective for an opening and closing when you have credits or titling up on the screen.

There are a million different things you can do with lighting, but these three types are enough to get started on. Master the normal, three-point lighting first, then start playing around and experimenting and see what you can come up with.

If you have to light for more than one subject or one location, you still use that three-point set-up, but you have to include more sets of three in order to cover more areas. Make sure the areas overlap slightly so you don't get disastrous

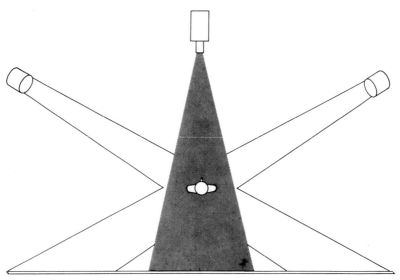

*FIGURE 1.28*   Lighting for cameo

drop-offs of light from one location to another. Your goal should be an even amount of light over the entire area you have to cover. Remember simple things like high lights cause long shadows going down. Pull the lights down lower and you'll have less problem with shadows from noses reaching down below chins. Remember that anything in front of a light will cause a shadow on the set. If, for example, you have a mike on a boom, and you position it in front of a light, you'll get its shadow in what are usually inconvenient places. It seems as if a boom shadow always falls across the star's face. Either move the light up and thus lower the shadow or move the boom so the shadow falls somewhere else. Remember that if you put a light on a floor stand (to illuminate a flip stand, for example), cameras may hit it. So make sure it's as much out of the way as possible. By the way, a title card with white letters on a black background needs less light than the rest of your set. Allow about two-thirds as much but spread it out evenly. If one side is brighter than the other, you'll have trouble. Remember to keep your backlights up high so they don't shine into the cameras. Use a light meter to check levels, but use your eye as well to make sure the lighting looks natural as well as technically acceptable.

Now comes the matter of what you will be able to see with all this light. People, of course, but where are they? Do you see the wires and light board and props? Generally not. You have some lightweight, movable panels to hide all the piles of junk, and the fronts of these panels look like anything from a flat wall to an ornately carved Gothic church. That's your set, the next area of our concern.

## SETS

Every shot you take is in a certain setting. That setting may be an ornate representation of a Victorian living room or it may be just a plain curtain stretched tight, but it has to be there. It has to hide the stuff you don't want seen behind the performers, and it has to help convey the impression you are trying to build. The setting may be as insubstantial as a total lack of light creating a black background, or it may be as solid as a grand piano showing behind a singer. Whatever form it takes, the setting has to be an important concern to you.

Generally, you'll want something fast and easy to set up. You'll have to think in terms of pools of light and representations of objects and flat surfaces. For example, that large curtain that's stretched smooth across a couple walls of the studio is called a *cyclorama*, or *cyc* for short. You can use it for a background by throwing some light patterns on it. Shakespeare, after all, got away with just asking his audience to imagine immense battlefields and armies. But you will want some particular sets in particular styles upon some occasions. So what will you do about those?

First of all, you have to decide what you want the scene to look like. If you are doing a drama, you may need a very realistic set of a lawyer's office. For an opera of the 1700s, a stylized candlestick, an ornately framed picture, and a Queen Anne chair can be enough. Your background could be just a blank curtain. But in getting the pieces and the flats for various settings, you need to decide on your approach. In the first example, for instance, the books on the lawyer's shelves would have to look very real. In the second example, however, the candlestick could be very ornate and very two-dimensional, even down to the flame on the candle. The designs are determined by the decision to be realistic in one case and representational in the other.

Your major problem, though, will not come from the little items you put into the setting, but from the flats that make up the walls of the setting. They are the biggest part of the scene you are creating and usually take the longest time to prepare. So how do you go about building them?

First of all, remember you want them to be easy to handle. Then remember they have to stand up, so you must have a way to keep them upright. And last, you may want to use them later in another set, so make them in a standardized way.

To make a flat which is easy to handle means you have to keep it lightweight. Build a frame out of one-by-three lumber. You can nail it together or you can use one of the super-strong glues available. Figure 1.29 shows how the frame goes together. Notice it is reinforced at various key points. Anything lightweight and moved around a lot takes a lot of wear and tear, so it needs extra protection in some areas. Hence the reinforcement. Once you have the framework, you cover it with un-

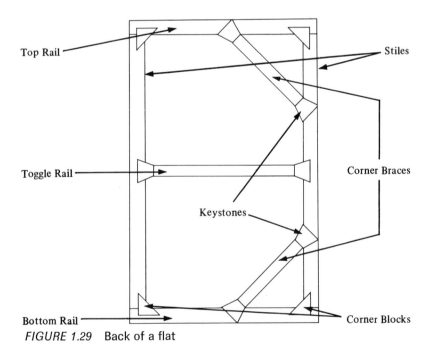

*FIGURE 1.29*   Back of a flat

bleached muslin. That's cheap and useful. This too can be glued on with one of the white, water-soluble plastic glues. Let it dry. Then thin out some of the glue with a lot of water and paint the muslin. It shrinks and stretches tight. Now you're ready to paint whatever you want on it—a few columns and a scene in the Roman Forum or the wood-panelled wall of the lawyer's office. Generally, flats like this are ten-feet tall, although you may find eight feet to be more convenient for a studio with low ceilings. Just remember to stay away from long shots if your flats are only eight-feet tall, as you will probably shoot right over the top of them.

There's another sort of flat that's heavier and more solid than this style. The covering, instead of being muslin, is a fiberboard like masonite. You build a different frame for this and use less bracing.

You can also nail wood panelling to frames like this and have that wood-panelled office for real. Remember, though, that dark panelling will absorb a lot of light and give you a very

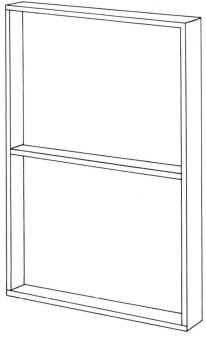

FIGURE 1.30   A rigid flat frame

dark setting or a very hot one if you throw enough light on it to make it bright.

Now, how do you get either sort of flat to stand up? You can build a triangular leg as shown in Figure 1.31. If you put a couple of hinges on it and put the other halves on the flats, you can attach the leg to any flat just by dropping the pins into the hinges. Just be sure you put the hinge pieces at the same height on everything you build. Then put a sandbag over the bottom part of the leg, and the flat will stand by itself. If you fasten two flats together, you can move them into an angle, and they will support each other. The problem is to fasten them together.

Those pieces sticking out from the stiles are called *lash cleats*. If you fasten a cord to the top of a flat, run it behind the lash cleat of another flat, then tie the cord to the bottom of the first flat, you will have fastened the two flats together. This works fine for the muslin-covered flats, but a better way to attach the more solid flats is to have holes through the stiles and put bolts through there. You can quickly tighten a nut and bolt sufficiently to hold the flats together, or you can use C clamps to hold them together.

You may want to cover up the seam between flats once they are up. First be sure they are securely fastened together in back, then run a strip of masking tape down the seam in front. Next paint it with the same paint you used on the flats. You will still be able to see exactly where the seam is, but the television camera is not so sensitive as your eye. It won't see the seam at all.

After you go to the trouble of making a flat, you will want to have a place to store it where it won't get accidentally

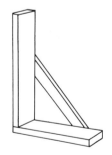

*FIGURE 1.31*   A flat leg brace

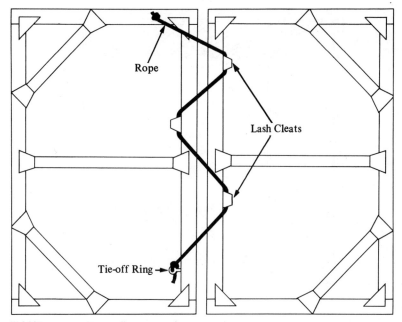

Rope

Lash Cleats

Tie-off Ring →

*FIGURE 1.32*   Tying flats together

destroyed. This may vary from a storeroom with areas marked out on the floor to a regular scene dock. If you just have a marked floor area, at least put the flats face to face so they don't get scarred. Also, try not to lean too many together. A better way is to have what looks like a file drawer turned on its side. At the top and bottom (on the ceiling and floor) there are strips of wood, generally 1″ x 1″, to separate the various flats and to help hold them upright. Between any two strips of wood is generally enough space to slide in four or six flats. Again, put them face to face to protect them. A scene dock offers a lot of protection and doesn't take up much more space than the flats themselves. Just be sure you don't build it too short.

Flats, of course, are full-sized to give you the entire scene you need. But some of the shots you need to take involve only a small area—only what you can see on a piece of cardboard about eight inches high by twelve inches long. That can be a title or the director's name or information like "Meanwhile . . . ." These cards are referred to as graphics, or title cards, or art cards, or flip cards, but under whatever name, you'll have some to use for every show.

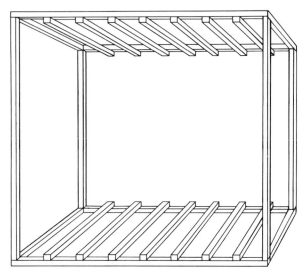

*FIGURE 1.33*   A scene dock

## GRAPHICS

Take a look at a television monitor (or set) that's turned off. What is it? A rectangle, longer than it is high, and with rounded corners. That's simple enough, but many, many people forget that when they start to make up a title card to be shown on the air. Now turn the monitor on. Look for the smallest detail in the picture. Are there a lot of small details? Are those details very small in comparison to the major object in the picture? Chances are the picture is fairly simple with few detailed objects, and the small details are not all that small. Television doesn't very well show small stuff that is intricately decorated. Lots of people forget that too in making title cards.

So when you start thinking of making title cards, think of a rectangle without much on it and not very decorated. Now, let's get a bit more specific.

Any title card or written, printed, or painted sign or any static piece of art work that's only two-dimensional is referred to by the catch-all term *graphic*. Usually these graphics are on pieces of cardboard and hence get the supplementary name of *title card*. The two terms are pretty interchangeable. Notice I said "two-dimensional." A small piece of statuary which you would have to show would not be called a graphic. Graphics and graphic art refer to flat works. That doesn't mean the scene presented on a piece of cardboard can't look three-dimensional. You may, indeed, be trying to create that effect, but you are, nonetheless, dealing in only two dimensions.

The pieces of cardboard that graphic work goes on are roughly in the same proportions as the television screen. Those proportions are three units high by four units wide. Those used to be the proportions of movie screens back around the time television started, so the new business just took over the old form. So anything you put on a card should fall inside a box that's three by four. That box can be three inches by four inches or three feet by four feet or three miles by four miles, as long as it's still three by four. Remember too, this is a *proportion*, so the box can be six inches by eight inches, or nine inches by twelve inches, and so on. The important thing is the three by four relationship rather than the actual numbers.

Immediately, this excludes those tall pictures of sky-scrapers, or a view up a mountain or a picture of someone standing. Now, I know you have seen all these things on the air. So have I, and sometimes they look fine. But you can't put them on just as they are. You have to fill in those sides with something so the overall picture comes out three by four, and that's not hard to do. Sometimes you even get added emphasis to the height of a building by showing the lower buildings at its sides. Or in a picture of a model, the price of the outfit and the name of the store can go in the space at the side and so make the whole thing three by four. But somehow you have to maintain the television screen's proportions.

You also don't want to fill up the card. What the studio camera shows in its viewfinder is more than you see on a control-room monitor, which is more than the transmitter sends out, which is more than the home receiver shows. So after all these losses, you are minus about 10 percent of what you can see when you look at the graphic. So to be sure the viewer sees everything you want seen, confine your material to a center area referred to as the *safe area*.

Obviously, you can have parts of your graphic running out of the picture. As long as what is lost isn't essential to the sense of what you show, that's fine. Material can run all the way to the edge of the card, but it won't be seen by the home viewer. Normally, you want to leave some borders on the card

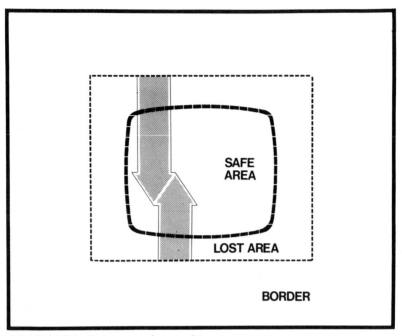

*FIGURE 1.34* Safe area of a graphic

though, and not have anything on them at all. That way your camerapeople won't shoot the whole card. They will move in to a tighter shot and just show the center part. That way, if anything happens while you're on the air and the camera gets moved, it won't suddenly be shooting part of the stand the card is on and part of the studio floor and the floor manager's foot. Also, if the card isn't done quite right or quite to your satisfaction, you have some room to have the camera move around and frame up to a better shot, one you find a bit better composed. Or you may find you have to super a name or a price over part of the card. If the margins are there, you can unbalance the shot of the graphic, super the price (or whatever) and get an overall balanced picture. Without margins, you can't unbalance the shot at all. So leave blank borders, and put all the essential information in the safe area.

Your next concern is to keep the graphic from looking cluttered. Don't use eleven different typefaces, and a border of little pink flowers and a draped curtain on a graphic announcing your afternoon movie. That might look lovely on a poster (I doubt it), but it certainly won't on the television screen. Keep it simple. A single rose on a long stem with a couple leaves and one typeface for the title can be just as effective and much less distracting.

This point of keeping it simple is good to remember if you have to show a group of stills of countryside, cityscapes, or the like. Generally, these pictures have a great deal of material in them. The view down the valley shows the river, the houses of the village, the road going up the mountain side, the peak which was climbed. . . . Put that on the screen and only a jeweler with his eyepiece will be able to pick out anything. . . . Pick simpler shots and use more of them. One shot of the river followed by a few close-ups of houses in the village and the town square, then the start of the road, etc., will make a more understandable presentation, and certainly one a lot easier to see. That's not to say all outdoor shots are bad. A view of the rocky coast with waves breaking into foam can show a lot of area and still be understandable. That's because there are only two *sorts* of things in the picture—the ocean and the rocks. Even if all the detail is lost, the impact of the picture remains because people can see what's happening. Again we have come back to the point of keeping the picture simple.

If you are dealing with pictures not done on a piece of cardboard, as will often be true for outdoor scenes, be sure you fasten these pictures to a piece of cardboard. If you don't, the heat from the lights will make the picture curl over and fall off the stand just as you put it on the air. But don't put another picture on the back of that card if you can avoid it. Sure as you do, the floor manager will confuse a command and turn around

*FIGURE 1.35*  Bad and good graphics

the wrong card or have the wrong side up to begin with. In order to avoid as much confusion as possible, put a number in the upper corner of each card you're using so you can say "Change to card 3" and everyone will know what you mean. Also, if the cards get dropped, they can quickly be put back in order.

There's a special sort of graphic you will deal with a good deal. That's a *super card*. These are the black cards with white letters on them, and you generally use them to matt or key a name or title over another shot. Just like all graphics, the letters should go in the safe area. If you want the letters to come out centered on the screen, place them in the center of the safe area. If you want them on the lower third of the screen, as is true with many names, then put them in the lower third of the safe area.

Of course you can adjust the framing by moving the camera, but prepare the card the way you intend to show it and you will have greater flexibility in adjusting. That is, don't put a name in the center of the card figuring you can always have the camera tilt up and put it in the lower third of the shot. The cameraperson may have to tilt up so far s/he shoots over the card, and then you can't use the card at all. There's one other thing to remember in preparing super cards. Use a plain, solid typeface. Fancy letters lose their fine lines and points and decoration when you try to matt or key them. Thick, heavy lettering runs together in matts and keys and becomes unreadable. Leave good space between words and letters, and use an open, simple typeface. The point is to be readable, not ornate.

Someone in the studio has to be in charge of all these cards. Further, someone has to cue the actors so they know when to start talking. Someone has to get props out of the way.

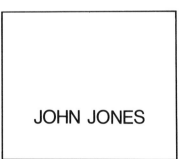

*FIGURE 1.36*   Printing positioned on graphics

Camerapeople aren't free to do all this, neither are the actors. So we have a special person charged with all these jobs. That person is the *floor manager.*

## FLOOR MANAGING

The floor manager is the director's mobile link to the studio. The director can and does talk to the camerapeople, but they are tied to their cameras. For getting things done, often at the last minute, s/he has to depend on the floor manager. When s/he has advice to give the talent, or questions to ask them, s/he has to go through the floor manager. S/he gets cues relayed by the floor manager. S/he finds out if there are problems because the floor manager is often the only one free enough to talk. Further, the floor manager makes sure nothing gets in the way of a moving camera. The cameraperson looks only at the viewfinder, not at the surroundings, and so may be headed right for a light stand or a prop. The floor manager is responsible for moving them. The floor manager makes sure the talent knows how much time remains till the commercial or the end of the show, so they will be able to come out on time. The floor manager, in short, makes sure the studio runs smoothly during the production. And yet, because the job seems easy, many floor managers will not give it their complete attention. However, the job is only easy if you know enough about all the production jobs to be able to remove the obstacles to a good performance. If you don't know that much, then you *become* one of the obstacles to a good performance.

Let's suppose a talk show is about to begin and you are the floor manager. The director is making last minute preparations, so you take that time to look critically at the set and the talent. Is everything where it should be? Are the flats firm and not in a position where they might fall over? Is the talent's make-up right? Are they sweating from the heat of the lights? Are they nervous? It's up to you to correct any of these situations. Some are easy—a flat can be braced, the air conditioning can be increased. But it takes a diplomat to calm down excited guests. You need to put them at ease by making them feel everyone is there to help them. Don't spend your time talking over the headset to the audio person just to pass the time. One-sided conversations, especially if you're joking and laughing, can really upset the talent. They can be paranoid enough without thinking you are laughing at them. Check to see the mikes are all in place, and tell the talent which camera the director will be starting on. Once the director has the tape rolling, or has said something like "thirty seconds to air time," pass this on to the talent. Just a simple phrase like "Tape is rolling, coming out on camera one," is very consoling to them, as they then know the program is about to begin. Then, about ten seconds before the show starts, announce, in a loud voice, "Stand by." This lets everyone in the studio know it's time to shut up. The mikes will be opened soon and no extra noise should be made. Also, stand next to the camera the director is starting on and raise your arm. The talent who will begin talking will watch you, and when the director says "Cue," bring your arm down and point at the talent. S/he should start talking, unless s/he's suddenly scared, and you can't do much about that. If the director is about to switch from one camera to another, stand between the two and point at the one that's now active. As the director goes to the other camera, swing your arm around and point at the other camera, the one that's now been put on the air. Make the gestures, both cueing and changing cameras, big and obvious because you are in the dark and the talent is facing bright lights. If you don't make an obvious movement, the talent may never see it. While the program goes on, you may have to move obstacles out of the camera's way, pull the cable around so the camerapeople don't get their feet tangled in it, change the lighting at the right instant, take a mike as a singer goes off the set, change the title cards on the stand, or any number of other things. It's these details that you and the director have discussed during the rehearsal, so you should expect whatever comes up. You should even expect an emergency. There's always one per show, generally of a totally disastrous nature. You're the only one free enough to prevent it from ruining the production. When a mike suddenly dies, you have to scurry around and plug in an extra and get it on the set. When a costume splits, you have to find the safety pin.

If you get through the show without major problems, your next, and final, concern is to get the talent out on time. The director will be giving time cues like "Five minutes." You relay this to the talent by holding up five fingers right under the lens of the on-air camera. Then get in the line of sight of those not

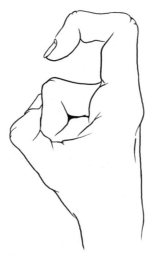

*FIGURE 1.37*　A half minute

on the air just then and show them the five-minute cue too. Then comes four, three, two, one, and thirty. How do you show thirty seconds? That's half a minute, so you show half a finger. When the director says "Wrap them up," make a fist and rotate it back and forth. The talent should stop almost immediately, but gracefully. If they don't, the director will end up saying "Cut," and you run a finger over your throat like a knife to indicate STOP. The talent ought to stop immediately without another word.

If you are out on time, you might think the show is finished. But stay on the headsets because if you were videotaping, the

*FIGURE 1.38*　Wrap up

director will quickly spot-check the tape to see if everything is all right. If it isn't, you'll have to call everyone back into places so the show can begin again. But if everything is fine, you can announce "Let's strike the studio." That's the signal for everyone to put away the sets, turn off the lights, get out of costumes, and generally get the studio cleaned up. It's your responsibility to see the studio gets struck properly and completely before anyone is allowed to leave. But once that's done, and you have returned graphic material to the director and props to the props person or the storage area, you are through. Simple job, yes, but only if you know enough about all the other jobs to handle them as well. It's only by knowing the other people's jobs so well that you can help them from your position as floor manager.

That takes care of the jobs and materials in the studio. What of the control room? Everything is run from there, so you might consider the control room to be the brains of the outfit. So let's talk about what goes on in there.


## VIDEO SWITCHING

The control room contains the monitors and the switching console, which the director uses to see and select the video portion of the production. Each camera will have a monitor here showing its shot. Next will come a monitor to show slides and another to show film. If there are additional slide projectors or film projectors, there will of course be additional monitors. Next will be a monitor for every VTR (video tape recording) machine. A monitor will show what is currently being broadcast, hence is generally referred to as the *air monitor.* Another monitor will show the output of that particular studio and control room and is generally called the *line monitor.* Another monitor will be a *preview monitor*, used to look at a shot before putting it on the output line of that studio. At stations with a network affiliation, there is a monitor showing what is running on the network. Other extra monitors may show the output of another studio, the program being broadcast by another station, or any other such thing which station personnel have decided is necessary. These final monitors are, logically, referred to as *auxiliary monitors.* The line-up of monitors might look something like the set-up shown in Figure 1.39.

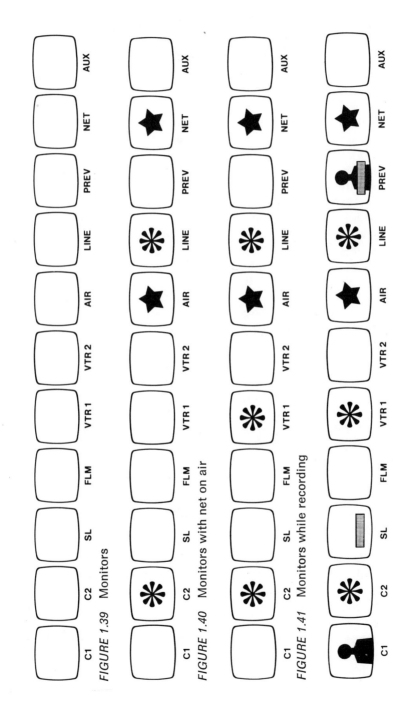

C1  C2  SL  FLM  VTR 1  VTR 2  AIR  LINE  PREV  NET  AUX
FIGURE 1.39  Monitors

C1  C2  SL  FLM  VTR 1  VTR 2  AIR  LINE  PREV  NET  AUX
FIGURE 1.40  Monitors with net on air

C1  C2  SL  FLM  VTR 1  VTR 2  AIR  LINE  PREV  NET  AUX
FIGURE 1.41  Monitors while recording

C1  C2  SL  FLM  VTR 1  VTR 2  AIR  LINE  PREV  NET  AUX
FIGURE 1.42  Monitors showing an effect

Obviously, not all control rooms have, or need, all these monitors. Some need even more. But the monitors are the primary video sources in the control room, and obviously a lot of these monitors might be showing the same thing. Let's look at an example.

Suppose you are in the control room of a network affiliate some evening at 8:15. There is a show being videotaped in the studio while the network is broadcasting a movie. The director has just called for the shot on Camera 2. See Figure 1.40 for what the monitors would show.

Camera 2 and the Line have the same shot and Net and Air have the same shot. If the director wants to see the output of the videotape machine s/he's recording on, VTR 1 might show the same picture as Camera 2 and Line.

Let's go a bit further. Suppose the next shot is to be Camera 1 with a name put over it, and the name is on a slide. The director wants to preview this, so the monitors would look like Figure 1.42.

We could go on adding elements, but you can easily see how much there is to look at on the control room monitors. Yet people in the control room learn to look at them all at a glance, see everything, and even call for minute corrections without losing track of all the other things going on.

These monitors represent the multiple eyes of a television production. If something looks bad here, you can bet it will look bad if it gets broadcast to the people at home. Yet if the scene is fine on the monitor, even though the out-of-sight edge of the setting is on fire, those folks at home will think everything is fine. Generally then, the control room people need only look at the monitors—they don't need to see the burning flat because they can still show the audience a good picture. Let the studio crew handle the fire!

Next we come to the switcher itself. Here is the device which enables you to put one of those monitor pictures on the line. The switcher may be operated by the director or by a technical director. In either case, its operation is based on a simple one-two choice. We can elaborate on that one-two choice, and go far beyond it, but right now let's consider the basics.

Suppose you have one camera. You can choose to be on or off the line with it. If you are off, you are in what is termed black—no picture at all. If you are on the line, you have what-

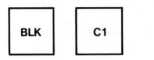

FIGURE 1.43   Switcher buttons

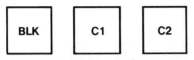

FIGURE 1.44   Switcher buttons

ever picture that camera has showing. To make this choice, you will have buttons to push. One will be marked "Black" and the other "Camera 1."

Push whichever one you want and that's what shows up on your line monitor. If you add another camera, you can choose either no picture (Black) or some picture (Camera 1 or Camera 2). If you choose some picture, you can choose Camera 1 or Camera 2. So you still have a one-two choice.

Now suppose you add a film chain. You have the picture–no picture choice, then a camera-film choice. You can guess we can add other buttons to match the various monitors we have discussed and that takes us away from our basic one-two choice, so let's set up an example row of buttons and talk about what we can do.

In Figure 1.46 we can have no picture on the line, or Camera 1, or Camera 2, or Film, or a Slide, or a VTR just by pushing the appropriate button. Each button except BLK will have a corresponding monitor for people to look at. In Figure 1.47, for

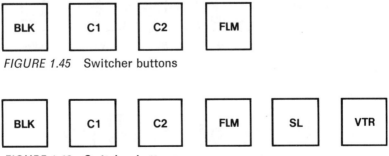

FIGURE 1.45   Switcher buttons

FIGURE 1.46   Switcher buttons

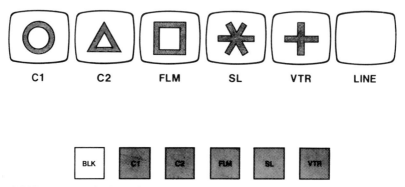

FIGURE 1.47 Black on line

example, BLK is pushed and the line shows nothing. Push the Film button and you have the situation in Figure 1.48. Now push the C 1 button and you will have the picture shown in Figure 1.49. These instantaneous changes of picture on the line monitor are called *cuts.* In this sequence, we cut from black to film and we cut from film to Camera 1. One way, then, to change what a viewer sees is to cut from one source to another.

Besides adding more buttons, how else can we add to the capabilities of the switcher? Suppose, instead of one row of buttons, we have two, as in Figure 1.50. Next, let's add a way to activate first one row, then the other. There's our basic one-two option again: you can have either the top row or the bottom row active. The way we will choose is with a *fader bar.* You'll see why it's called that shortly. Right now, the fader bar is opposite the top row (generally called the top *bank)* of buttons,

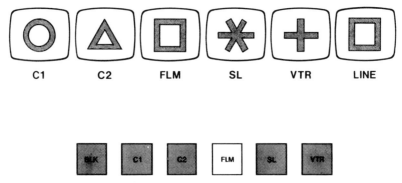

FIGURE 1.48 Film on line

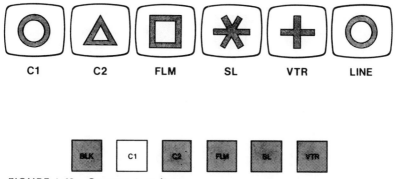

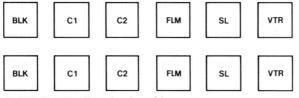

FIGURE 1.49   Camera 1 on line

so they are the ones which are active. Just as when we had only one bank, we can cut between sources to change what's on the line monitor. The lower bank, however, is not active and whatever we push on it does nothing to affect what's on the line monitor. If we move the fader bar down opposite the lower bank, it becomes active and we can cut by pushing buttons there, and this will now change the picture on the line monitor. But the top bank is now inactive and causes no changes.

Let's take an example. Suppose Camera 1 is punched on both banks as in Figure 1.52. You have Camera 1 showing on the

| BLK | C1 | C2 | FLM | SL | VTR |

| BLK | C1 | C2 | FLM | SL | VTR |

FIGURE 1.50   Two banks of buttons

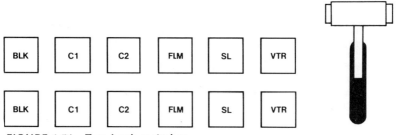

FIGURE 1.51   Two bank switcher

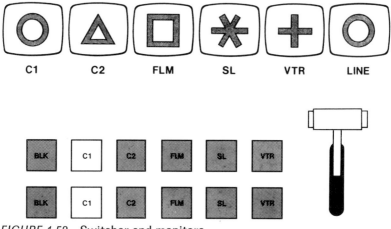

FIGURE 1.52   Switcher and monitors

line monitor. If you move the fader bar to the lower position, you still have Camera 1 on the line monitor. (See Figure 1.53.) Suppose now you push Camera 2 on the upper bank. That won't change anything on the line monitor as shown in Figure 1.54. Now, if you move the fader bar to the upper position, the top bank becomes active and Camera 2 shows up on the line monitor.

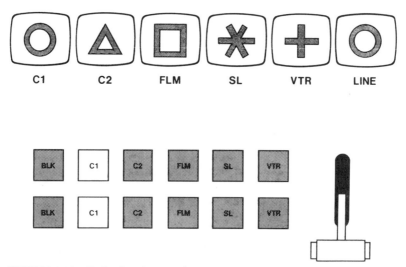

FIGURE 1.53   Fader bar lowered

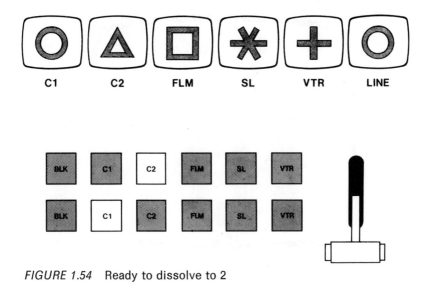

FIGURE 1.54   Ready to dissolve to 2

But what happens as you go from the lower position to the upper position? The scene on the line monitor was Camera 1, and it got dimmer and dimmer. At the same time, Camera 2 very dimly appeared and got brighter and brighter. It's as if one picture was dissolving away while another was "dissolving" in. Hence, this kind of picture change is called a *dissolve.* When the fader bar is halfway between the two banks, you see one

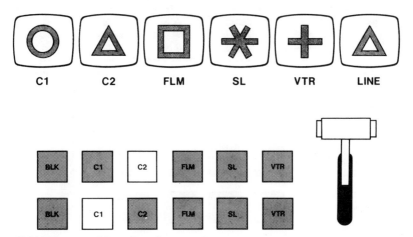

FIGURE 1.55   After dissolving to 2

*FIGURE 1.56*    A super

picture superimposed over the other. This is called a *super*, which will sometimes be useful to you. Remember though, you can "see through" a super; if a hand is supered over a face, you can still see all the features of the face.

There's one other picture change, much like a dissolve, that we will use. Look at Figure 1.57. If you move the fader bar to the lower position so black is on the line monitor, the picture from the slide will slowly fade away to be replaced by—

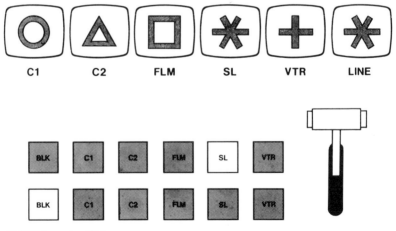

*FIGURE 1.57*    Slide on line

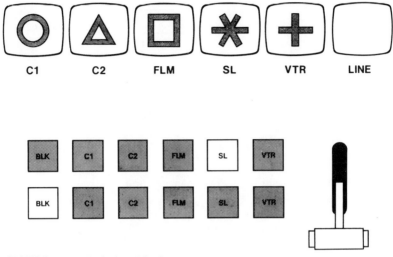

FIGURE 1.58   Faded to black

nothing. This change into black is called a *fade*. The reverse, moving from black to a source, is also a fade. In the first instance, you are fading *from* a slide *to* black, and in the second you are fading *from* black *to* Camera 1. It's this move, a fade, which gives the fader bar its name.

The basic switcher, then, has two banks, buttons for a variety of video sources, including black, and a fader bar to get

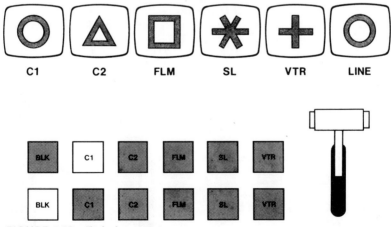

FIGURE 1.59   Faded up on 1

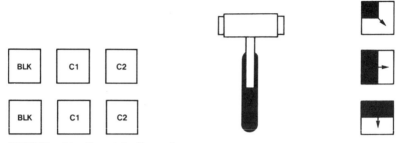

FIGURE 1.60   Special effects buttons

from one bank to another. You can change the picture on the line monitor (which is the output of your studio and control room) by cutting, dissolving, or fading.

Now let us add some sophisticated equipment which lets us electronically change our pictures. Simplest of all are *wipes.* We know we can go from one video source to another by cuts or dissolves, but there are also decorative and sometimes functional ways to go between sources. For example, suppose your switcher looks like Figure 1.60. Those three buttons on the side show you what sort of picture change you will get. Suppose you push the buttons illustrated in Figure 1.61. Because the fader bar is at the top, the line monitor will show Camera 1. Now move the fader bar toward the bottom and watch what happen in Figure 1.62. The picture from Camera 2 starts

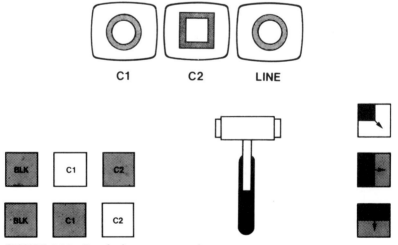

FIGURE 1.61   Ready for a corner wipe

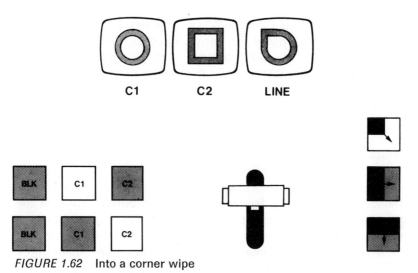

FIGURE 1.62    Into a corner wipe

to come into the upper left corner in exactly the pattern shown on that top button of the column of three. The farther you move the fader bar, the more that corner moves over the picture from Camera 1 until finally, with the fader bar all the way at the bottom, the corner fills the whole screen and you see only Camera 2's shot.

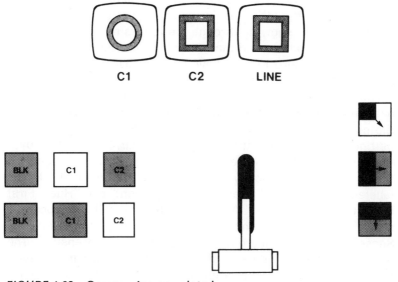

FIGURE 1.63    Corner wipe completed

You have *wiped* Camera 2 over Camera 1. Push the fader bars back to the top and the corner retreats, revealing Camera 1 again. Likewise, the other buttons in the column of three give you wipes moving down across the screen or from left to right across the screen.

Obviously, there are other shapes which you can have for wipes—stars, circles, checkerboards, etc., but they all work on this same principle. Often, too, you will find an extra switch which makes the wipes always go in the same direction. That is, in our example above, the corner descended from the upper left and showed Camera 2. With this extra switch thrown, even though you move the fader bars from the bottom bank to the top, Camera 1 would reappear in a corner descending from the upper left instead of being revealed by a retreating corner. Obviously, too, you can have many more buttons and many more video sources, and they can all be put into wipes like these. A word of warning here. Use a wipe *only* if you have a good reason. An example might be a shot of a pitcher with a corner inserted at the upper right to show a runner off first base. But without a reason, wipes look phony and are clearly gimmicks.

Next let's look at matts and keys. First, though, remember what a super is. It shows two pictures at once but lets you see through the elements of each. Suppose you have a shot on Camera 1 of a man whose name is unknown to the audience. And suppose you have a slide with his name on it. You can super one over the other as illustrated in Figure 1.64. But notice you see the man showing through the letters of his name. There are devices to get around that. First let's consider a *matt.*

Notice in Figure 1.65 we have no fader bar, but we have the addition of several new buttons and dials. This is a special portion of the switcher, called the special effects board. To get a matt, we push the button labeled "mat" and the shot of the man on Camera 1 and the name on "S1." Now, instead of getting things showing through, we get clear, solid letters over the man, completely blanking out whatever is behind them. All this is done electronically. We control it by turning the knobs labeled "Key Sense," "Intensity," "Saturation," and "Hue." First let's turn "Key Sense." Notice the letters will disappear or spread out like blotted ink to cover the whole picture. Set "Key Sense" to get the clearest letters. Next turn "Intensity." The letters go from very dark to gleaming white. Now turn "Saturation." The letters go from a muddy black to a very vivid color.

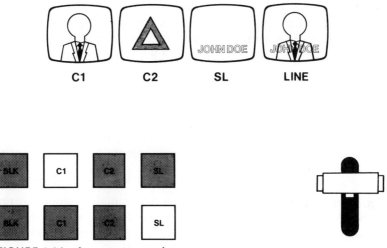

FIGURE 1.64   A name supered

Turn "Hue" and you can change that color. By manipulating these last three knobs, you can make the letters any color you want. (On black and white equipment, you can only change the letters from black through shades of gray to white and so will not have the knobs for saturation and hue.) But you get clear letters with nothing showing through, and that's better than a

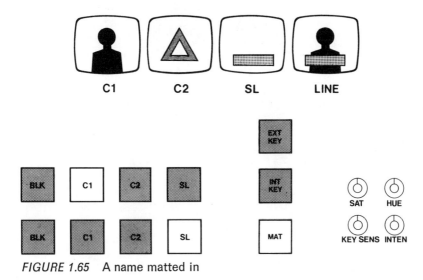

FIGURE 1.65   A name matted in

super. Quite often, though, the edges of a matt "fry." Look closely and the edges of the letters appear to be moving back and forth. To avoid this, we can use an *internal key.*

The internal key is set up exactly the same way as a matt except you push the "int key" button instead of "mat." Again, key sense controls how clear the letters are. But in this instance, saturation, hue, and intensity have *no* effect on the letters. The letters are exactly the color they are on the slide, but the edges are clean, stable, and unmoving. That's an advantage, but now you can't change colors. You gain a little, you lose a little.

It's time for a pause to discuss the "name" slide. First of all, it must be white letters on black. In a pinch, I'll admit a very dark background with very light letters will work, but not as well as white on black. You need white letters because electronically the black is being ignored or dropped out. Once it's gone, another picture can come through where it was, but not where the white letters still are. That way you get clear titling.

Now back to the keys. You noticed the "int key"—"ext key" difference. We have done something with internal key, but what does it mean? This special effect uses material "internal" to its closed world of person and name slide; it uses those two video sources and that's all. *External key* adds something "ex-

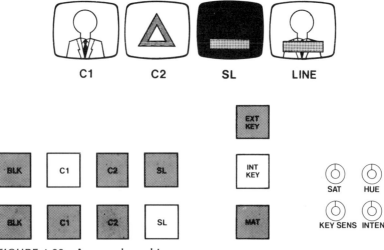

FIGURE 1.66   A name keyed in

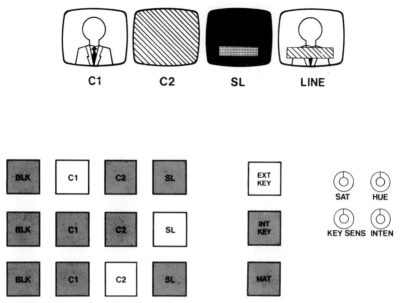

FIGURE 1.67    Another sort of key

ternal" to that set-up. Let's see what. And to do that, we need another bank.

In Figure 1.67, as before, we have the letters over the man, but now we have something new showing in the letters. By adding a third bank, a place where we can push another button without losing those already pushed, we add an "external" element to the picture. In this case Camera 2 shows up in the letters. We took away the black to let the person show through. Now we are taking away the white of the letters to let something else show through. We didn't take away the *shape* of the letters, just their color. And as you add more buttons, you can show more things in the letters. Suppose you have a host introducing a movie. Suppose you have "MOVIE" on a slide with the "O" all filled in with white. Push the buttons as in Figure 1.68 and the movie itself will show through the "O" of the word. Remember, though, only that portion of the movie which is on the "O" portion of the screen will show; you won't see the whole movie picture.

What if you had a person against a black background? Could you drop out the black and thus make the person look

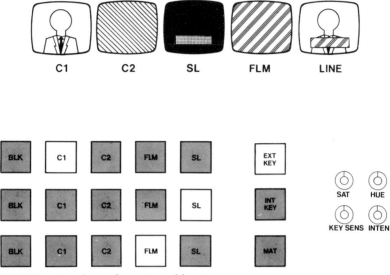

FIGURE 1.68   A use for external keying

like s/he was in front of some scene? Yes, you can, but in color television, we find it easier to work from a color other than black. And that brings me to the last of our special effects.

   *Chroma-key* is, as you can guess, a type of key, an external key to be exact, that deals with color. It is a way to remove any color you want from the scene so something else can be inserted. Quite often you need a special button to activate it, so let's add a "Chroma" button and see how it's set up.

   First, we push "ext key," as it is an external key. Next we activate chroma key by pushing the "Chroma" button. Then we push "Camera 1" on the middle bank, if that's the camera on

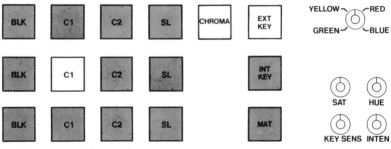

FIGURE 1.69   Chroma-key

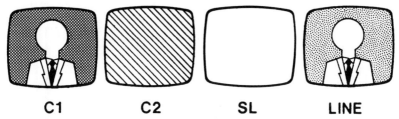

C1            C2            SL            LINE

*FIGURE 1.70*    Monitors in chroma-key

which we will lose a color. Adjust the key sense knob so the color is cleanly taken out. Right now we are in a very similar position to an external key when the white of the letters has been removed but nothing put in its place. We have a scene with some things saved and some shapes saved. The monitors might look like Figure 1.70.

Now when we push "Camera 2" on that lowest bank; that's like adding something into those empty letter shapes of a normal external key. Here, however, it goes into the space where we've taken a color out. Now the monitors look like Figure 1.71.

How about that extra knob in Figure 1.69 pointing to blue? That's where we pick the color we want to lose, and generally we pick blue because there will be less blue in the picture than any other color. As a matter of fact, only 11 percent of the camera's response is blue, while 59 percent is green and 30 percent is red. And since every item of the color we choose will disappear, including clothing or eyes, we want to disturb the picture as little as possible. Blue, then, works best. If you choose red, and a redhead walks on the scene . . . .

Those are the basic effects of a switcher. One problem remains. Figure 1.72 shows the basic switcher from Figure 1.51.

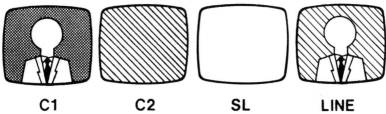

C1            C2            SL            LINE

*FIGURE 1.71*    Final chroma-key effect

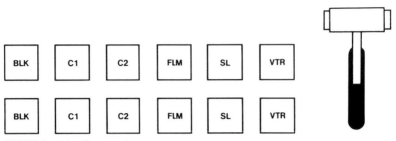

*FIGURE 1.72*   A switcher

How do we get to these special effects, and where do they come from? We have to add a button for "Effects," and a whole other board to handle all the effects. It might look like Figure 1.74.

Normally, we would work off the lower two banks, but for an effect, we would push the effect button and then we would get whatever was set on the effect board. Wipes would be controlled by the fader bar on the effects board; keys and matts would be controlled by the buttons and knobs to the right of the three banks of buttons. If we add an effects button to the effects board, and add another effects board, we could set up an effect within an effect. Such a switcher is called a *double re-entry switcher.* As we increase the number of buttons and sources and boards, you can see we can increase the functions of the total switcher till it gets too big for anyone to handle. But it all works off the basic ideas we have talked over here.

One last word about monitors. You will, of course, have one for each video source. But what of special effects? You will also have one called "preview," and on it you can look at the effect you have set up and see if it's really what you want. Always check an effect on a preview monitor before you put it on the line.

We have, of course, been discussing a general situation. Not all switchers will be arranged as I have shown. Some will have special capabilities not touched on here. Not all control

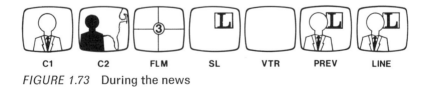

| C1 | C2 | FLM | SL | VTR | PREV | LINE |

*FIGURE 1.73*   During the news

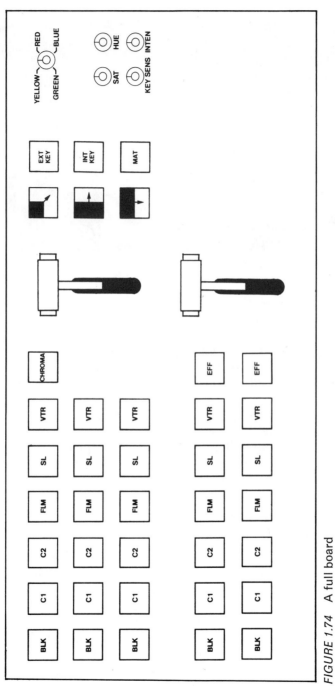

*FIGURE 1.74* A full board

61

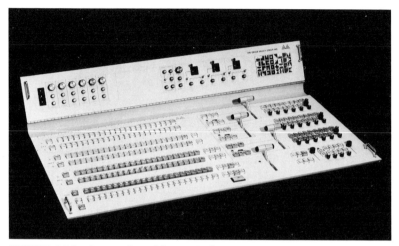

*FIGURE 1.75*    A complex video switcher

rooms will have the monitors I have mentioned. Yet everywhere the ideas will remain the same. Know the ideas and you
can master any switcher you encounter.

The switcher, however, deals only with video, and that's
only half the story. Audio is vitally important to the television
personnel. To understand how important, think back to times
when the sound has gone out during one of your favorite television shows. You can't really follow what's happening. If the
picture goes and you can still hear, you can stay up with the
story line and know where you are when the picture returns. So
the audio console in the television control room is a very important piece of equipment.

## THE AUDIO CONSOLE

Everything you find out about audio for radio can be used in
television. I can add a few things that are seldom used in radio,
but audio remains pretty much the same in both fields. You will
still be concerned with a clear, true pick-up and with the
proper mike for the particular condition. You will still be using
an audio control panel like the one in radio. So instead of
duplicating the material from radio, let's assume you can
refer to it and go on from there.

As audio person, it's your responsibility to run down the script and determine what your sound sources are. You will have people in the studio, a theme on a record or a cart, perhaps something on reel to reel tape, a constant tone on one pot by which you can set the levels of your VU meters, and one thing you don't have in radio. That's the sound track from VTR or films. But that's like any other recording; it comes in on a particular pot and you handle it just like all other sounds. So once you determine what your sound sources are, it's up to you to get ready to handle them. You'll cue up the records, check levels for carts, and set all the right switches on your board. The people in the studio need mikes, just as in radio, so you have to get the proper ones and place them properly.

It's in the placement that television generally differs from radio. In radio it doesn't matter where the mikes go, so long as they pick up the sound properly. In television, you sometimes have to worry about the mikes not being seen at all, and you always have to worry about whether or not the appearance of mikes will look bad. Viewers are quite used to seeing mikes on desks during talk shows and newscasts. They are also used to seeing people like singers and reporters holding mikes. Even the lavalier mike is accepted around the necks of hostesses on women's shows or personalities being interviewed. But in a drama or a comedy, the viewers don't expect to see guests sitting at a dinner table and trying to keep lavaliers from falling in the food. So let's talk first about the mikes you don't see, and then about those you do.

By looking at the script (if you don't know before that) you can tell if you are working on the type of show where you have to hide the mikes. If this is a big dramatic presentation, you may have to work with the set designer some days before the rehearsals start just to find places for mikes. A flower pot may be specially designed to hold a mike. A pile of books on an end table may cover a mike. A mike may be attached to a side of a window which always faces away from the cameras. Each set presents its unique places, and it's up to you and the set designer to find them. These places, of course, must be near the action or the words will sound distant and muffled. As the action moves around, there have to be other mikes close enough to pick up the changing sound patterns. That's no easy trick, so you may use a *boom mike.* Here you have what seems the perfect answer. It's a movable mike, capable of following the actors wherever they go. What if they go in opposite directions? Then maybe you need two booms. That's awkward, and hard to manage in the congested space of a studio in production. And what if the major actor moves to a spot where the long arm of the boom is between him and a light? He ends up with this long horizontal shadow across his face. Boom shadows are probably the biggest disadvantage. They always fall in places you don't want. There are ways to handle the shadows, and sometimes they work well enough even if not perfectly. One way is to bring the boom straight in from in front of the set. That way the shadow can be avoided by a simple step to the right or left. If the boom comes in from the side, an actor has to move a long way forward or backward to get out of its shadow, and that's seldom possible. Another way is to have the lights up high, particularly the ones causing the shadow. That puts the shadow down on the floor instead of up on the set. Usually only one or two lights really give you bad shadow problems, so they can often be raised. Sometimes, though, they are your major lights and simply can't be budged. Then you have no choice but to move the boom. Or move the set. Move the set, though, and you'll probably have to change the lighting.

So as audio person, you'll have to work closely with the set designer and the lighting crew to get exactly what you want, or at least something close to what you want. Sometimes, in desperation or in a rush, you will end up throwing an omni-directional mike like a lavalier over the light grid and letting it hang down to pick up whatever sound is below it. That does create a sort of cone of sound for that mike. The only problem is that this arrangement picks up *every* sound in the cone. Feet shuffling on the floor, pencils rolling on desk tops, script pages turning, and sometimes the sounds of cameras and the floor manager moving around. So if you have to use this set-up, tell everyone and warn them to be extra quiet.

Now what about the mikes you do see? Most often, you will be using a *lavalier*. These mikes either hang from a cord around the neck or have a small clip for fastening them to clothing. The major point to remember is to keep the mike from rubbing against clothing and to keep the cord from swinging free. Both movements will create strange, loud sounds like static. You may have to tie a knot in the cord so as to make the mike hang higher, or clip it to a different piece of clothing, but keep it away from coat lapels, neck scarves, and so on. Then tuck the

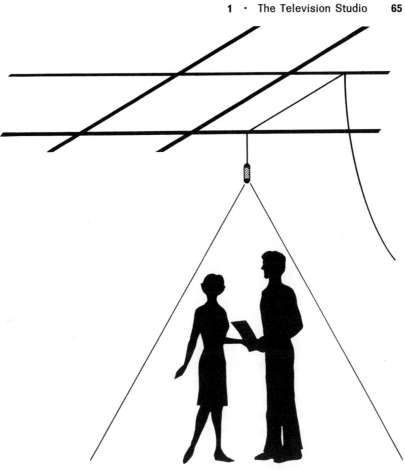

*FIGURE 1.76*  A cone of sound

cord under a belt or even fasten it with masking tape behind the performer's back to keep the cord from swinging. Also, don't put the mike under any layers of clothing. This lets the clothing rub over the mike and make noises, and it muffles the sound.

Other mikes which are visible are *desk mikes* and *hand mikes*. The desk mike should be off to one side and low so as not to be distracting, but not so far away that you can't pick up sounds. When you're placing the desk mikes, think about which way the performer will face when s/he talks, not about where the front of the set is. Quite often the performer will be talking to someone at the side and not out to the front of the set. So the mike should go off to the side. Hand mikes don't present you with this problem, as the performer holds them.

If your talent is inexperienced, you'll want to explain how to hold the mike and where to point it and how far away to hold it. But generally its use is so obvious you'll have no problems.

If you are placing mikes for a performer who won't be holding them, that's generally because s/he is fairly static but with both hands occupied, for instance with playing a guitar. Think about where the sound comes from. You'll need a mike pointed at a singer's mouth, and you'll need one pointed at the hole of the guitar. Don't be misled by instruments; mikes should go where the sound comes from. The keys of a piano don't produce the sound, the sounding board does, and it's at the back of an upright or underneath a grand. And in general, you'll want a mike for the instrument and a mike for the performer. That way you can balance the two for the clearest sound. In placing mikes around a performer, talk with the director. You don't want a mike and its stand right across one of the key shots. Support for a mike can generally be angled a dozen different ways so as to clear the shot s/he wants.

Here's a simple word of warning—be sure you know which outlets the various mikes are plugged into. That saves you a lot of trouble when you get back in the control room.

Once all your mikes are out and all the other sound sources are figured out, you'll want to get levels. Over the headset or over a studio loudspeaker, ask a particular person to say something or to play something. Open that one mike and set a level. Then go on to the next. Be sure you check them all because you know the one you don't check will be the one that isn't working. When you ask people to say something, stop them if they start to count. That won't give you the same level as talking. Insist they talk. You'll get very tired of hearing people ask, "But what do you want me to say?" but try to bear up. Tell them to recite a poem they know or repeat part of the *Gettysburg Address.* Generally, mike checks like this will be a bit softer than they will be on the air. But you can make adjustments to compensate for that in the rehearsal. If you have a lot of mikes and other sound sources, you may want to write down the pot number, what that pot controls, and what the level settings should be. This can be particularly useful if you have three different records to work with, and each one runs at a different level. Jot down what each level is, and you can cue the right one up at the correct level much faster. Also, if for some reason you take a mike under, you don't have to remember what the original level was. You can just look at your list. That's an advantage when you have fifteen other things to think about and remember.

Most of the concern in the control room will be with the audio console and the video switcher. These two, after all, control the great bulk of the program. But an absolutely indispensable addition is the *film island*. It's called an island because it's off separated from everything else. From that island you can run slides or motion pictures to add to the events you are seeing with your studio cameras. You thus have another video input.

## PROJECTION

In order to see anything on a television screen, there has to be a television camera involved. So just like the studio cameras, you have a camera to look at slides or film. It isn't mobile, and it doesn't require a cameraperson. First of all, let's look at the set-up for slides.

Television uses 35-mm slides, which are just like the ones your friends have taken on their vacations which show Aunt Tillie in front of the Taj Mahal. As a matter of fact, the slide projector which your friends use to project their slides on a screen is just like the projector used to get slides on a television screen. There is some sort of drum to hold the slides (and the types of drums vary a good deal), a lamp which shines light through the slides, and a lens arrangement to project and focus the image of the slide. The major difference is in where this image goes. Your friends throw this image up on a large screen in front of everyone so the slides can be seen. In television, the image is thrown at a camera. By adjusting both the lens of the projector and the lens of the camera, the image can be focused on the pick-up tubes of the camera. That way you get a good, sharp picture of the slide on a television screen. Now, it may seem this violates the rule about shining lights into the camera, but remember you have to have a certain amount of light in order for the camera to see. So really, you are always letting light of some sort into the camera. Only

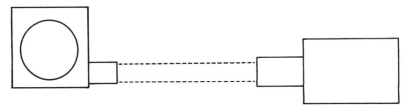

*FIGURE 1.77* A slide chain

straight, undiluted light can injure it, and in this situation we have a slide between the light and the pick-up tubes, so there won't be any injury to the camera.

Let's go back to Aunt Tillie. Remember the black on the screen as you friend changed from her picture to the next one of Uncle Fred arguing with the rickshaw driver? In television, you don't want to have that black as you change from one slide to the next. So there is a way to have the second slide all ready to be shown and capable of being put on the air instantly. Like magic, it's all done with mirrors. Suppose you have one drum showing its slides right into the camera. Put another drum off to one side, put in a mirror at a 45 degree angle across the straight path from the other drum, and suddenly the camera is seeing the slide from the side drum. It's a simple matter now

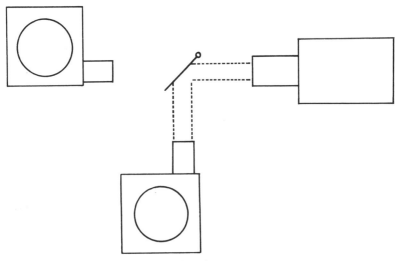

*FIGURE 1.78* Mirror for second slide projector

to make the mirror swing in and out of that straight path so the camera sees first the side drum, then the straight drum, then the side drum . . . . All you need is a switch somewhere within easy reach of the director or the technical director, and that mirror can let you see one slide followed immediately by another. While you are seeing the slide on the straight drum, the side drum can be rotated to the next slide. When you go to the side drum, the straight drum can move to its next slide. So you can have a continuous showing of all the slides in order and have no black on the air in between.

Film works a good deal like the slides. If your friends take home movies, they may show you Aunt Tillie and Uncle Fred falling into the moat of an old castle. The projector they use is very like the projector used in television, but again the image is focused on the camera's pick-up tubes rather than on a screen. The projector will most likely be for 16-mm film at the television stations instead of the 8-mm size of your friend's home movies or the 35-mm (or bigger) size used at the local movie house. There's little reason why television stations couldn't use other sizes as far as technical considerations of projectors go, but larger film is too expensive and smaller film doesn't always give as clear a picture. So most stations use 16-mm film.

There's one further difference between projectors for television and those for home use.

The ones at home (and in movie houses, for that matter) show you twenty-four pictures in one second. But for television, since our electricity works on sixty cycles a second, we have to use a number related to sixty. The projectors, then, have to be rigged to change from twenty-four to sixty. Now follow closely, because here's how they do it. They show the first picture for a sixtieth of a second. Then they show that same picture again for a sixtieth of a second. Then they show the second picture for a sixtieth of a second, again for a sixtieth of a second, and a *third* time for a sixtieth of a second. That's two pictures shown for five-sixtieths of a second. Then the cycle starts all over again—twice, then three times, twice, then three times. You can get twelve packages of five-sixtieths of a second into a full sixty-sixtieths of a second (one second), and each of the twelve packages has two pictures in it, so you get twenty-four pictures into a second cut up into sixtieths. Neat, but not simple. So home projectors won't work perfectly in television.

If you bring one into the studio, show a film, and put a regular camera on the image, you'll get funny bars and black showing on the television picture. Put the film on a television projector, and everything's fine.

Suppose you want to show a full-length movie on television. It may very well be on three or four separate reels. You can do one of two things to cover the time when you run out of one reel, take it down, and load up the next one. You can cover by breaking for a commercial, or by going to the host in the studio who ad libs till you are ready, or even by punching up a slide which says, "We'll be right back . . . ." Obviously, there are times when you won't want to cover with anything. So the best thing is to go back to "magic"—put in mirrors. Then you can, just like with the slides, go directly to another projector which already has the next reel loaded and set.

The mirrors, just like the projectors, are special for television, both for the slides and the projectors. Most mirrors have the reflective silver coating on the back of the glass because that protects it from scratches, smudges, dust, and so on. But that puts a flat surface between the silver and the viewer, and that flat surface is the front of the glass itself. The glass surface can reflect some images you don't want in television, so the mirrors are silvered on the front. That exposes them to damage pretty easily, so you want to be extra careful around them. With front-silvered mirrors, you get only one image but you have to clean them carefully, keep objects away from them that might scratch them, etc.

I haven't said anything yet about how to load slides or film because I can only speak generally. Slide drums and film projectors work in similar ways, but each model seems somewhat different from the next. Generally, though, slides need to be turned upside down and backwards before they go in the drum.

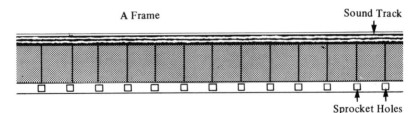

FIGURE 1.79   Film

Film is a bit more complex. Those holes in one side of the film are called *sprocket holes*, and they fit over toothed wheels on the projector.

First the film comes down off the feed reel. Then it goes to a toothed wheel, is locked onto it with a cover, makes a loop, goes behind the lens, makes another loop, goes over another toothed wheel, goes down to a sound head (to pick up the audio), then to a last toothed wheel, then around to a take-up reel. The crucial spots are the loops before and after the lens, and the distance from the lens to the sound head. On 16-mm film, the sound track is twenty-six frames (small pictures) ahead of the action. So while the action is at the lens, the sound has to be exactly twenty-six frames ahead of it at the sound head.

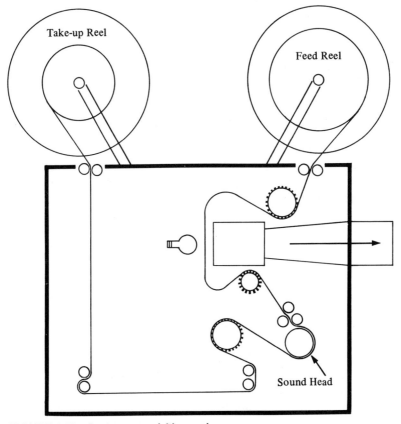

*FIGURE 1.80*   Projector and film path

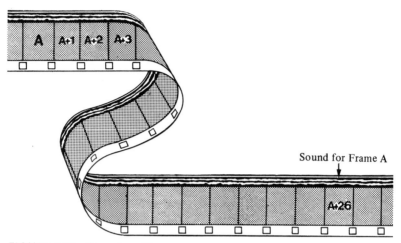

*FIGURE 1.81*   Sound on film

If the sound is twenty or thirty frames away from the action, you get lips moving with different sounds coming out. We've all seen that and know how silly it looks and how distracting it is. So that twenty-six-frame distance is very important, and each projector will have some method to get exactly twenty-six frames from lens to sound head. As to those loops I mentioned, they can be of differing sizes as their purpose is to add some slack to the film. Film doesn't pass smoothly behind the lens, but moves down in jumps, one frame at a time, so you need some slack to allow for the jumps. Without these loops, the film pulls, gets scratched, or even tears. It can also jump on the air, giving that blurred, up-and-down jumble we have all seen from our local stations.

There's one other thing to mention about film. You have seen those countdown numbers before a film starts. That's called *academy leader*, and it gives you a visual reading of how many seconds till the picture starts. Generally, the director will have the film stopped on 3 or 4 so s/he knows s/he has to roll the film three or four seconds before s/he wants it on the air. That's to allow the projector to get up to speed so the sound and picture match up. The point is to roll the film and not put it on the air till the numbers disappear, which they do at 2. Then you know the film is up to speed.

Film isn't the only source of moving pictures that you have. Viedotape provides the same sort of thing, but in a different way. It, like film, is another video input you can use, so let's talk about what it is and how it works.

## VIDEOTAPE

A videotape machine works a lot like an audiotape machine—it uses bits of rust glued on a long strip of plastic to remember both pictures and sound and reproduce them later. I don't suppose anyone in his right mind can tell you why this works. They can give you all sorts of information about oxide particles and impulses and magnetic fields, but the fact remains that you get full-color pictures and high-fidelity sound out of bits of rust, glue, and plastic. The "how" it works is easy; the "why" is nearly impossible.

That's OK though, because all we need to know is the "how." The "why" might satisfy our curiosity, but the videotape will go on giving us pictures and sound whether or not we know why. So let's talk about "how."

Videotape looks a lot like audiotape, except it's generally wider. Some systems have been designed that work off the one-quarter-inch tape we generally think of as audiotape, but the pictures aren't the world's best. They can't be used for broadcasting because they simply do not have enough clarity, Someday maybe they will, but not now. The size of tape for broadcast quality is now generally considered to be two inches. For years that has been the standard size in the industry because that much tape was needed to get sufficient information recorded to allow a good picture to be reproduced. It's like writing home for money. If you're limited to two words ("Send money."), your parents probably won't get the full picture and probably won't send you any. But if you write a complete letter telling all your problems, they may see what you're talking about and send you at least some of what you need. So with videotape, a certain amount of information just plain needs a certain amount of space. Suppose, though, both you and your parents had some sort of magnifying device so you could write on smaller pages and still get as much information across. You'd get the same reaction but use less space. Videotape is developing the same way. More and more, ways are being found to put the essential information on one-inch tape. Lots of places, including some broadcast operations, are using one-inch tape now. It's less bulky, easier to store, and just as useful. So you will probably work with both sizes. And you will undoubtedly encounter three-quarter-inch and maybe even one-half-inch tape. Three-quarter-inch tape is being used in video cassettes for fast recording of news events. These video cassettes are boxes of small lengths of video tape, generally enough to run for several minutes, although cassettes running a half hour, or even longer, are also common. The entire cassette slips into a recorder so you don't have to thread the tape through any long pattern. Once the recorder is loaded with a cassette, all you have to do is punch buttons to get it to run, to record, to playback, and so on. These three-quarter-inch and one-half-inch sizes of tape don't give you room enough to get as high a quality picture as two-inch tape; but various additional machines in the system, like processing amplifiers, will allow you to broadcast from a three-quarter-inch cassette, and the home viewer won't be able to tell the difference. Besides, the recorder for cassettes can be much smaller and lighter than anything used for two-inch tape. News can now use this size of videotape as well as film. Someday, you may even find one-quarter-inch tape good enough, or one-eighth-inch, or . . . . But right now, you will most likely face two-inch, one-inch, and three-quarter-inch tape.

What is videotape? It's a thin strip of plastic with oxidized metal particles glued to one side. When it is on a recorder, it passes by magnets which rearrange those particles into certain patterns. At one point, the magnets rearrange to create an electronic representation of a picture, and at another point, the magnets rearrange to create an electronic representation of sound. So videotape is a way to save certain patterns of metal particles. It's these patterns that can cause electricity to be varied and modified later on, and these modifications can create the pictures and sound we want. Now we have the metal particles, the magnets to put particles in patterns, and a machine to pass the particles by the magnets. What else do we need?

We need pictures and sound coming into the machine. The cameras and mikes turn what we see and hear into electrical signals which are varied and modified as the pictures and sound change. If we send those modified electrical signals into the machine, it can get the signals to the magnets, which can then use the modifications to make the patterns in the metal particles. Later, if we do that in reverse, the patterns in the metal will make the magnets modify an electrical signal so it can affect something very like a camera (but at this point called a receiver) to create the pictures and sound we originally had in the studio. It's all very neat, even if it is incredible.

The upshot is that a videotape recorder will store pictures and sound on videotape and will reproduce those pictures and sound when the videotape is played back on the recorder. As you might guess, the machine is pretty sensitive and has a lot of fine adjustments. Changes in temperature and humidity affect it, kicking it in the side affects it, and dirt affects it. Tobacco smoke puts particles in the air which settle on delicate parts and mess up reactions. Bits of metal oxide from the tape get rubbed off on the magnets and cause them to make bad patterns. So you need to respect the machine itself and the room where it operates. Keep the place clean, keep it cool, and keep it relatively dry. The magnets are located in the recording heads, so clean the heads every so often. Keep the tapes away from heat and dust and *other magnets.* Since the patterns were put on by magnets, any other magnet can re-arrange the patterns. If you put a tape near a magnet, you will lose some of the picture and sound you need. It sounds easy to avoid magnets, but remember that every electrical current flow creates a magnetic field. Even around a light cord there will be a weak magnetic field. So you want to be sure you store tapes away from main power lines or heavy pieces of electrical equipment. The weak fields around light cords won't do much, but it's safer to avoid them anyway.

Now comes the question of what to put on that tape. Obviously, you will want to put on something worth saving. It may be a show to be aired later, or it may be a commercial, or it may be a bit of material which will be used as part of a live show later on. In all of these cases, you simply have a reel of tape on the recorder, start the recorder, do your bit, then stop the recorder. Those are the bare bones, but what about the flesh?

Suppose you are recording a thirty-second commercial to be aired over and over on your station. The reel of tape is on the machine, an engineer is standing by waiting to start the

*FIGURE 1.82* A videotape recorder

machine and be sure it's recording properly, and you have a
studio full of people who know what to do to make an advertise-
ment for underarm neatness.

What do you do first? You ask the engineer to start the
machine recording. When s/he says it's recording, you put what
are called *bars and tone* on the line. Bars are a series of dif-
ferently colored bars making up a picture you can put on the

line. These bars look different to an engineer; s/he sets the adjustments of the recorder to certain points judging by how those bars look technically. S/he does the same thing with tone. Tone is an audio signal of a certain loudness which s/he needs in order to set adjustments. So both bars and tone are references for the engineer—points s/he refers to in making sure everything is running right. So the first thing recorded on the tape is a certain time period of bars and tone. When the tape is played back, this time period lets an engineer get adjustments that match those used in recording. That way, everything works together.

The next thing you put on is *slate*. The purpose of slate is to identify the subject matter so an engineer later doesn't have to watch the whole recording to be sure s/he has the right one. So slate is a listing of the title (or content), the director's name, the date recorded, and whatever else may be pertinent, like the time the recording lasts. In this example, that's thirty seconds. Where does slate come from? It may be a formal piece of equipment on which this information is written, or it may be as informal as a piece of paper with everything on it. You get it on the recording by having a camera shoot a picture of it. Quite often, slate is accompanied by a sound of someone counting backward from eight or so to two. This, too, can be formal and be a flashing number of 8, 7, 6, etc. accompanied by a beep at each number. The point is like that of academy leader in film—it lets you know how many seconds till the picture starts. At 2, as with film, you lose all picture and sound. Then at zero, the commercial, or show, or insert starts. At the end, you have no special series of things to do. You fade to black, kill the audio and ask the engineer to stop the recording. Always be sure you at least get an immediate spot check to see if everything really did get recorded. Machines being what they are, everything can seem perfect but for unknown reasons nothing will be recorded, or it will be recorded badly. If you are doing something short, like our thirty-second commercial, you can watch it all. If you just did an hour show, you may want to check three or four random spots in the show just to see if everything looks right. You can be pretty sure from a random check how the recording went. It's unlikely the machine would stop recording, then start again between the spots you randomly pick.

But suppose something does go wrong. Suppose the machine dropped out of record during a crucial scene. Or suppose part of the set fell over at the end of the show, or you accidentally called for the wrong camera and got a swish pan. What can you do?

You can edit. It used to be people actually cut the tape into pieces, left out the bad part, and pasted the remainder back together. This has a number of drawbacks, not the least of which is its difficulty. Since you can't see a picture on the tape, nor even very clearly the patterns in the metal, it's almost impossible to cut at exactly the right spot. And once the tape is pasted back together, it's thicker where it's joined than anywhere else. This extra thickness does bad things to the heads. So a process has been developed that allows you to edit electronically, and no real cutting is involved.

The trick is all in the electronics, because you have to go out of playback at a specific time and into record. You have to save a portion of a scene and that requires playback. Then at a particular instant you have to put something new in the scene, and that requires recording. So somehow the machine has to switch functions in an instant without adding any extra electronic bumps or wobbles. This switchover is done in one of two ways—by *assembly editing* or by *insert editing*.

Assembly editing is the assembling of bits and pieces that aren't electronically related. What does that mean? Well, normally a videotape recording has the picture, the sound, and a third part called a control track. That track is like the sprocket holes on film except it's all electronic. Imagine it as a series of beeps evenly spaced. The machine moves the tape along smoothly so a beep comes up every second, let us say. If a beep is slightly over a second in arriving, the machine knows it is running slow and so speeds up the tape. If the beep arrives in less than a second, the machine slows down. Think of a record running too fast, or too slow, and you'll instantly have an idea of what a fast or slow videotape would be like. Now, in assembly editing, the pieces are put together without regard to where the beeps are on the control track.

The pieces weren't made together, so they can't match control tracks or much of anything else. At the spot where the machine changes instantly out of playback and goes into record, it adds a new piece of material with a new control track that may have its beep a second and a half away. After that point, the beeps will come at the normal interval of a second apart, but it's the first one that's rough. It can throw the machine off,

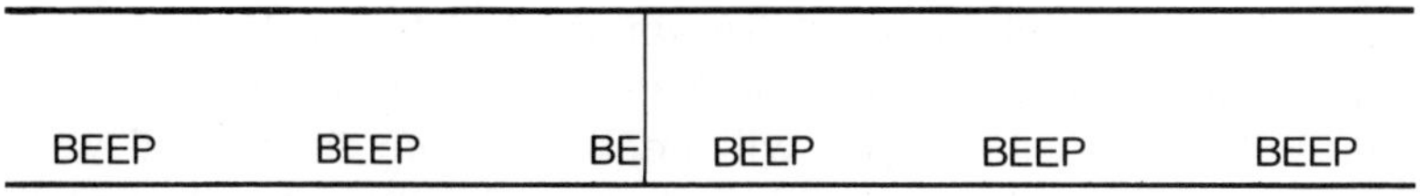

| | | | | | |
|---|---|---|---|---|---|
| BEEP | BEEP | BE | BEEP | BEEP | BEEP |

*FIGURE 1.83*   Assembly editing

the picture can roll, lose color, or any number of bad things. A good machine, a good engineer, and a good bit of planning can minimize these problems; and with a bit of good luck, the initial beep will be very close to the right time. That way, the edit looks fine and the machine doesn't get thrown off.

Insert editing gets around that. Instead of changing totally to record, the machine only changes the video and audio parts into record. That way, the control track remains the same throughout. At the edit point, the machine still has a constant reference of beeps so the picture won't roll, the color won't drop out, and so on. That sounds ideal and makes you wonder why anyone bothers with assembly editing. It's cheaper. The machine that just does assembly editing isn't as complex so it's cheaper. And the edits, if properly done, look just as good. Assembly editing takes more time and care, but it works well for a lot less money. Of course, if you can afford it, insert editing is preferred. Sometimes you must have it. If you expect to do videotape animation, which is a matter of shooting a number of different scenes in one second, you have to be able to get good edits every time. That's got to be done by insert.

So there are ways to correct mistakes made in taping. Remember that editing takes a lot of time, even if everything goes well. You'll never have enough time for what you do, so try to do as little editing as possible. Never depend on editing to create a show for you.

You don't put any material down on tape spontaneously, fresh out of your head. Some time, someone has to sit down and write out what's supposed to happen. That writing gives you a *script.*

## SCRIPTS

What do you want in a script? That depends on what you're going to use it for. If you have to learn the lines and do the acting, you'll need the lines plus indications of what moves you'll have to make and where you'll have to go. If you're the audio person, you'll want a clear indication of how many mikes you will need, where you will need to place them, and what other sound sources you will have. As a director, you'll need all that information, plus indications of what camera is doing what. So somehow we have to pack all that stuff into one form.

I say "one form," but there is no standardized form everyone follows. Some characteristics are common to all scripts, but the variations are endless. That's true of television in general; nothing is set into a rigid pattern. The best way to judge whether or not an approach is right is whether or not it works. So what I'm going to say about scripts is a guideline to follow. Once you have the guideline down pat, feel free to improvise, to change, and to improve.

At the top of the script will go some information about time, date, writer, etc. This varies a great deal from place to place, but it ought to include the title of the script, the time length, the date, the airing date (if known), and the writer's name. Other things included might be the sponsor, the advertising agency involved, the program name, and so on. The heading will look something like this.

```
Title: A Long Day     Air Date: 1/22/77
Time:  14:30          Writer:   Smedley
Date:  1/14/77        Sponsor:  P & G
```

Next will come a brief indication of what the set looks like and what significant action is involved. This helps the director know what to plan for and lets the audio person know where s/he has to place mikes. The directions might run something like this.

```
Two men in L.R., one in chair, one on couch.
Man on couch moves upstage left to desk.
```

Then we get into the major portion of the script, and from here on, the script is divided into two parts. The column on the left is for video information, and the one on the right is for audio. After all I said about no hard and fast rules, this page division can almost be said to be such a rule. Perhaps somewhere there is a station which doesn't use this left–right division, but it's pretty unlikely. So let's assume that script division is one thing you won't change.

The right column is for audio and includes directions, spoken lines, music, and whatever else is heard. There are a couple nonaudio things which get thrown into this column because there is nowhere else to put them, but we will get to them later. Suppose the show starts off with music. The identification of the music source goes into this column. It may be a record and get identified by album name, side, and cut number. It may be on a cart, and the name and number of the cart will be shown. It may be reel to reel tape, and the cut number will be given, and so on. Somehow the sound source has to be identified. Also, the audio person has to know what to do with the music. Does s/he fade it up? Does it start out full? So some directions will be given explaining what the sound does.

```
MUSIC: ("SUNSET SCENES," SIDE
2, CUT 3. UP FULL, ESTABLISH,
THEN UNDER.)
```

We can tell by this that the music is on a record, an album entitled "Sunset Scenes," that the selection is on side 2, and the selection is the third cut on that side. We also know the music starts at full volume, plays long enough to make sense as a theme, then is reduced in volume. So next we would expect something else to come in over the music. Suppose it's an announcer giving a welcome to the show.

```
THEN UNDER.)
ANNCR: It's time now for
another episode of "The
Couples."
```

Here we again identify the sound source, and then we give the lines to be spoken. Notice the difference in spoken and nonspoken information. To make things easier for the actors, the announcers, and anyone else who has to read this script on the air, we make a difference between the spoken and nonspoken parts, and the easiest way to do that is with capital letters and small letters. Whatever is *not* to be read is written in all capitals. Now let's suppose the action is to start. What do we do with the music? We have another couple lines of instructions.

```
                    another episode of "The

                    Couples." George seems to be

                    concerned.

                    MUSIC: DOWN AND OUT.

                    FRED: It seems to me . . . .
```

The music fades out altogether and the actors begin. Once more we identify the sound sources (by using their names in capitals) and separate the read from the non-read.

If there are stage directions for the actors, they get thrown into this audio column. These directions might be: "(FRED MOVES TO THE DESK.)" or they might be: "GEORGE: (WITH CONCERN) Now Fred . . . ." In any case, they go in capitals.

Notice also that directions get separated from the identification of sound sources by being put in parentheses. That way the audio person can spot all the sound sources s/he has to deal with by scanning through the script looking for all capitals out of parentheses. This speeds up figuring out what mikes s/he needs, what channels s/he needs on the board, etc.

Let's switch over now to the video column and catch up with the audio column. At the beginning, when we have music for our audio, we need some picture on the screen. It would be logical to assume we start out with a title, so let's assume that.

```
T.C.                MUSIC: ("SUNSET SCENES," SIDE
(The Couples)       2, CUT 3. UP FULL, ESTABLISH,
```

"T.C." stands for "title card," but that doesn't mean such a card will always have a title on it. That's a general name for a card with *something* on it which will be shot by a camera. That *something* may be a picture, a name, a price, a title, or any of a number of such items. And it gets called a great many things—title card, art card, flip card, graphic card, camera card, and so on. I arbitrarily chose the name "title card," so that's what my "T.C." means. Beneath that abbreviation, in parentheses, is an indication of what's on the card. The indication may be exact, as in this case, or it may be a general description of what's there. A general description is necessary when the T.C. has a picture—"woman posing in fur coat." Notice that this bit of video information goes directly across from the portion of audio it goes with. As the music starts, so does the picture. It stays on till the audio changes to Fred saying his first line.

```
Cover                    FRED: It seems to me . . . .
(George & Fred)
```

Then we have new video directions. The abbreviation "Cover" is short for "cover shot." That means to show everything that's important in the shot. In this case, according to the directions under "Cover," that's George and Fred. Later on, we get a close-up of the two actors, and that will be indicated in the video column like this.

```
CU                       GEORGE: Now Fred, she
(George)                 wasn't . .
```

Now that we have an idea of the basic elements of a script, let's look further at this one and see what else may come into it.

```
T.C.                     MUSIC: ("SUNSET SCENES," SIDE
(The Couples)            2, CUT 3. UP FULL, ESTABLISH,
                         THEN UNDER.
                         ANNCR: It's time now for
                         another episode of "The
                         Couples." The party's about
                         to begin, but George seems to
                         be concerned.
```

| | |
|---|---|
| Cover<br>(George & Fred) | FRED: (LOOKING OUT WINDOW) I hope Helen gets back before the first guests arrive.<br>GEORGE: I'm sure she will, Fred. She's never late. |
| CU<br>(Fred) | FRED: (SMILING) Yes, you can always depend on Helen. |
| CU<br>(George) | GEORGE: (WITH CONCERN) But what if she is late just this once? How will we explain that to the guests? |
| Cover<br>(Fred & George) | FRED: (MOVING TO DESK) Maybe she left us a note saying where she went. I'll look in the desk. |
| T.C.<br>(The Couples) | ANNCR: We'll be back to the exciting action right after this word. |
| SOF<br>(Sunshine Soap) | SOF: :30 (Has your skin . . . . be sure you pick up the beauty bundle of Sunshine Soap today.) |

First of all, notice the script is double spaced. Sometimes, it's even better to triple space the copy. That makes it easier to read and easier to mark up when you make corrections or indicate changes. The only parts not double spaced are the explanations under the video directions. Next you notice the video column doesn't give the director any indication of how to get from shot to shot. Generally a script won't. If transitions are important, or as the writer or producer acquires more control over how the show is done, directions like "Dissolve to . . . ." or "Box wipe in . . . ." will appear. But a director is expected to be able to get from shot to shot without help, so quite often the listing is simply of what shot follows what. For example, on this script the director would probably fade to black after Fred says he will look in the desk and then fade up on the title card. From there s/he would cut to the film.

What new information does the video column have? Those abbreviations. CU is close-up, and SOF is sound on film. Silent film is generally indicated SIL. You also have the length of the film—in this case, thirty seconds. I've put it in the audio column here and not in the video column, but it fits equally well in either column. Where it goes depends on the habits or preferences of each individual station. There are a lot of other abbreviations. Most are obvious if you think about them. ECU or XCU both mean extreme close-up. LS is a long shot. MS is medium shot. Some samples are illustrated in Figure 1.84. But when T.C. is listed, there is no other indication of the size of the shot because the only way to shoot it is so the screen is filled. Now how about the audio column?

The only new thing here is in connection with the film. The source is identified (SOF), and all that in parentheses is part of what is said. No one, neither the actors, the director, nor the audio person, needs to know every word on the film. But several do need to know what the first few words are and what the last ones are. We know from the video column it's a film about Sunshine Soap, but there are dozens of different films it could be. By having the first few words, we will know instantly if we are running the right film. If not, then there's a problem to work out, but if it's the right film, we also want to know the ending words. Sure, we have the time of the film, but it's often easier to listen for an ending cue than to watch time. So for any recording, whether on film or videotape, the script should have the time, an indication of content, a few words as an in-cue and several words as an out-cue. The more words you can give as an out-cue, up to a limit of about a dozen, the better off the director will be.

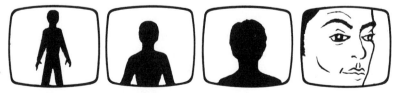

*FIGURE 1.84*   Various shots

When you come to the end of a page, never split a sentence. Even if you have to end with the bottom third of the page empty, never split a sentence. Try not to split a paragraph or a speech if you can avoid it. When you come to the end of a line, never split a word. At the end of a page, put "(MORE)."

```
                    no more to be said about that.

          (MORE)
```

At the top of the next page, put an indication of what the script is about and a page number.

```
                              "Couples" Page 2
```

Sometimes you will find the second page listed as ADD 1, the third page as ADD 2, and so on. That's just an indication of the addition of one or two to the first page. Since the numbers don't match the actual number of pages, this is not my favorite form, but it is commonly used.

At the end of the script, and centered like (MORE), put a symbol to indicate you're through. The most commonly used symbols are -0-, # # # # #, -30-, $$$$$, ¢¢¢¢¢, and sometimes even -END-.

This script form is used for commercials, dramas, musical reviews, situation comedies, talk shows, and every other sort of show except one—news. News shows have a particular script format like no other, so let's see how it differs.

The major difference is that everything to be read is in CAPITALS and everything *not* read is in normal upper- and lower-case letters. The reason is to make it easy for the newsperson. News copy comes across wire machines like AP or UPI in all capitals. If a newsperson is on the air when a fast-breaking story hits the wire machines, the copy will be ripped off the machine and slipped onto the desk while s/he is on the air. If it matches the look of the on-air script, s/he will be less likely to falter and stammer on the air and sound foolish. So news scripts are typed in capitals to match the wire copy.

Another common difference is that instead of identifying

the newsperson each time, since s/he generally doesn't change from night to night, the video column will just list "Live On."

```
Live On              IN THE WAR TODAY, THE WEEKLY

                     REPORT OF PROGRESS WAS

                     ISSUED . . . .
```

Notice too that the audio column doesn't list the newscaster's name. If there are two anchorpeople, this won't work, and they will be individually identified in the video column.

```
Smith                AND WAS RELEASED.

Jones                BUT THE ATTORNEY GENERAL'S

                     OFFICE
```

Still, though, the names do *not* appear in the audio column. That's a reverse situation in news copy.

The end symbol like "-0-" is used at the end of every news story, not just at the end of the script. This helps the newspeople know how to emphasize sentences while reading. Also, only one news story at a time goes on a page. A news story may run to several pages, but if it finishes at the top of the third page, never put another story on the bottom of that page. That's because the newsperson and director have to confer and make changes over an intercom system in the very short bits of time while a commercial is running or a news film is on. It's faster and more certain to say "Kill page 3" than to say "Kill the story at the bottom of page 3."

A particular T.C. also appears in news scripts quite often, and sometimes in other scripts. That's the super T.C.

```
Slide                PRESIDING AT TODAY'S

(Wilson)             CONFERENCE WAS FRED WILSON,

Super T.C.           PRESIDENT OF THE AMERICAN

(Wilson)             ASSOCIATION OF . . .
```

In this case, the basic picture is of "Wilson." Another camera will shoot a black card with white lettering "Wilson" on it. As you know, that can be matted or keyed over the picture. So the total picture you get is illustrated in Figure 1.85. Obviously, this "super T.C." idea can be used over a film, a videotape, a reporter in the studio reading his copy, and all sorts of other shots. But a super T.C. is always a bit of white lettering on a black card.

News also uses chroma key quite a bit. Generally, a particular camera will be the only one which can be used for chroma-key effects. So the script will have to indicate when the news-person turns to the other camera as well as what goes into the chroma-key shot. It may be listed like this:

```
                       (Turn)
Chroma                 AND IN IRELAND TODAY, THE
(Map-N. Ireland)       GOVERNMENT REPORTED A SERIES
                       OF . . . .
```

Because all scripts are to be read, you will want them clear for easy reading. So if a word is hard to pronounce, especially a foreign name, you will often find a pronunciation given right in the script just like this: ". . . and Prime Minister Cholmonde-ley (CHUM-LEE) announced . . . ." Also, because you are writing to time and because you will get in the habit of judging

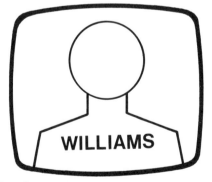

*FIGURE 1.85*   Identification in news

time by the amount of copy you write, it's safer to write out all numbers, especially in commercial copy. That more closely approximates the time it takes to say the numbers. If your copy is full of "$1.98" and "only $3.49," and you write only a half page of copy, you may still find it takes longer to read this than a normal full page of your copy. Even write out the numbers for something like "Born in nineteen fifty-three, he . . . ."

Following are two sample scripts containing a great number of the situations you will be faced with. The first script is the normal dramatic variety, and the second is a news script. If you come upon a situation you don't find handled here, remember the point of a script is to convey clearly what needs to be done. Figure out a common-sense, plain way to write it.

```
Title: Puttmobile        Sponsor: Puttmobile
Time:  :60               Writer:  Brubaker
Date:  1/15/77
```

```
First set is Mary sitting in chair, John on arm.
Plain background. Second set is car on shiny floor
with varied colors lighting up background.
```

| | |
|---|---|
| Cover | MUSIC: ("FANFARES," SIDE 1, |
| (Mary & John) | CUT 2. HOLD UNDER.) |
| | MARY: Have you heard about the |
| | new Puttmobile? |
| | JOHN: It's all new for this |
| | year, with all the features |
| | you're looking for. |
| | MUSIC: (FADE OUT.) |
| Cover | MARY: The grand sweep of its |
| (Puttmobile) | design is sure to please. |

(MORE)

Puttmobile Page 2

CU
(Front bumper)

MS
(John & rear of
car)

SIL    :08
(Car hitting wall)

MS
(John in driver's
seat)

Slide
(Instrument Panel)
ECU
(Oil gauge)

From front bumper to rear
lights, it's all new this
year. (WALKS INTO PIC AT HOOD
OF CAR.) These energy-
absorbing bumpers protect you
from damage for anything up to
ten miles an hour.

JOHN: And at over ten miles
per hour, they help hold
damage down to a minimum. This
helps hold down your insurance
costs.

MARY: Here you can see the
new Puttmobile demonstrating
how safe it is. Notice there's
no damage at all to the car.

JOHN: And surrounding the
driver are all the controls
and protections he could ever
want. This shoulder belt
(PICKS UP BELT) will help
keep you in place no matter
what happens. And up where
the driver can see everything,
the Puttmobile has instruments
to tell you how well your car
is doing. There's even a gauge
to tell you when the oil is
low!

(MORE)

Puttmobile Page 3

| | |
|---|---|
| Cover<br>(Mary, John, Car) | MARY: But don't just take our word for it. Listen to these satisfied owners. |
| VTR<br>(Bald Man) | VTR:  :09 (It's probably the finest . . . you get what you pay for in a Puttmobile.) |
| Slide<br>(Woman) | CART:  :07 (This is the easiest . . . my driving safer and more enjoyable.) |
| SOF<br>(Man & kids) | SOF:  :08 (I feel safer . . . for a big family, it's ideal.) |
| Cover<br>(Mary, John, Car) | MUSIC: (REEL 4, SIDE 1, CUT 1. UNDER AND HOLD.)<br>JOHN: You'll be just as satisfied as these people were when you own a Puttmobile.<br>(TURN AND PRETEND TO TALK WITH MARY.) |
| Super T.C.<br>(Jones Bros.<br>Puttm.) | ANNCR: Drop in soon at Jones Brothers Puttmobile and look at the ideal car. You'll be delighted!<br>MUSIC: (UP AND OUT.) |

-0-

West Virginia mine
15 Jan. 1977
Bell

Live On

THERE'S BEEN ANOTHER MINE
DISASTER TODAY IN THE HILLS
OF WEST VIRGINIA. IT ALL
BEGAN WITH THE MORNING SHIFT
COMING TO WORK AT UNITED
COAL'S NUMBER SEVEN MINE.
(Turn)

Chroma
(Map showing town)

THE MINE IS OUTSIDE TWO
WHISTLE, WEST VIRGINIA AND IS
THE ONLY INDUSTRY IN THE
LITTLE TOWN OF TWENTY-ONE
HUNDRED. AT EIGHT THIS
MORNING, THE NEW SHIFT WAS
ARRIVING FOR WORK. WHAT
HAPPENED NEXT IS REPORTED TO
US BY JEFF BELSKY OF STATION
WSAB IN HUNTINGTON, WEST
VIRGINIA.

VTR
(Belsky)
Super T.C.
(Jeff Belsky)
Live On

VTR:  2:02 (As the first men
arrived . . . .trying to
rescue the trapped miners for
over ten hours now.)
THE EXACT CAUSE OF THE
EXPLOSION IS AS YET UNKNOWN,
BUT WE WERE ABLE TO TALK TO A
COMPANY SAFETY ENGINEER ON THE
PHONE THIS AFTERNOON. HE GAVE
US HIS OPINION ON A POSSIBLE
CAUSE.

(MORE)

West Va. Mine Page 2

| | |
|---|---|
| Slide<br>(Engineer)<br>Super T.C.<br>(D. N. Perkins<br>Mine Engineer)<br>SIL    :24<br>(Outside Mine)<br>Slide<br>(Engineer) | Cart:  1:03 (It's possible the<br>engine . . . of course we<br>won't know until an<br>investigation is completed.) |
| Live On | DICK MELODY TALKED TO SOME OF<br>THE FAMILIES OF THE TRAPPED<br>MINERS, AND HERE IS HIS<br>REPORT. |
| SOF<br>(Melody interview) | SOF  1:41 (This sort of<br>disaster . . . can only stand<br>by and pray now. Dick Melody<br>at Two Whistle, West<br>Virginia.) |

-0-

As a director, what do you do with these scripts? Obviously, they will work as a guide for what to show on the air, and they will let you know what should be coming up next in the way of sounds. You'll want to make various marks on these scripts to remind yourself what to do when. The more you have written down on the script and the more you do automatically, the less you have to think about during the show. That leaves more of your mind free to concentrate on how to overcome the mistakes that happen, or how to get from place to place more smoothly. You'll have enough going on around you without having to figure out all over again when to give time cues or where you had decided to cut to another shot. So let's talk about some ways to mark up a script.

For many scripts, you won't need to write in anything about the content of individual shots. That's done for you with something like "CU (Fred's face)." You may, however, want to write in sometime to indicate a slow dissolve or a cut or a corner wipe. A symbol will work better than words as the script already has enough words on it. You can make up your own symbols, but something like ↓ directly above a direction like CU might mean "cut to a close-up." A symbol like ⟨⟩ is used in film for dissolves, and you might find it handy. Drawing a box wipe is probably the best bet for that symbol ▣ . In commercial scripts, I've found it handy to mark right in the copy at the point I want to change shots. That's because the commercial copy is often written with only vague relation to the visual elements. So I've done something like this.

| | |
|---|---|
| Slide | Or you may want to choose |
| (Evening Dress) | from the large and elegant |
| | collection of couturier styles |
| | for evening wear. Set off that |
| | sparkling dress with the proper |
| Slide | accessories, ⌐the evening |
| (Ev. bag & shoes) | bag, and the right shoes. No |
| | outfit is really complete |
| | until . . . . |

The change ought to come in the middle of a line, so I put half a box over the word where I change to the next slide. In this case, I dissolve to the next slide because the copy needs the slowness and lack of abruptness of a dissolve.

Until you know your preparatory commands so well that you are calling them by habit, you may want to write them and the commands of execution into the script. Eliminate them as soon as you can, though, for the script's sake. It gets jumbled. But one command of preparation you may want to retain. If you are going to a videotape, and you must have a six-second roll to get up to speed, you may want to mark a spot in the copy where six seconds comes and write in something like "roll

VTR." All of this will get you from shot to shot at the right time and in the right way. How can you be sure that the shots are there?

If you think you might forget to ask a camera to move to a new shot, or if you think the cameraperson might forget to make the move, even though you have rehearsed forty-seven times, you may want to write in on the script something like "Camera 2 move to the two shot." This might be abbreviated on the script as "2–2 shot," which would be enough to remind you to give the command.

You will want to have some indication on the script of which camera gets which shot, as well as reminding yourself to tell a camera to move. Let's take the situation of the "2–2 shot" and see how to indicate the camera numbers.

CU

(Electric Skillet)

*2*

can't go wrong with this wrapped in that special paper and given to that special person on your list. And it comes with our famous two-year guarantee.

MS

(Mary)

*2–2 shot*

MARY: I know I'd like one, John, and so would any woman. Christmas is so much nicer with a present from Brown's Department Store.

Cover

(John & Mary)

*2*

JOHN: So come in soon. Remember, only forty-eight more shopping days till Christmas.

-0-

The camera numbers go in the video column near the description of the shot. Write them in with pencil if you can. That way you can change around the order and not mess up the script with scratch-outs. If you want to take a camera on a particular word, as we did here with Camera 2, you can indicate exactly where with a half-box over the word.

A good deal of your directing may be commercials and news. These can be the staples of many stations. So you may find it convenient to make marks at the bottom of a page indicating whether there is more on a following page or if it's the end. I know I've talked about symbols like "-0-" but only in reference to that one topic. Suppose you are directing a station break with three commercials in it. Each commercial has a "-0-" at the end to indicate that *one* spot has no more pages of script. But you may have more spots to follow. So you may want to adopt something like an arrow to show there's another spot. An arrow with a couple lines in front of it can indicate that's the end.

You may want to adopt marks very like those shown in Figure 1.86 in marking a news script to indicate where the commercial breaks come. An arrow with a couple lines at the bottom of the page on *both* your script and the newsperson's will indicate that's where the break comes and s/he is to stop reading.

Any special audio cues or changes you may want to underline in the copy. That makes them stand out even more than the capitals they are typed in do. If you have special things you

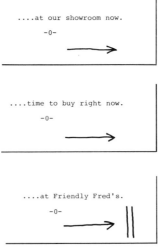

*FIGURE 1.86*   Director's marks

are doing with audio, you may want to write them into the video column rather than jumble up the audio column further. But it's generally smart to run at least an arrow from the audio column out to your extra command so you won't overlook it as you follow down the audio column.

Don't keep your eyes glued on the script, however. Television is a visual medium so you have to watch the monitors. Take a glance at the script, run your finger along with the copy so you have a rough idea where the place is, but don't follow every word. You will soon learn to listen, hear three or four words, and scan a page to pick them out. You'll do that fast enough to keep up. Know what the last words are on the page so you'll know when to go on to the next page. But keep your eyes up.

You now have the script with its markings, the films and slides loaded on the film island, the carts and records in the audio person's hands, the cameras ready to go, and the actors on the set. How do you know when to start? Where do commercials go? How much time do you have? This and dozens of other questions are answered by a glance at the daily log.

## TV LOGS

Logs are the road maps prepared by the traffic department. They tell exactly what events happen at what times throughout the entire broadcast day. Because of that, everyone involved in production ends up regularly looking at the log. Engineers check to see what videotapes are to be played and when, film editors look for films and film numbers, announcers see when breaks come and if anything is to come from the announcer's booth rather than from audio carts, and directors check to see what commercials come up and whether they are live, or on tape, or on film. After the day is finished, the log goes to the accounting department, which uses it to bill sponsors for the commercials which ran. Much later, at license-renewal time, the FCC looks at certain days' logs to see how the station has performed. Obviously, the log is quite useful and valuable to the station, so we need to take a closer look at it.

Suppose you are directing an afternoon talk show, done live from your studios. What information must the log give you?

First of all, if you are directing the break before the show begins, you will need to know exactly when the preceding show, a soaper named "Life and Happiness," ends. Then you will need to know what commercials go into the break. So the log will start something like this:

```
         Life and Happiness
3:58:58  Boch Oldsmobile
3:59:28  Stop & Shop Supermarkets
3:59:58  ID
4:00:00  The Virginia Douglas Show
```

But you need more information than this. You need to know if the Oldsmobile spot is live, on film, or on videotape. Probably it's on VTR. But which one? So you need a number. There's also a possibility the announcer will have to say something at the end, so you need to know where the audio comes from. You'll have two columns, one for video and one for audio. The FCC will also want to know what sort of announcement this is—for pay, for free, as a public service, and so on. A separate column will list the type of spot. Below is an example of a typical log entry.

|         | Title | Audio | Video | Type |
|---------|-------|-------|-------|------|
|         | Life and Happiness | Net | Net | Net |
| 3:58:58 | Boch Oldsmobile | VTR #4 | VTR #4 | CA |
| 3:59:28 | Stop & Shop Supermarkets | F #38 Annc. Tag | F #38 S #12 | CA |
| 3:59:58 | ID | C #7 | C #7 | ID |
| 4:00:00 | The Virginia Douglas Show | Live | Live | Var. |

The video column lists what's going on (VTR for videotape, F for film, S for slide, L for live, etc.), plus an identification number (videotape #2032, slide #42, etc.). The audio column lists where the sound comes from (for example, from the film with a tag live from the announce booth over a slide at the end of the spot). In the column for type we are told these are commercial announcements (CA) or public service announcements (PSA) or station identifications (ID) or whatever. All the abbreviations will be explained on the bottom of the page.

Because things don't always go the way they should, the log also has room to list comments and to list the actual time any event goes on and goes off. That way, if everything gets delayed by a machine malfunction, but still goes on, the right time can be listed along with an explanation for the delay. Furthermore, the spots listed within a show itself aren't listed with a time.

```
4:00:00   The Virginia Douglas Show
          Milady's Frocks
          Thompson Jewelers
          D & H Drugs
          Etc.
```

These come whenever the hostess pitches for them, so no set time can be given. So the log has to have a place to list when they ran. The on and off columns allow for that. You will, in addition, have a column listing the length of spots so in situations like this you can tell how long they should run. On other spots, you could subtract the times listed for when the spots run, but here that maneuver is impossible, so the log will provide a run-down of all lengths, just to make sure everything is covered.

These are the major categories any station needs on a log. Some stations may want other columns for specific purposes, like a column for checks by the official log keeper (generally the booth announcer) to verify that spots ran, or a sign in–sign off column for announcer changeovers, but these columns provide at least the minimum of information needed.

A companion to the log is the book. Every event on the log also has a page in the book repeating some of the information and giving even more. The book is intended primarily for the director and the announcer. Let's look at that film spot for Stop & Shop Supermarkets. It has a booth tag over it, but how is the announcer supposed to know what to say? S/he will have a page in the book like this:

```
Stop & Shop        END CUE: (:20) (. . . YOU CAN
Film #38 :30       DEPEND ON.)
Slide #12          ANNCR: Save this week on Stop
(Logo)             and Shop's special on round
                   steak. Be sure to stop at
                   Stop and Shop.

                   -0-
```

Now the announcer knows what to say and when (after twenty seconds and the end cue), and the director knows how to end the spot. The film can't just run out, the announcer has to read his copy. If a particular slide were to be matted over the end of the film, it would have been listed, *and described*, with a phrase like "14¢ a lb." and directions like "Over film." The log gives only a number; it's the book that tells you "This week, 49¢ a lb." That's a good double check in case the number gets mistyped on the log. The director checks his slides before going on the air, so he can spot possible errors.

So between the book and the log, both prepared daily by the traffic department, everyone in the station knows what to do and when to do it. If any changes have to be made, they must be made in ink and dated and initialed because the log becomes a legal document once it's finished. After all, the FCC uses it to check on what the station's doing, and the accounting department uses it as proof that commercials really did run. The log and the book are not only useful, they are essential.

Now you have all the materials assembled for a show. What you need next is a director to make things happen.

## DIRECTING

So the day arrives when you have to walk into the control room, put on a headset, and tell everyone on the crew what to do and when to do it. You are the *director*! You know you have to tell two camerapeople what shots to get while giving information to the floor manager to pass on to the talent, while telling the audio person what mike to hit or what record to start, while telling the technical director (T.D.) how to go from one shot to another while watching fifteen monitors, while . . . . How will you ever have time to follow the script? To listen to what the actors are saying? To check on the next slide? To figure out how much time is left, and so on? Every member of the crew has a lot to think about, but as the director, you will have to cover your own concerns, plus everyone else's, and sometimes come up with answers before anyone else realizes there is a problem. That's what the director is faced with, but how do you handle it all?

Let's set up a sample situation and see just what the director has to do to make it work right. Suppose you're directing a local talk-variety show. The host has just pitched by saying "We'll be right back after these messages." You have to run a :30 film commercial, a :30 live studio spot, and a :30 VTR spot with a live announcer tag, then get back into the show. You have a band in the studio for the show and it plays music as you leave for the break. The film spot has a three-second roll (check the end of the *Projection* section), the live spot has two close-ups, a cover, a music bed, a price matted in at the end, and all the audio from the booth announcer. The VTR spot has a store name matted over the last seven seconds, has a six-second roll, and has a booth tag. Then it's straight back to the host. His show is over at 5:28:30, so you'll have to tell him how much time he'll have left after the spots finish. No one else will be talking on the headsets, so here is how it goes.

*Host:*   We'll be right . . .

*Director:*   One, zoom out. Two, break for your close-up. Stand by to roll the film, and stand by to hit the film sound.

*Host:*   back after these messages. (Music starts.)

*Director:*   Stand by to fade to black. Stand by to hit the film. Roll the film. Fade to black. Take the film. Hit the sound. (Director starts the stop watch and notices real time on the wall clock. It is 5:13:38.) One, break for your close-up. Plus 1:30 (length of spots) is 15:08. From 28:30 is 13:22. Tell Bob (host) he'll have almost thirteen and a half coming back. (S/he checks monitors to see if shots are right—they are.) I'll want a matt of that slide (the price) over two at the end of this. Music cued? (Audio says yes.) Seven seconds left in the film. Ready booth. Stand by to cut to two. Ready to bring music under. Take two, music under, booth. (S/he resets the stop watch. S/he looks at the script to see when the next shot should come.) Ready to dissolve to one. Dissolve to one. Two, break for your cover. Ready to dissolve to two. (S/he checks the script again.) Dissolve to two. Ready to dissolve in a matt of slide over two. Stand by to roll VTR. Dissolve in effect. Roll VTR. Ready to bring music up, then down and out. (Announcer finishes reading.) Bring music up, down, and out. Hit VTR. Hit sound. Change slide. (S/he resets stop watch.) One, break for cover of Bob. Two, break for close-up of guest. Stand by to cut to matt of slide over VTR. Ten seconds left. Ready booth. (Floor manager relays ten-second cue to host. Cut to effect. Booth. Stand by to fade to black. Stand by to fade up on one and stand by to open Bob's mike. (Floor manager gives a stand-by cue to the host.) Fade out, up on one, open his mike, and cue him.

It's over. The host is back, the spots ran, and everyone knew what to do. The director controlled eight other people, gave each of them the information s/he needed just as s/he needed it, and kept the pieces together as a unified whole. The director's language was quite specific, with few extra or wasted words. Some preparation beforehand made things easier; s/he had rehearsed the shots for the live spot so each cameraperson knew what s/he was to get. The director and the audio person had checked out the record which was to be used for music in that spot. S/he had gone through the slides before the show started to see they were in the right order. But let's take a closer look at what s/he did, because it still seems pretty miraculous that everything worked.

Let's start with the language. The crew won't do anything until s/he tells them to, because they assume s/he knows better than they what needs to be done, so they don't want to risk a mistake by doing something s/he doesn't ask for. So s/he has to tell them precisely what to do. But s/he wants them forewarned, so s/he starts off with a "ready" command, or a "stand by" command, before s/he gives the "action" command. That is, s/he says something like "Stand by to cut to one" so that the T.D. gets ready to punch the right button and so one's cameraperson gets a steady shot. Then s/he can say "Cut to one" and both the T.D. and the cameraperson are set to give the director what s/he wants exactly when s/he wants it.

The exact language isn't important. S/he can say "Stand by to . . ." or "Ready to . . ." or "Prepare to . . ." or anything else that works so long as s/he warns everyone rapidly and accurately. With very few exceptions ("Change slide."), a ready command always precedes an action command.

Keep the commands short because you don't have much time, and be sure they are accurate. If you say "Ready to go to one," your T.D. can dissolve or cut or even fade out and fade back up on one. But if you say "Ready to cut to one," there's no doubt what sort of transition you will get, unless your T.D. goofs up. Likewise, if you say "Stand by to start the audio," you may get the record when you want the cart or the studio mike, and the sound may fade in instead of starting full. If you say "Stand by to hit the cart," everyone knows what s/he should hear. There's also a concern of accuracy in talking to camerapeople. Don't say "One, get me a better shot." Tell that person to dolly in or tilt up or pan right or whatever you think will work. In talking to camerapeople, start out by giving the camera number, so they know who you're talking to. "One, pan left. Two, break for a cover shot." Don't confuse *pan* and *tilt*. A good cameraperson starts tensing the right muscles at the first sound of a command. "One . . ." A particular cameraperson's ears and brain perk up. ". . .p" s/he gets ready to go left or right. ". . .pan up." The muscles get confused and reaction time is slowed. If s/he's on the air, you'll miss a bit of the shot you wanted. Say, "One, tilt up," and you'll get faster, slicker, more professional production.

Having said all this about language, let's go back to that spot break and follow the director's conversation. S/he knows, by the host's comment, that a break is coming up.

HOST: We'll be
right . . .

DIRECTOR: One, zoom out.    *S/he has camera one on a close-up of the host and tells that camera to zoom out to a cover shot so s/he'll have a little time to get everything going.*

Two, break for your close-up.    *Camera two has been on a close-up of the guest and needs to be told what the next shot will be, so s/he says it is a close-up and the camera-*

*person knows to go over for a shot of one of the products being sold in the upcoming commercial. The director and the camerapeople have run through this spot before the show, so both camerapeople know what to get.*

Stand by to roll the film, and stand by to hit the film sound.

*Next, the director tells the projectionist to get ready to start the film and tells the audio person to be ready to hit the film sound. Automatically, the audio person will kill other sound sources, such as the music coming over the mikes in the studio.*

HOST: back after these messages.

DIRECTOR: Stand by to fade to black. Stand by to hit the film.

*S/he tells the T.D. to stand by to fade out from the studio, then cut directly to the film. At this point, s/he has warned the audio person, the T.D., the camerapeople, and the projectionist. These are the "ready" commands. Now come the "action" commands.*

Roll the film.

*Because the film has to roll before s/he can take it, s/he calls for that first.*

Fade to black. Take the film. Hit the sound.

*Then a fade, a cut, and a sound cue. S/he has to know how long the film will run, so as soon as it starts, s/he starts the stop watch. That way s/he'll know when the :30 is up. S/he also checks the time on the wall clock, and tells the other cameraperson where to go next.*

One, break for your close-up.

Plus 1:30 is 15:08. From 28:30 is 13:22. Tell Bob he'll have almost 13 and a half coming back.

*S/he quickly figures time cues and passes the information on to the floor manager so the host will know what he should do, and whether he should stretch or rush.*

I'll want a matt of that slide over the end of this.

*At this point, s/he's no longer thinking about the film. S/he's worrying about the next event, which starts when the stop watch gets to thirty. This is always true. Once an event gets on the air, don't waste any more time on it. Go on to the next item. Even if what's on the air is wrong, go to the next thing. If something is wrong, and you are properly preparing the next item, you have something to go to which will cover the error now showing. You have to stay anywhere from three to thirty seconds ahead of what's on the air. If your time and air time match, you're in trouble. You have no idea where to go next. That next event is the live spot. It has two close-ups of products, then a cover of both, plus a matt, music, and the announcer reading the commercial copy from the booth. But take it one step at a time. The first shot is ready, as the camera broke for it way back before the film started running. The second shot is ready. A monitor check shows that, plus the slide for use at the end. The director has told the T.D. what s/he will do with that slide later on.*

Music cued?

*S/he asks audio about the music, and because they rehearsed earlier, audio knows what music s/he is referring to. Now the director knows the elements s/he needs are there, so s/he starts on the "ready" commands.*

Seven seconds left in the film. Ready booth. Stand by to cut to two. Ready to bring music under.

*S/he warns the announcer.*

*S/he tells the T.D. what s/he will want.*

*S/he prepares the audio person. By implication of what s/he says to the T.D., the cameraperson on two knows s/he should get ready.*

| | |
|---|---|
| Take two, music under, booth. | *The time on the film runs out, and the "action" commands start. A shot, music, and copy.* |
| Ready to dissolve to one. | *S/he warns both the T.D. and Camera one of what's next.* |
| Dissolve to one. Two, break for your cover. | *S/he gets to the next shot, and immediately tells the now free camera two what to do next. One, of course, holds its close-up.* |
| Ready to dissolve to two. | *While that's on the air, s/he goes on to the next thing, and gives a "ready" command. To the T.D. and camera-person s/he announces the transition to the next shot.* |
| Dissolve to two. | *S/he gives the action command, and goes to the next item.* |
| Ready to dissolve in a matt of slide over two. Stand by to roll VTR. | *S/he tells the T.D. what s/he wants next and warns the projectionist about the upcoming VTR. S/he has to roll it six seconds before this spot ends so it will come up right on time.* |
| Dissolve in effect.<br><br>Roll VTR<br>Ready to bring music up, down, and out. | *S/he calls for the final shot in the live commercial,*<br>*rolls the tape,*<br>*then warns the audio person with a "ready" command of what s/he wants to do with the sound.* |
| Bring music up, down, and out. Hit VTR. Hit sound. | *The announcer finishes, the director calls for the music change, gets into the VTR, and uses "action" commands to do it all. Now s/he gives a command which needs no "ready" command.* |
| Change slide. | *"Ready" commands are to prepare people to react fast. With this slide off the air, it really doesn't matter how fast the reaction time is, so long as the next slide gets up within the next few seconds. If it were a slide change on the air, the director might indeed give a ready command, but off* |

*the air doesn't matter. That's true of off-air camera moves as well. Now we are into the tape spot. Next s/he worries about what happens at the end of the spot and afterwards.*

One, break for cover of Bob. Two, break for close-up of guest.

*S/he tells both cameras what shots to get.*

Stand by to cut to matt of slide over VTR.

*S/he gives a "ready" command to the T.D. about the end of the VTR.*

Ten seconds left.

*Time cues, like other off-air activity, need no ready commands, so s/he just announces the time. This is a very important cue, however. Without this indication, the studio situation may not be in control so the director can come back to the host. Time is of vital importance in broadcasting, so treat it with respect.*

Ready booth.
Cut to effects. Booth.

*S/he prepares the announcer. After two "action" commands, the tape spot goes into its final part.*

Stand by to fade to black.

*Three "ready" commands, one to the T.D.,*

Stand by to fade up on one, and

*one to the T.D. and cameraperson,*

stand by to open Bob's mike.

*and one to the audio person, and the director's ready to hit the show again.*

Fade out, up on one, open his mike, and cue him.

*Four fast "action" commands in one sentence and the director is back into the show and already thinking of what s/he will do next.*

Those eight people, the T.D., the two camerapeople, the audio person, the projectionist, the floor manager, the booth announcer, and the host, have all been told what to do one at a time and in a working sequence. They were, most of them, first warned to get ready and then told to start. The director kept them all in mind, plus checking scripts, clocks, monitors, and speakers. S/he worried first about the video portion of an event, then the audio. For example, s/he talked of fading to black, rolling the film, then hitting the film sound. For the next spot, s/he got the camera shots set first, then worried about the music and the booth announcer. S/he tried to give everyone as much preparation time as possible. S/he told the camera-people where to go next as soon as they were freed from an on-air shot and as soon as s/he had time. That way they didn't finish a shot, hang around not knowing where to go, and then learn they had to get all the way across the studio in two seconds flat. There were gaps where s/he had nothing pressing for a few seconds, as when the film was running and everything was set for the second spot. So s/he used that time to figure the time cues.

Let's summarize what happened. S/he lives in the future— from three to thirty seconds ahead of what's showing up on the home screen. S/he gives "ready" commands to prepare every-one to act. S/he gives "action" commands in order to get things done. S/he worries about video first, then audio. Orders are clear, short, and precise. S/he times accurately, and gives all necessary time cues. And s/he uses all of his or her senses totally.

That's the technical side of what the director does, but there's also a more creative side. Let's go back to that live spot with the two products and the cover shot and the matt of the price. Most likely, all the director is given is the copy to be read and the products themselves. How the spot looks on the air is pretty much up to the director. S/he can set the two items on a tabletop, shoot them, and let it go at that. If the table top is shiny, the engineers may have to take the shading down so far you can't read the labels. Or the labels might be turned away from the cameras. Or the background may be so busy you barely notice the products. Or, if the background's plain, they may be so close to it that their shadows get as much attention as they do. Any of a dozen other things may be wrong.

Strange as it may sound, anyone can learn to give the com-mands necessary to get through a break like this. Some directors may be a bit better than others, but anyone who can walk through a door and chew gum at the same time can master the sequence of commands. The appearance on the air is what distinguishes a good from a bad director. The appearance of a live spot like this one is a giveaway to the skill and value of the director as more than just a button-pusher. A director who consistently uses the shiny tabletop is rapidly picked out as a second- or third-rate director. S/he won't go far. S/he will end up directing the 6 A.M. sign-on news or the Sunday afternoon public affairs panel show. The good director, on the other hand, handles all the commands easily and in good time, *plus* having an attractive setting for the spot, covering the shiny tabletop, and getting all the labels facing the cameras. S/he will consistently produce clean, attractive commercials. S/he will have well-composed, informative shots during the live show. S/he will have an ear for the right music for the right mood. S/he will have a feel for when to pause and when to hurry. In other words, s/he thinks about the content, not just the outer form, of the material s/he puts on the air.

For example, if that live spot is for perfume, s/he may use a bit of gauze and some flowers (use plastic, as the camera can't tell the difference) to surround the bottles. Softer, gentler lighting is called for, plus perhaps a colored spot hitting the background. The music should probably be a soft, romantic instrumental with lots of strings. On the other hand, if the products are aerosol sprays for athlete's foot and the copy speaks of locker rooms, the music may be of marching bands, the lighting will be harsher, the cans may sit on some artificial grass, and a football may rest in the background. It's the director's awareness of the different appeals of these products that creates different spots even though the basics—two items on a tabletop—remain the same.

In dealing with people, the director is aware of the composition of the pictures too. S/he knows s/he needs to leave a bit of space above a person's head, but if s/he goes in very tight, s/he should chop off the top of a head rather than the chin. S/he knows that when a person is looking to the side of a picture, s/he should leave a bit more space in front of the face than behind. That's called "leading" the face. S/he knows that one rule to follow is, "Show the viewer what s/he wants to see when s/he wants to see it." S/he therefore cuts a split-second before an object is named or shown. If the detective mentions the dagger, the cut is to a CU of the dagger just before the detective says the word, so the viewer sees it when s/he wants to see it. S/he knows a dissolve can be part of the effect in a dream sequence. A dissolve can also be used to indicate to viewers that something else at a different location is happening at the same time. Cuts generally show something within the same area, like a shot of the eavesdropper behind the curtain in the same room where we have been watching a conversation. The director, then, worries about composition and effect as well as the mechanical process of getting shots on the air. And this worry lasts as long as s/he directs. S/he develops a sharp eye for the composition and form of shots, and constantly thinks about how to better the productions. Walking in the control room that first time and starting to tell a crew what to do is only the beginning of the constantly changing demands on a director's abilities.

# 2
# THE
# RAdio
# STudio

## THE RADIO BOARD

When you walk into a room, one of the first things you might do is flip up the switch on the wall to turn on a light. Then you may walk over to a box and turn a knob which starts the radio. If it's a hot day, you might push a button to start the air conditioner. During the course of the day, you push buttons or flip switches in a steady stream, and each time some one specific thing happens. If you could collect in front of you all the switches you touch in a day, you would probably be amazed and a little overwhelmed at the number and at their apparent complexity. So when you first face a radio control board, you may likewise be amazed and a little overwhelmed. But it's just a collection of a bunch of switches, each one of which does one specific thing. And just like the lights, the radio, and the air conditioner are different things serving one purpose (that of satisfying you), so the radio board takes a number of different things, like records, tapes, and microphones, and pushes them into one output—the sound on the air. You know how to handle all the switches you encounter so as to satisfy the one person you are, so now let's approach the various switches on a radio board and see how to satisfy the one sound we want on the air.

Do you know of any machine that doesn't have an off-on switch? That, then, is where we start with an audio board. Somewhere on the board will be a switch we have to activate in order to hear anything which goes through all the other switches. It's called the *master gain switch* because it controls

*FIGURE 2.1* Radio board

the gain, or volume, of everything else. But the switch may not look like the sort of thing you are used to. Remember that on your radio you turned a knob to turn on the set. You may be facing an array of knobs here too. Or you may have knobs which move back and forth in a straight track. Both types are switches. The turning knob is called a *pot*, short for *potentiometer*, and works just like the knob on your radio. As you turn it clockwise, the sound level goes up.

The other knob is called a *slider*, for obvious reasons, and will generally have a numbered scale printed alongside it. Needless to say, the zero position is for no sound at all. Locate the master gain switch, whether it turns or slides, and put it about halfway up. You've just turned on the board. However, that doesn't mean you'll hear anything. You have some switches to turn on yet. Find a knob labeled *monitor gain*. Turn it about halfway up. That turns on the speaker, or monitor, so you will hear what goes on the air.

What you hear over this monitor that's now turned halfway up will depend on another switch more like the types you're used to in that it's like the light switch on the wall. It's just labeled *monitor*, and it clicks into positions like a wall switch but generally has more than just two positions. It can be off or in *program* or in *audition*. Flip it into program; we'll talk more about what these two names mean later on. Next, locate a switch called the *output switch*. Like the one we just flipped, this one has three positions. But this one controls the entire

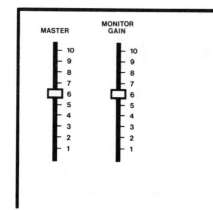

*FIGURE 2.2*   Radio board

board, putting everything on the audition or the program line instead of merely on the monitor. Again, put it into the program position.

Switches like these, that work like light switches, are generally referred to as *keys*. So you flip the key into program, audition, or whatever you want.

So now you have turned up the master gain control, the monitor gain control, and put the monitor key and the output key into program. But you still don't hear anything. All you've done so far is get the board ready to put sound on the air. Now

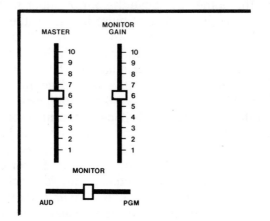

*FIGURE 2.3*   Radio board

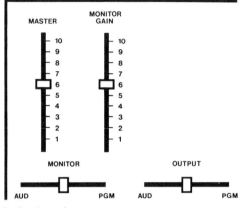

*FIGURE 2.4* Radio board

we have other switches to move so as to allow sound to come into the board.

Where will the sounds come from? You can have someone, even yourself, talking into a microphone, or have a record playing, or have an audiotape running. Those, in essence, are all your sound sources, but they can do a great variety of things for you. Let's start with a microphone.

On a bendable metal tube above the audio board a mike is pointed at you. Generally, the switches which control it are the first ones to the left. If you turn the pot or push the slider up halfway, will you then hear yourself talking into it? No, for a couple reasons. The first is because there is yet another switch to click on. That's the key above the pot or slider that can click to the left or the right and that must be put in the "program" position, generally to the right. To the left is "audition," and in the middle is "off." The second reason is that, even with the key on program, that particular mike won't be heard over the control-room monitor the way other sound sources will be. If that mike could be heard, the mike would pick up its own sound from the monitor, feed it back to the monitor, pick it up again, and so on. That's *feedback*—more on that later. But if there is a speaker outside the control room, people listening there can now hear you talking into the mike. So for one simple sound you had to handle six switches. But for each additional sound, you will need to handle only a couple more switches. Those two will be the one at the top, which must be put into program or audition, and the pot or slider. Let's simplify at this

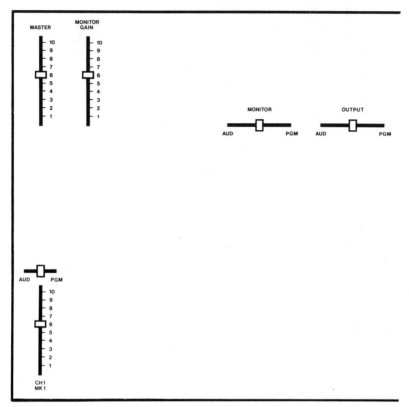

*FIGURE 2.5*    First channel

point and talk of sliders only, even though what we say will refer to pots as well. Technically, both the turning and sliding knobs are pots because both are potentiometers. They both can vary the electrical potential of a circuit, but in conversation, most people call the turning knobs "pots" and the sliding ones "sliders." So that's what I'm doing.

As you talk into the now working mike, you notice a needle on a gauge jumping around. That gauge is called a *VU meter*, for volume units. As your voice gets louder or softer, the needle goes higher or lower. You see the red portion of the scale. The needle isn't supposed to go over into that red portion except very quickly and very seldom. How can you stop it? Move the slider back toward zero, and the needle drops down. I said "the slider" because there are two you can move—the one for the mike and the one for master

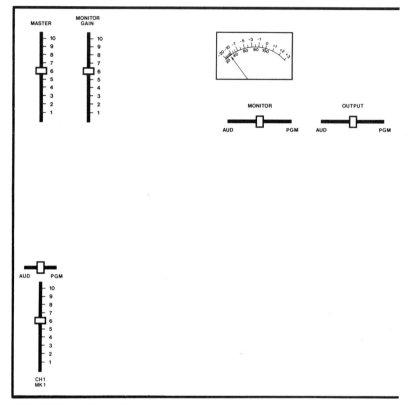

*FIGURE 2.6* VU meter

gain. If everything on the board is running loud, pull the master gain slider back. If the one mike is too loud, pull just that slider back. Obviously, the reverse is true too. If the person talking has a soft voice, push the mike slider up. If it's up all the way, push the master gain slider up. That move can be a problem though. Suppose you have one soft voice on a mike and you push up the master gain slider. Then the other mikes, the records, and the tapes will be louder. So each individual slider for the other sources may have to be brought back. Always remember you change everything when you change the master gain. Generally, try to keep the peaks of sound from voices no higher than 100 on the scale of the VU meter and the sound of music no higher than 80. That's because so much sound energy goes into music that it will seem as loud at 80 as voices do at 100. Sounds that go over 100 get dis-

torted, so except for a sudden cough or drumbeat, keep everything under 100.

The next three sliders on the board are also for mikes, but
these are for the studio, not for the person at the board.

The board with the mike is in the control room and is
separated from the other mikes, which, for a couple of reasons,
stay in the studio. First, you may want to set up any number of
actions or activities in the studio while someone else goes on
the air. Since the mikes are in a separate room, you can talk
and arrange things while the technical control and the playing
of records or tapes goes on in the control room. Second, the
mikes in the studio would cause feedback if they were brought
into the control room, but the mike in there has been specially
prepared not to do that. What is feedback? It's that loud squeal
we've all heard over loudspeakers. What happens is that sound

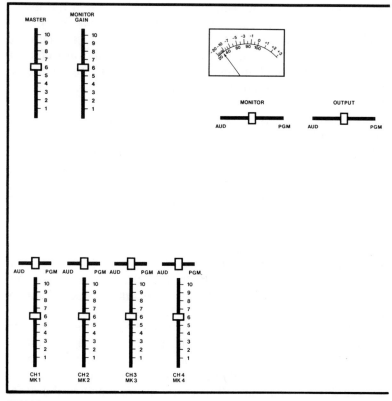

FIGURE 2.7    More channels

goes into the mike and is sent out to a speaker, in our case, the monitor in the control room. Then the mike picks up that sound (its own) and sends it back to the speaker, which sends it out to the mike, which picks it up and sends it back to the speaker, which sends it out to . . . . It feeds back upon itself and gets louder with each cycle. The mike in the control room, though, feeds into a special circuit which kills the monitor. So when you use that mike, the monitor doesn't play anything. That breaks the cycle. The studio mikes break the cycle by being in a room where they don't pick up the monitor. But as far as the board is concerned, there's no difference from one mike to the next. They all operate the same way: flip a key and move a slider. There's an advantage to you, though, as the board operator. You can talk into the mike there and introduce the people in the studio. Then you can kill (shut off) your mike, signal the people in the studio through the control-room window, and turn on their mikes. Now you are free to watch the levels on the VU meter. If you were part of the discussion in the studio, you couldn't do that, and the sound might get distorted or be too low to hear. If the people in the studio are doing a drama, you can sneak in the sound effects from the mike over in the corner and bring it in just till it's loud enough, something you couldn't judge from the studio.

The next slider is for a turntable. If you're going to play a record, you have to have a turntable, and so you have to have a slider. This slider operates like the others—flip the key at the top and move the slider to the proper level as judged by the needle on the VU meter. The turntable itself is generally located to one side or the other, and just far enough away so you don't bump it with your elbow. Now what's the next slider? Another turntable, and that explains why there are two of them sitting there. With two sliders for two turntables, you can do things like start a record on one, push the slider up, start a record on the other, and push its slider up while pulling the slider for the first one down. That way, the sound gradually shifts from one record to another. That is called a *segue* (segway). You segue from one piece of music to another by having the sounds overlap for a bit in the middle. Or you can cut instantly from one record to another by having both sliders up but only one key on top flipped. To change, close one key and open the other, and you will instantly go from one to the other (provided your reaction time is fast).

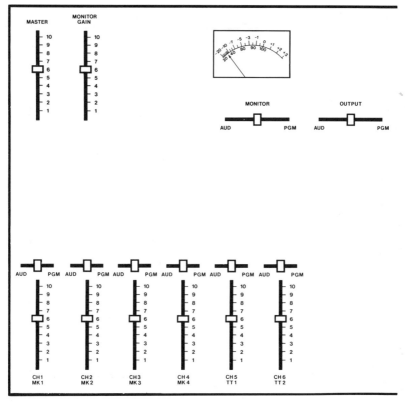

*FIGURE 2.8*   Turntable channels

At this point, what can we do? With the control room mike open, we can introduce a record, have it playing in the background by holding the slider low, then bring it up full as we quit talking. Be sure to close the mike key so you don't say something you shouldn't after you're through with the intro. That's a familiar pattern we have heard on a lot of music and talk stations. The D.J. intro's a record, then plays it—all by using just a couple of switches.

The rest of the sliders are easily explained now that we have the pattern down pat. The next two, sliders 7 and 8, are for the two tape decks. For reel to reel tape, we have two machines we can play on, and each one has its own key and slider. The next two, sliders 9 and 10, are for the two tape cartridge machines. They are somewhat like cassettes in that the tape is totally contained inside a plastic case, but unlike

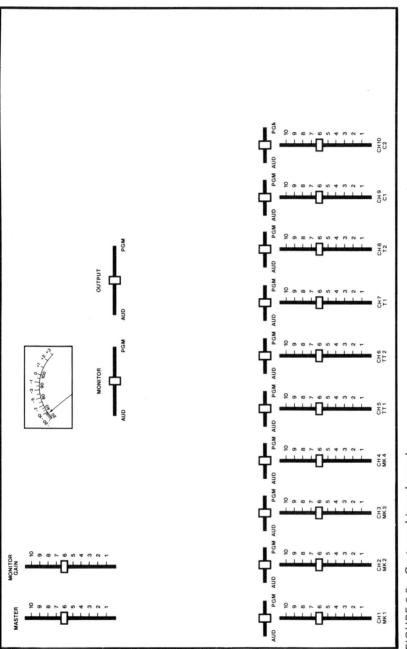

*FIGURE 2.9*   Cart machine channels

cassettes, the tape is in a continuous loop. By putting electronic beeps on the tape, you can get it to stop automatically so it doesn't go on running. These *carts*, as they are called, have varying amounts of tape on them, enough for :20, :40, :70, 3:00, 5:00, or really almost anything you want. And as with a single 45 record, just one thing is recorded on them. You may have a jingle ID on a short :20 (or even a :10) cart, a :30 commercial on a :40, and so on. With the two cart machines, we can go directly from that jingle ID to the :30 commercial without stopping to pull one cart out and put another in. We just go to the other machine for the second cart.

That leaves the last two sliders and keys. They are all-purpose and can control a number of things, depending on what you select. If you have a second studio, its output may come through one of them. If you carry news from a national network, those reports will probably come in through them. A field reporter at election headquarters downtown may be on one slider or the other. But which one? Up above these two sliders and keys you will see five more switches. On some boards you have push buttons, and on some others you have dials that click around to five numbered positions. But on this board, it's five keys. The first key controls network news, let's say. The second, studio B. The next is the downtown remote line, and so on. Flip any key up and the sound it controls goes into the first remote slider, number 11. Flip it down and the sound goes into the second, number 12. So you can get two remotes at once on the air. Or, depending on what's happening, you could put all five keys up and get all five remotes on slider 11. Chances are, though, that would result in chaos.

As you pushed these various sliders up and down, you may have noticed some of them move farther down than zero. With a bit of a pop, they click into a position below the fully off position. That's a *cue* position, and when the slider is moved that far, regardless of whether the key is in audition, program, or off, the sound for that particular channel is sent into a separate system called the *cue system*. You'll even spot a slider called the *cue slider*, and as you push it up, any sounds coming through that cue system will be made louder.

You'll hear them through a speaker located generally to the side of the board or directly in the middle of the front. Here's the point. If you have one record on the air, you will want a way to be sure you are at the beginning of the next one you will

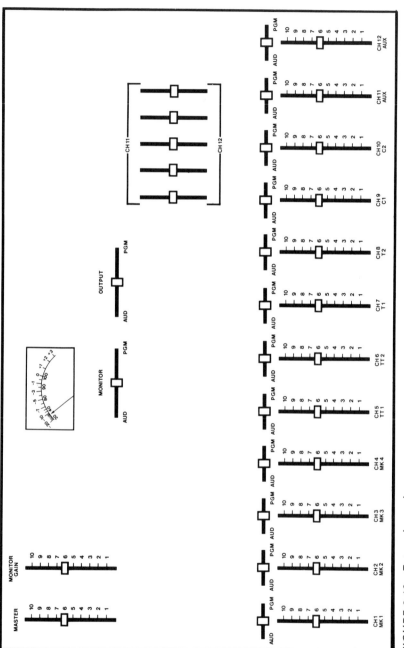

*FIGURE 2.10*   Extra channels

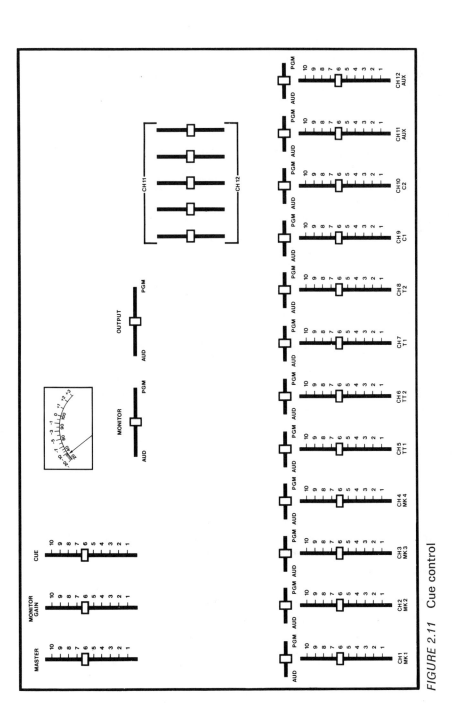

*FIGURE 2.11* Cue control

play. You can't use the normal program position for this second turntable as that would send the sound out on the air. So you have a second channel called a *cue channel* to allow you to cue up the record while it's off the air. Click the slider for that second turntable into the cue position, push up the cue slider, and the sound comes from its own speaker. If listening to another speaker could cause problems (you might have to have your mike open for some reason), there is yet another way. There's a *headset jack* on the board, plus a slider for its volume, plus a switch to let you feed the program, audition, or cue line into that headset. That way, you alone can listen without any sound going out into the control room.

You know what cue is, but what's the difference between program and audition? I've mentioned that the key should be put in the program position. So long as the output key for the entire board is in program, that's the line that will go out on the air. However, now go to the monitor selector key and put it in "audition." The control room speaker goes dead. Flip a key to "audition" and whatever is on that channel will now come out over the monitor. The original sound will still be going out over the air, but you are hearing a different sound source over the speaker. That's somewhat like the cue system except you now control the loudness by pushing up the specific slider, not the one slider in the cue system. Even without the use of a VU meter (which is still giving a reading of what's on the air), you can come pretty close to setting a good level just by using your ears. Here's an example of why this set-up might be useful.

Suppose you know a major news story was to be fed down one of your remote lines in the near future, but you don't know exactly when. You announce over the air that you will shortly cut to Reporter So-and-so giving the report. Then you put on a record. You flip the remote line on audition, change the monitor over, and set the slider at a good level by listening to what sounds right. When the report comes on, you merely flip the key to "program" and kill the key for the music. Your level is preset. Had you done it through the cue system, you would have had to move the slider up, thus getting a weak start. Or suppose something goes wrong with the electronics of the program line. You can flip the output key to "audition," reverse your keys, and still go on the air. Sometimes, audition can be a lifesaver.

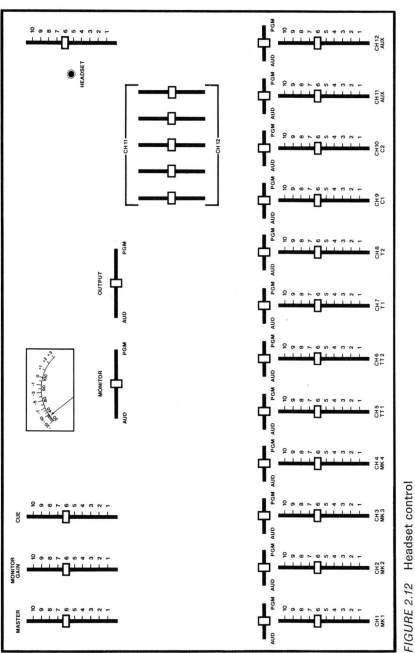

FIGURE 2.12  Headset control

One key remains. Not all boards will have it. But any board for an FM station probably will. It's the *stereo-mono* key. Up till now we've been talking about mono sound—one sound going through one channel to one speaker. For stereo, almost everything doubles. Flip this key into stereo and suddenly you can send out two channels from stereo records or tapes. You'll get different sounds from left and right speakers. As for records and tapes, you need do nothing else for stereo sound but flip that one key.

But what about the microphones? With records and tapes, someone else has already set the balance of loudness between the two channels, but with microphones, you're responsible for that. So you'll need another set of keys, one above each mike.

By putting the key to the left, that mike's sound goes in the left channel only. Put it to the right and the sound goes to the right. Leave it in the middle and the sound is evenly split between the two channels. So with the board in stereo, you can "place" a person on a mike to the left, right, or center of the sound spread. If you were recording a symphony orchestra, you would need a board more complex than just this three-spot arrangement, but for most stations, you'll find this gives you all the flexibility you'll need.

A stereo board will have a second VU meter, so you can read the level for each individual channel. So with a little sharp listening and proper slider settings, you can get a good stereo sound. Each channel can be individually controlled by you, and can be balanced just as you like. After all, you're running the show.

And just what kind of show can you run? Suppose you work for a local radio station and you are just coming on duty. The preceding show comes from another control room. You have a live news special coming from your studio, so you'll handle the station break and the show from here as soon as an engineer gives you the signal your studio has been put on the line. So you have to set some things up in advance. Here's what you have to have ready to go on the air. You start with a commercial, :30, for Icy Cola. That's all on a cart. Following that is a :30 spot for a local merchant running a sale "this weekend only." It's got music in the background and you will be reading the copy over it, so that means you'll need a record ready for the music. Next is an ID, and that is also on a cart.

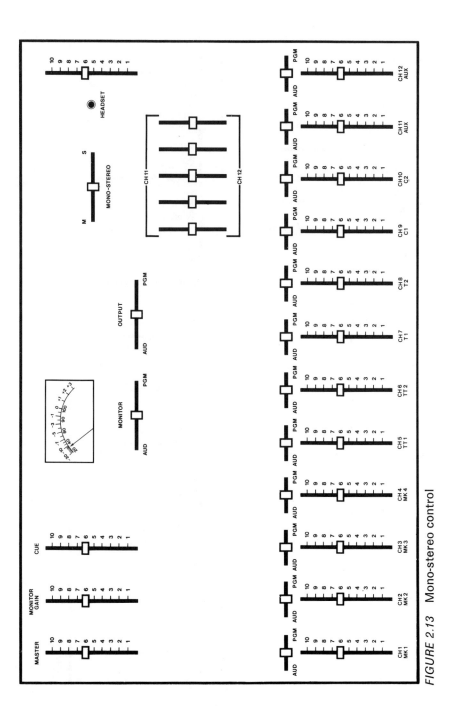

*FIGURE 2.13* Mono-stereo control

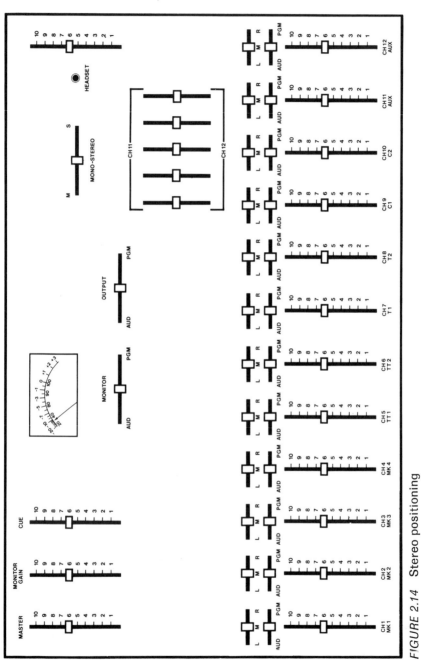

*FIGURE 2.14* Stereo positioning

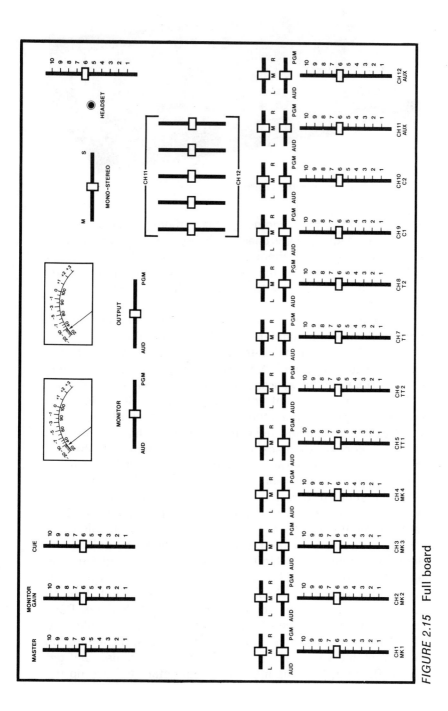

FIGURE 2.15 Full board

*FIGURE 2.16* A mono radio board

Then the news special begins. It has a theme, also on a cart, but the introductory copy changes every week so you will be reading that over the theme. Then the news person in the studio starts in. Part of the special includes reel-to-reel tape which has been edited by the news department. So where do you start?

Come into the control room early, so you can check everything out. Push the master gain up about halfway. Flip the monitor key to "program." Push up the monitor slider. Flip the output key to "program." Now you can check out the levels of the various sound sources, but nothing will go on the air as the engineers have not yet made this studio live. Have the newsperson go into the studio and sit in front of the mike. Check to see where the mike is plugged in, that is, into line 2, 3, or whatever. Go back in the control room, flip the key for that mike to "program," and move up the slider. Give a signal for the newsperson to start reading the script, and adjust the slider to give the right level. Remember the moving needle of the VU meter should go no higher than 100. Shut off that mike by flipping the key to the middle and by signaling the newsperson to stop reading. Don't kill the mike by pulling the slider down unless you also mark the level by putting a grease pencil mark on the board or write the level down on a piece of paper. Otherwise, why check for a level at all? Next, turn on your mike: slider 1, key to program, slider pushed up. Read part of your copy and check your level. Shut off the mike and put on the record. That will be on slider 5 or 6, depending on which turntable you use. Flip the key, move the slider, and get a level. Then put the tone arm back to the start and cue up the record. We'll discuss exactly how to do that when we discuss turntables in detail. Once that's set, you can leave the key either off or on "program." No sound will come through till you start the record, so you are safe either way. You have three carts to play, first the Icy Cola, then the ID cart, and then the theme music. But you have only two cart machines. That's OK though, because one plays at the very first and the third one plays quite a bit later. So put the Cola cart in one cart machine, flip the key and push up the slider, start the cart, and check the level. Again, we will talk more about carts a bit later on. Now you are just worried about getting through a station break and a program opening. Put the ID cart in the other machine, flip the key to "program," raise the slider, and check the level. Carts will run after the recorded material on them is finished, that is, until they get back to the beginning. Let them go to that point; that automatically cues them up again. Then remove the Icy Cola cart and put in the theme music cart. Check it for level. The two carts will probably have two different levels, so you will want to make a note somehow of what each level is. If you are marking the board with a grease pencil, a "C" for Cola and a "T" for theme would do it. The same holds true for a written note. The Cola cart may have a level of 6 (the slider is pushed up to that number on the scale beside it), while the theme runs at $7\frac{1}{2}$. This is information you will need. Once you have set the theme level, let it recue, then take it out and put in the Cola cart again, as it runs first. Be sure to set the right level. Now put the reel-to-reel tape up on the tape deck. (Once more, we'll get into tape deck details later on.) Here, the newsperson may be able to help you, or hopefully you can read the script the news department gave you to tell what part of the tape you are to use and what it contains. Flip the key, open the slider, turn the tape deck on, and check the level. Once you have it, go back to the start and cue up the tape. You are set for all your levels. Now you wait for an engineer to tell you your studio has been put on the air. That may be by a headset line, a red light going on, a hand signal through a window, or any number of ways. But once the signal is given, here's what happens.

Flip the first cart machine's key to "program" (if you didn't leave it there) and start the cart. The Icy Cola commercial runs. You take a look at the clock so you will know when it will run out (:30). Check to see the turntable key is in "program." Put one hand on the turntable off-on switch and the other on the key for your mike. When the Cola commercial stops, start the turntable. Move the slider down now, open your mike, and start to read the local merchant's copy. The music started full, but it has to be a good deal softer so you can be heard. Therefore, you have to pull the slider down. The two sounds together —your voice and the music—should not total over 100 on the VU meter. While you are reading, the Cola cart will recue to its beginning. Keep reading, but reach over and remove it from the machine. Put in the theme cart and reset the level on the slider. Now get ready to kill the record and hit the ID cart machine. Be sure the key is in "program." Don't worry about your mike, as you can simply shut up. When you finish the commercial, kill the music by flipping the key off, and hit the ID cart machine. While the :10 ID in running, check the other cart machine. Is the key right, and the level up? That's the theme for the show. When the ID finishes, start the other cart machine. Don't worry about the ID cart, as there's no sound on the rest of it anyway. The theme music is up full, so take it down the way you did the record and read your opening copy over the music. Your mike has been open since the commercial you read, so you don't have to worry about keys. Get ready with one hand to signal the newsperson in the studio and with the other to take out the music.

But how will you get the studio mike open? You can assume that once you give a signal to stand by, the newsperson won't be talking, so open the mike. If, before the show, you have told the person you will open the mike as soon as you give the standby signal, you can be reasonably certain you won't catch any extra sounds from out there. Now you have that essential second hand free. When you finish reading the introduction, signal the newsperson and kill the music. Now kill your mike, as you have nothing left to say. Follow the script so you will know where the reel-to-reel tape comes in. Check to see the key and level are right and get set to start it. At the right moment, start it and kill the mike in the studio. If you don't kill that mike, the monitor in the studio won't work (that's to prevent feedback) and so the news person won't hear what's going on the air. As long as a mike in the studio is live, the monitor is dead. Hence no feedback, but also the people out there can't hear the show. In an instance like this, hearing the show is essential, so when the newsperson stops talking, kill the mike. The monitor will come on, and the show can be heard. Also, coughing or clearing the throat might be essential, so give the newsperson a break.

And so you got through maybe as much as 3:00 of material. It's all a matter of switches and dials.

I've been talking about a particular radio board as if all boards were exactly the same. They aren't. What I've described is generally the same as all boards, but the details of almost every board in existence are different. Each station or radio operation will have specific things the board should do which other operations won't need. So the boards either get modified by the manufacturer or by an engineer working for the buyer so as to fit particular requirements. Many stereo boards, for example, have not only a stereo-mono key, but a stereo-left or a stereo-right position as well. That is, the sound you pick up in stereo right may be only the right channel and that's all you would send out. Or it may be that stereo right puts all sounds into the right channel, which is being broadcast. It depends on what is wanted. All boards will work basically in the fashion I have described. So basically you can work any board you walk up to. The only way to find out about the peculiarities of a particular board is to have someone familiar with it point them out to you. They will all be in the "flip a key, move a slider" tradition though, so you'll feel right at home.

Now let's take a closer look at some of the elements which feed into this radio board. First off, let's see what microphones are like.

MICROPHONES

Broadcasting equipment is almost always involved in the changing of energy from one form to another. Sound, for example, is a movement of molecules in the air. Radio gear changes that movement into a form of electricty. That electrical energy gets changed around, sent out as "electromagnetic waves," picked up by your receiver and changed back into electrical energy, and then changed back to a movement of air molecules. So the whole process is changes from one form of energy to another. The technical concern is that the changeover creates as accurate a pattern as possible. If the changeover takes a note, say B-flat, and changes it to an electrical wave one-inch high once and one and one-eighth inches high the next time, then the changeover isn't giving an accurate pattern. You might end up with a B-flat and a C when both notes are supposed to be the same. All the transformations from one form of energy to another are called by one name—*transduction.* Change air molecules into electrical energy and you have transduced the sound into electricity. Engineers are concerned that transduction be clean, accurate, and introduce as little extra material as they can manage.

In audio, the first step in this transduction process is changing the sound, those moving molecules of air, into electrical energy. That's done with a microphone. Microphones are machines that move with the air, and that movement creates an electrical flow. That seems impossible, but it works. There are four different types of microphones, all of which can do exactly this. They are called *dynamic, ribbon, crystal,* and *condenser.*

Crystal microphones are cheap and not very good in sound quality, so you seldom run into them in any situation where good sound is a requirement. They work like this: a diaphragm is fastened to a small piece of a crystal—not glass, but a crystal like a crystal of salt. The diaphragm is very thin, and when the moving air of sounds hits it, it moves too. That movement twists the crystal a bit. Certain crystals give off electrical impulses when one side moves and the other doesn't. So the sound moves the crystal, which twists a bit and gives off electricity. More sound, more twisting, more electricity. Less sound, etc. Certain ceramic elements have been made that act like these crystals, so you often run into ceramic mikes now instead of crystal ones. The principle is the same, and unfortunately the quality is about the same, although that may improve with a bit of research. With either one, it's a way to change sound into electricity.

The next way is with a dynamic microphone. Again, sound moves a diaphragm. This time the diaphragm is connected to a small coil of wire. A coil of wire moving in a magnetic field will give off an electric current. So you put this small coil between the poles of a magnet and you can once again change sound into electricity.

A ribbon microphone, in essence, combines the diaphragm and the moving coil. A thin ribbon of metal is put between the poles of a magnet. It moves as sound hits it, and just like the coil of wire, it gives off a current. Once more, sound is converted into electricity.

Finally, we have the condenser microphone. Here you feed electricity to the mike. The diaphragm is not very far from another metal plate, and electricity can flow across the diaphragm to the other plate. As sound hits the diaphragm, it moves closer or farther away from the plate. That makes it easier or harder for the flow of electricity to continue. So sound here creates a difference in the flow of electricity, and that creates as good a pattern of changing sounds as any of the other systems.

Each system has some advantages and some shortcomings. Crystal, as I mentioned, isn't too strong on quality. But the low price is a particular advantage for some situations. Most home recordings don't need great fidelity, and most people won't lay out hundreds of dollars for a mike, so crystal is perfect for the home sound movies or a small cassette recorder. It's also subject to humidity changes, to heat, and to shock (like being dropped). So it's fairly fragile.

Dynamic mikes, on the other hand, are rugged. You can't pound nails with them, but an accidental drop probably won't destroy them. It may, but it probably won't. They respond to frequencies in a particular way, though. They pick up low notes from all around them, but high notes will only be picked up from one particular direction. If a dynamic mike were turned slightly away from a soprano, you would lose much of the value of her voice. A baritone would be fine though.

The ribbon mike can carry this one step further. For sound sources close to the mike, bass notes are emphasized. All the other frequencies are reproduced very well by ribbon mikes. Sopranos and violins sound very good over a ribbon mike. So do bass drums. But put an announcer with a thin voice close to this mike, and the bass qualities get more emphasis than is realistic. That, of course, can be an advantage to the guy with the not-so-hot voice. Generally, though, the good fidelity of these mikes is their strong point. They are somewhat more fragile than dynamic mikes, and if you have them outside, they respond a lot more to wind noise. They are generally pretty bulky mikes too.

Finally, we come to the condenser mikes. Their frequency response is quite good, good enough that they are very popular for accurate music recording. But they are fragile. They never belong outside, and they should be protected from shocks and bounces. But being careful is a small price to pay for their accuracy.

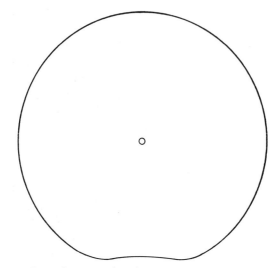

*FIGURE 2.17* Omnidirectional pick-up pattern

I've made some reference to how microphones pick up sounds—high notes from one direction only, bass notes emphasized from close in. The areas from which mikes pick up sounds is another of their characteristics. This is referred to as their *pick-up pattern,* and the basic patterns are named *omnidirectional, bidirectional, cardiod,* and *unidirectional.* If you know a little Latin, the meaning of all these patterns will be obvious. "Omni" means "all," so that pick-up pattern is from all around the mike. Crystal and dynamic mikes often have this pattern.

"Bi," of course, means "two," so these mikes pick up in two directions, generally from directions opposite each other. This is a common pattern for ribbon mikes.

"Cardiod" is related to the heart, so the pattern is heart-shaped. Condenser and dynamic mikes often use this pattern.

Finally comes the "uni," or "one" directional mike. Ribbon and dynamic mikes can be unidirectional. If the mike is ex-

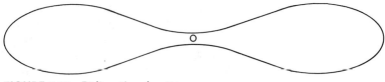

*FIGURE 2.18* Bidirectional pattern

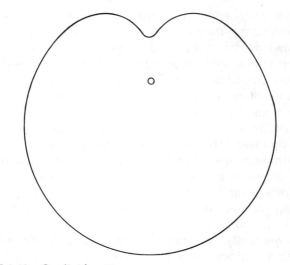

*FIGURE 2.19*  Cardioid pattern

tremely unidirectional, it is sometimes called a *shotgun mike* because it looks like a shotgun and has to be aimed right at the person speaking in order to pick up the sounds. You probably have seen these long mikes at presidential news conferences where one reporter is picked up from way back in the crowd just by aiming the mike toward that specific location. That's one advantage of a shotgun mike—you can pick up someone from quite a ways away.

No one type of mike has a monopoly on a particular pick-up pattern. Mikes can be built on various principles and with various pick-up patterns so as to meet certain requirements. On the other hand, not every type of mike can have every pattern. A ribbon mike will inevitably lose fidelity as a person walks around to the side of it and is then talking to the edge and not the flat side of the ribbon. It can't possibly move well

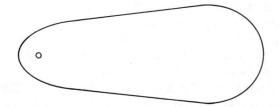

*FIGURE 2.20*  Unidirectional pattern

with a voice from edge-on. That's why ribbon mikes are generally bidirectional; they work off both sides of the ribbon.

By knowing what setting you have, where people will be, what other sounds will be around, whether some frequencies need to be damped down or others emphasized, and whether high demands of accuracy are essential, you can pick the mikes or mike you need to use. You can tell people where to stand and where to move. You can make someone seem a long way off by having them "off mike." Have a person stand at the edge side of a ribbon mike when s/he starts talking, then move around to the front side of the mike, and s/he can sound like s/he is walking up from yards away when in reality s/he is only moving a couple feet and is never any farther than a foot away from the mike.

Mikes generally are mounted somehow. We've all seen speakers on a platform raising and lowering a mike stand; that's one sort of mike support. A heavy base directly beneath a mike is common for a desk support. The reporter's hand is the most common support for the interview mike. In any case, all these mikes have a cord running from them to a connection somewhere. In the studio, it's in the wall. Out in the field, the reporter's mike cord goes into the portable tape machine. This cord can be disconnected from the wall or the tape machine. Quite often it can be disconnected from the mike itself. One end or the other of the connection will have a series of pins in a metal sleeve. They are arranged in a particular pattern. Don't try to cram together the cord and mike, or the cord and tape machine. Look at the pattern of the pins and line them up with the holes of the connection. When you are taking off the cord, somewhere there is a tab to push or a slider to pull back. That releases the tension on the connection and makes it very easy to separate the two. Also, after you have pushed the tab or slider, pull them apart by holding the metal sleeves. Don't pull on the wires as that only pulls apart the connection inside the sleeve and you're left with loose wires in one hand and the still-connected sleeves in the other.

Sometimes, if you place two mikes of the same type fairly close together, they will interact with each other and give you a boomy, hollow sound. Using different mikes that don't share the same pick-up patterns or frequency characteristics will eliminate the problem. So will moving the similar mikes farther apart. Other problems you should rapidly learn to avoid come

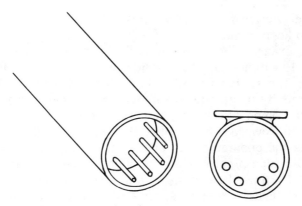

*FIGURE 2.21* Connector and outlet

from the clowns who whistle into mikes, yell, or tap them with pencils. These are all sudden, high-level sounds which cause the diaphragms to move rapidly and extensively. And that can tear them loose from their supports, thus destroying the mikes.

Mikes, with all their foibles, strengths, and problems, are only one source of sound for the board. They may be basic in that all other sources use them at the beginning, but by the time we come to the board, we encounter the tapes and records that were made using the mikes to pick up the sound. So as far as we are concerned, mikes are only one of our sound sources. There are others—records for example. Records are too familiar for me to need to say anything about them. You probably handle records regularly. But there is an aspect of the equipment that goes with records that we need to talk about.

TURNTABLES

Go put on a record, then come back and read this.

You just dealt with a turntable, and I'm sure it was a very familiar experience. You put a record on it and turned some sort of switch. That one switch may have started the record turning and at the same time started the tone arm over toward the first grooves. Or it may simply have started the record turning, leaving it up to you to place the tone arm on the record. The latter method is what you'll encounter in a broadcast studio.

The gear will be familiar, but with some few extra considerations to keep in mind.

For example, you'll never find a changer in a broadcast studio. The turntables there handle one record at a time, not a stack. The station's concern is double—both the quality and the durability of its equipment. With a changer, the tone arm has to accomodate differing heights. With one record, the arm may slant down a bit. With five, it may be tilted up. All this changes the geometry back at its pivot point. That can cause a lot of design problems, so it's simpler just to figure on one record at a time. That way, the arm always plays at the same angle. With fewer problems, fewer considerations have to be taken into account, and hence the design can be simpler. A simpler design means fewer problems with the equipment. Remember, this equipment is going to be in use in some stations as much as twenty-four-hours-a-day, seven-days-a-week. It has to be rugged and reliable. So one record at a time, and a tone arm you place on yourself, not some system that moves it over for you. Basic.

But an equally important consideration is the quality of the sound. Broadcasters know their signal gets degraded (their word) by passing through even the finest of equipment. Think of it this way. Take a perfectly clear piece of glass and put it between you and some object. You can still see the object plainly. Now add another pane of glass. And another. And another. And another. As you go on with this process, the object remains visible, but it does get dimmer and dimmer. Even the most transparent glass affects the "transmission" of sight. So the broadcaster figures the same way. S/he therefore tries to put out the best signal possible at every point in the system. As with any reach toward perfection, it's ultimately the little things that count.

So with the studio turntable and tone arm, you'll be dealing with a familiar piece of equipment, but one you'll probably have to regard a bit more carefuly in ways that may seem minor. But those are the little things that matter. Obviously, you'll want to be careful of the needle, or stylus, to see it doesn't get hit or dropped which might chip it or break it off. But don't do something like running a fingertip over it to see if you have sound. That puts a lot more force on it than even the loudest passage of music. It also leaves a deposit of oil which will then be transferred to the grooves of the record. You also have to be careful when you cue up a record—but more of that later on.

The turntable itself may seem like there's nothing you can do to hurt it. You either turn it off or on and that's it—but not quite. You can select one of three speeds (generally) at which it can run. Or you can leave it in neutral with the engine running, much like a car. It's getting into the right gear that's the problem. Think of the turntable as a wheel. Inside the rim of this wheel is a group of three smaller wheels. Depending on what speed you pick, one of these three wheels will be put in contact with the rim of this turntable-wheel. As the smaller wheel turns, the rim turns with it, thus giving you the speed you want. Now suppose the rim is sitting motionless but the engine is running. That means the three little wheels are all turning but not touching the rim. If you pop the turntable into a speed, one of the wheels will be put up against the rim. As with any moving object and stationary object, when they first meet, something slips. That means you wear a bit of the rubber off the little wheel (which is usually rubber covered) as it slides on the rim at first. So put the turntable in gear before you turn on the engine. Don't waste the durability this equipment is built for.

When you're through with the turntable, don't just turn it off. Put it in neutral so the little wheels aren't touching the rim. If you leave a wheel pressing against the rim, this can eventually cause flat spots on the wheel. The rubber gives, but the metal of the rim doesn't. So leaving rubber pressed against metal causes flat spots. That can cause an uneven turning of the turntable as the little wheel goes from flat, to round, to flat. Think about how smooth your car ride would be if your tires were square—an extreme example of flat spots—rather than round. That's the idea of what can happen with a turntable.

Now let's get back to cueing a record. You want to be able to start exactly at the beginning of the music. But since the first few grooves are silent, how do you get beyond them? Put the turntable slider down into cue, turn up the cue monitor loud enough, put the tone arm on the record, put the turntable in gear, and start the motor. The record starts to turn, but there is no sound yet. As soon as you hear the first sound, flip the turntable into neutral and stop the turning of the record with your free hand. Do this gently so the stylus doesn't pop out of that groove. You're very close to the first sound, but not exactly there. Since the turntable is in neutral, you can spin it backward. Do that until you don't hear any sound at all. When you think you are sitting on the first sound, and you can rotate the turntable back and forth to make sure, then go on back about one-third of a turn for a 33, a half turn for a 45, or a full turn for a 78. Turn the motor off and put the turntable in gear. Your record is now cued, ready to start on the first sound. But, you say, you're back from that first sound a little way. Yes, because the turntable won't instantly come up to speed when you start it. If you were resting on the first sound and started the turnable, you would get a "wow," a kind of wobbly, low-pitched sound that builds up to the proper pitch as the record gets up to speed. To avoid this, you give a bit of silence at the beginning so everything is up to speed by the time the sound is reached. The silence only lasts for a split-second anyway.

There are two ways to start a record once it's been cued. Move the slider up out of cue, turn the motor on; and since the turntable is in gear and ready, it will come up to speed and hit the music almost immediately. But some people believe they can shorten that "almost" by another method. With one hand, they gently lift the record by pressing an edge up a bit. The record is now off, but infinitesimally off, the turntable at one point. With the other hand, they start the motor. The turntable starts turning, but under the raised record. Yes, it does rub a bit on the record, but the record is tougher than the surface of the turntable, so nothing is hurt. The turntable is now up to speed, so to start the record they just release their hold. The record drops on a spinning surface and almost immediately starts turning at the same speed. It slips a bit at first, which causes a bit of a delay, but these people feel this delay is shorter than waiting for the whole thing, turntable included, to get up to speed. So they don't have to turn back quite so far when they are cueing up records. This method, for obvious reasons, is referred to as a *slip cue.* Try both ways and see what you think.

Now that I've told you all that, let me tell you that sometimes you can't cue a record at all. You have to be content with a bit of silence before each record. The reason goes back to those little differences that make for better quality. If you are working in a stereo set-up, the stylus and the cartridge it's in are more delicate than they are in mono. The reason is the record groove the stylus runs in. For mono, both sides of the

FIGURE 2.22 A magnified view of a quad disc groove. The small waves give third and fourth channel information; the major sidewall movements give stereo information.

groove are the same; as one side waves left, so does the other side. The stylus has to respond to this leftward wave and nothing more. But in stereo, the sides may be doing opposite things. The left side may be a singer's voice and may wave to the right. Meanwhile, the right side may be the orchestra and at that point may wave to the left. So the stylus has to move in opposite directions on its opposite sides. To pull off that trick, it has to be in an extremely flexible mounting and free to move a lot. If you try rotating a record backward under a stereo stylus, the poor thing will try to follow, but will just end up bending back its fragile support. Suddenly your stereo stylus is crumpled and angled wrong to play. So with a stereo pick-up, you just have to put the tone arm at the first of the record and suffer through the little bit of silence. Always check, then, to see if your stylus and cartridge are mono or stereo. Ask an engineer, the production manager, or the program director. But check first.

If you don't want the silence, you may want to record the music on tape, and edit it down to the first sound. Therefore, our next concern is with the various kinds of tape recorders.

## TAPE RECORDERS

How do you get sound out of rust and plastic? That, essentially, is what audio tape is. That ribbon of thin plastic, generally one-quarter-inch wide, is covered with rust. Rust is, as you know, oxidized iron, and the particles of iron, even though they are oxidized, can still be moved by a magnet. That's the secret. Each particle of iron oxide can point in a particular direction—up-and-down or back-and-forth or in any position in between. When you get a whole bunch of these particles together, as on a piece of audio tape, a magnet can cause them to move around in all sorts of patterns. If that magnet is an electromagnet, it can be made magnetic or nonmagnetic by turning its current on or off. So by varying the electricity going to the electromagnet, you can vary the patterns made in the iron oxide particles. Now, if you can convert sound into varying amounts of electricity, you can use an electromagnet to create patterns in iron oxide. Those patterns exactly represent the varying amounts of electricity from the sound but in a permanent record on the tape. Now reverse the process. Use the patterns in the oxide particles to make the electromagnet give off varying amounts of electricity and convert these varying amounts back into sound and you get back to where you started. A tape recorder is the machine we use to do this process in both directions. It feeds varying amounts of electricity to the electromagent when it's recording, and it picks up varying amounts of electricity when it's playing back. The conversion of sound to electricity, or electricity to sound, is the same process we talked about when we discussed mikes, so I won't rehash that here. However, there's one other thing the tape recorder has to do, and it is so obvious you may tend to overlook it. The tape has to be moved past the electromagnet. Obviously you can't have everything happening at one spot on the tape or you wouldn't hear anything useful. So you have a tape transport of some sort, which is a way to transport the tape in a continuous run past the electromagnet. For a tape deck, the tape runs from one reel to another. For a cartridge machine, the tape runs from the inside of a spool to the outside. For a cassette, the tape runs from one hub to another—the same idea as for reel tape. In any case, it gets moved past an electromagnet, referred to as the *head.* Let's talk of the reel-to-reel set-up first.

On the left is a reel holding the blank tape. That's called the *feed reel.* On the right is the *take-up reel*, and its function is obvious. The tape goes in a shallow curve down between the two reels and thus against a series of heads, and between a *roller* and a *capstan.* This roller and capstan squeeze against the tape and, depending on how fast they turn, pull the tape past the heads at 15 inches per second (ips) or 7½ inches per second, or even slower. Generally, broadcast operations use 15 ips, occasionally 7½, almost never 3¾, and never 1⅞. Home recorders, on the other hand, often do not have a 15 ips speed. Whatever the speed, the roller and capstan pull the tape past the heads. Even if the tape is not on a take-up reel, it gets pulled past the heads and will then just spill out on the floor, but at least it will be pulled past the heads at the proper speed.

Assume, though, you do have a take-up reel and you are running at 15 ips. The tape, coming from between the capstan

*FIGURE 2.23*   A reel-to-reel audio tape machine

and roller, goes around an *idler arm* before it goes onto the take-up reel. This arm will fall down unless the tape holds it up. So as long as tape is going from the feed to the take-up reel, the idler arm can be held up. What happens when it does fall? The machine shuts off. So when you get to the end of the tape, even if you do nothing yourself, the machine stops. If the tape should break while it's playing, that too lets the idler arm down and the machine stops. If that happens on the air, you may have to keep the tape playing regardless. Hold the idler arm up with your finger, and the machine starts playing instantly. You will also instantly be back on the air, but the tape will be piling up on the floor. Let it. You can take care of it later, but do it gently; don't fold it or crease it or mash it. Also, *clean* it.

Now, what about the heads? Generally, there are three. Think about what you want done with the tape. First you want to make sure nothing else is on the tape, so you won't be recording over other sounds. So the first head is an *erase head*, and its only function is to remove all sounds from the tape by putting all the oxide particles back in one pattern (all up-and-down or all back-and-forth, etc). Next, you want to put some sound on the tape. So the next head is the *record head*, and all it does is feed in the varying amounts of electricity and hence the varying amounts of magnetism. Third, you want to hear what you've recorded, so the third head does nothing other than *play back* the material now on the tape. The three heads are always in this order—erase, record, playback, or *ERP*. Sometimes, a tape deck will combine the record and playback functions in one head. That's especially true on home machines but is very seldom true on broadcast machines. With separate record and playback heads, you can listen to the recording almost at the same time it's being made. Quite often a broadcast tape deck has a circuit connected to a headset and gives the playback head only. That way, you can put a record on the turntable, start recording it on the tape deck, and listen on the headset for any problems you might not have anticipated. It's an instant check on the quality of the recording. But because the record and playback heads are separated by a bit of space, the sound from the disc and the sound from the tape will not be precisely together. The disc, of course, will come first, as that's what is going into the record head. Then it passes to the playback head, and so a split second later, you hear it over the headset. Suppose you have two tape decks. You set up both to record, but one you set up to record from the turntable and the other you set up to record from the output of the board. Now feed the playback of the first tape deck back into the board. What you'll now have going in to the second tape deck is the turntable, and a split second later, the same sound from the playback of the first tape deck. So you get an echo effect. Another gimmick on some tape decks is a switch to kill the effect of the erase head. That allows you to record over something already on the tape, so you get what's called *sound-on-sound*.

Just how do you go about making a recording, even a simple one? It's easy. The tape deck has a VU meter. As your sound source plays a record, for example, set the tape deck VU meter and the board VU meter so they read the same. You do this by adjusting the slider on the board for the sound source and the pot or slider on the tape deck for the VU meter. Then check to see you have turned the speed indicator to the one you want. Somewhere you may also find a switch which says "record–playback." Put it, of course, on "record." If you find no such switch, you will undoubtedly find a button which says "record." But if you push it, it won't stay down. Even if you had a switch which you turned to "record," you wouldn't be ready to record. You will have to do two things at once to get the tape deck going. This is a safety measure so you don't accidentally go into record when you don't mean to. Once you start to record, the erase head will take off whatever else is on the tape, and you don't want accidentally to erase the only copy of something important. So if you have a switch turned to "record," you will still have a button somewhere to hold down as you turn another switch to "play," or punch a button marked "play." The tape deck will start going, and it will be recording. Also, somewhere on it a red light will come on to show it is indeed recording. With all these warnings, it's hard to accidentally erase a tape, but you may do it someday anyway. What can I say except you'll hate yourself?

Obviously, the easy thing is to start the tape deck recording, then turn on the turntable. You'll get a little silence at the head of the tape, but you can take care of that later. Just remember, when you are recording, have the key to the tape deck turned off. Otherwise, the signal will be taken off the deck, fed to the board, which feeds it back to the deck, which feeds it back to the board, and so on. We're back to the feedback cycle. That will ruin your recording.

But what of playback? That's easier yet. If the deck has that "record–playback" switch, put it in playback. Open the key for the deck, push the slider up, and punch the deck's play button or turn the deck's start switch. Watch the VU meter on the board, and you have whatever is recorded on the tape. To cue up to the first of the sound, go either to the cue or audition positions on the tape deck's switches on the board. Then start the tape rolling. As soon as you hear the first sound, hit the stop button. Now with one hand on each reel, rotate them back and forth. You can hear a low growl of sound as opposed to the silence. Set the tape at the first note of the growl, or just a hair before if your machine takes any time to get up to speed. Now set the key in "program" and the slider at the right level, and you are cued and ready to go.

One other detail. The feed and take-up reels should be the same size. Big, medium, and small reels all have different-sized hubs, so the tensions can change on the tape as it goes from a small hub to a large one. If you are in fast forward or reverse and stop the tape, the changing tensions can stretch or even break the tape. So always use the same size. Also, be sure to put *stops* of some sort on the reels. Stops are the rubber or metal clamps that slip over the center spindle of the deck to hold the reel on. They keep the reels from wobbling up and down (or in and out) when you use fast forward or reverse. And that, obviously, helps to prevent the tape from being damaged. Tape decks, which can be mounted either horizontally or vertically, are better off with stops.

A second sort of tape player is the *cartridge machine*, or *cart machine* for short. These tape players very seldom have an erase head, so you have to bring a clean cart to them. Every broadcast operation will have a large electromagnet some-where which you can use to *bulk* tape. That simply means to erase all at once, or in bulk, all the material on the tape, in-stead of a piece at a time the way an erase head does. You turn it on, the electricity creates a strong magnetic field, you bring the tape to it, you take the tape away, and you turn it off. Now all the particles are aligned the same way. Be sure you take the tape away before you turn it off, because when the electricity is turned off, the magnetic field collapses and shifts in differing directions. So the tape picks up low-level, random

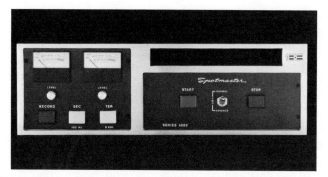

*FIGURE 2.24*    An audio cartridge record-playback machine

noise which will sound like a hissing noise on the tape. Other things cause hiss too, but this is one source of a small bit of it. Also, beware of having other things sitting near the bulker that you don't want erased or magnetized, such as other tapes, watches, etc. This erasing process is also called *degaussing*, in honor of Karl Friedrich Gauss, who worked a lot with magnetism. So, now that you know how to bulk or degauss a cart, let's get back to the cart machine.

The cart machine is a simple device, having generally only an off-on switch, a stop button, a start button, and a record button. Somewhere also will be a VU meter and a slider to adjust it. To record with the cart machine, put the cart in. Slide it in flat and up against the right-hand edge of the opening. Don't slam it in because the heads are at the end of the slot, and if carts keep getting slammed into them, they slip backward a bit and eventually can't maintain contact with the tape. Then you get no sound. So slide it in easy. Flip the off-on switch to "on." Start your sound source and set the board and cart machine VU meters to the same level. Then cue up your sound source. Push the cart machine record and start buttons together and start the sound source at the same time. You're now recording. At the end of the sound, push the stop button. Then push the start button *only*. This makes the cart play around to the beginning again, but it doesn't record anything. As with the tape deck, you must be sure the cart machine key on the board is off while you are recording, or you'll get feedback.

To hear what you've recorded, open the key on the board, push the slider up, and push the machine's start button. Whatever you recorded will play back, and at the end, the cart will keep on running until it comes back to the beginning. Whenever you start recording on a cart, the machine will automatically put an inaudible tone on the tape which tells the machine where the start is. Sometimes, if you start the cart and music exactly together, a bit of music gets on before the start cue. Then, when the cart recycles, you will hear a note or two of music before the cart stops. To avoid this, start the cart and then start the music. The difference can quite literally be less than a second, but you will avoid that extra beep of sound as the cart recues. Generally, you never push the stop button after a cart has started to play; you let it go around till it recues, so the cart is always ready to go. But if it's the wrong cart, or if you need the machine for another cart right away, don't hesitate to stop a cart and remove it. Just be very sure you later put the cart back in and start it so it can get around to the beginning again.

Carts seem to lock into the slot once they are pushed all the way in. That is, you can't pull them straight out. To remove one, put your fingers underneath, lift up, and slide it out. The lifting up releases the catch, and it takes no force at all.

Always label a cart when you record on it. Don't rely on your memory, as all carts look alike. A stick-on label on the

*FIGURE 2.25* An audio cartridge. The tape comes off the hub at the center, runs left to right across the front, and returns to the outside of the reel.

end, not on the top or bottom, is common, but every so often stop to peel off the accumulated seventeen or so labels which have been put on top of each other. I say not on the top or bottom because some machines use the top or bottom surfaces to hold the cart in alignment with the heads. If labels are there, everything is thrown off. Besides, a label on the top or bottom can't be read while the cart is in the machine, and sometimes you need to so you can figure out what happens next.

The final form of tape machine you will encounter is the *cassette player-recorder.* Like the cart machine, it accommodates a box containing the audio tape. The difference is that the tape runs in one direction and stops. It doesn't recue. You have to turn the cassette over to get more sound, and playing through on the second side automatically gets you back to the beginning of sound for side one. There are variations of this form which move the playback heads and automatically cause the tape to start running in the other direction so you don't physically have to turn the cassette over. These variations are most common in the tape machines we see in cars or in some home players. But most broadcasters deal with the sort which requires taking the cassette out. That's because the machine is primarily used by reporters out getting interviews. A cassette recorder and microphone are about the size of a couple large books and weigh about the same. The recorder is so perfectly portable that interviews and on-the-spot recordings become a snap. Once the recording is done, the cassette can be played back through a cassette playback unit permanently wired into the board, or on a unit put into the board through the patch panel. But more about the patch panel later on.

Cassette recordings are becoming more and more commonly used by stations as the quality of the sound improves. The tape in a cassette machine is only one-eighth inch as compared to the one-quarter inch of other systems, so for a long time everyone assumed the sound quality couldn't be as good. But engineers labored away among their wires and IC's and came up with eight tracks on one-eighth inch that sound fantastic. Now music recorded on cassettes is comparable in fidelity to music recorded any other way. So more and more broadcasters are using cassettes as a music source for their boards. This, of course, does not invalidate the uses of cassette recordings in news. That's still fast, easy, and of excellent fidelity.

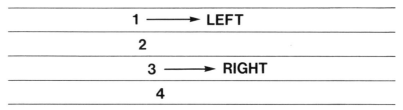

*FIGURE 2.26*    Audio tape tracks—first direction

## tape

What of the tape itself, now that we have talked of the machines it plays on? It's generally only one-quarter inch wide, but it can have a lot of information on it. In most broadcast operations, you encounter full-track or half-track recordings. Here's what that means. For full track, the entire width of the tape, all one-quarter inch of it, is devoted to a single output from the board. That one output may be as complex as a symphony orchestra, but it's still only one output. For stereo, you need two outputs, a left and a right channel. So broadasters go to half-track recordings. The left channel is put on one-half of the tape and the right channel on the other. Stereo playback still plays the whole tape width, but half goes to one side, half to the other. Most home recorders work with even less width. They are quarter-track machines and work like this. Imagine the four-quarter tracks as numbered 1, 2, 3, and 4 from the top down. Tracks 1 and 3 will have the left and right information on them. At the end of the tape, when you turn it over, track 4 is now highest so tracks 4 and 2 get the left and right information going back the other way. What would happen if you took this tape to a broadcast operation? Those machines would play the whole width and get some music running

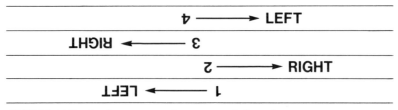

*FIGURE 2.27*    Audio tape tracks—second direction

backwards. So you generally can't record at home and use the recording in a broadcast studio. You can, however, if your tape is clean and you only record in one direction. But your equipment had better be good, or all the flaws will show up.

You can also cut this tape and add in bits of music or take out bits of bad or unwanted sound. You judge where you want to cut by playing the tape, and at the particular sound you want to eliminate, you stop the tape. See where the tape is on the playback head, pick it up and place it on another surface, and mark that spot with a grease pencil. Then thread it up again and go on playing till you get to the end of the part you want to remove. Again, stop the machine, see where the tape is, remove it, and mark it. Now, with a sharp razor blade and a metal block called an *edit-all*, fit the tape in the groove in the block. It's exactly one-quarter-inch wide. Put the grease mark right over the narrow slanted slit in the block and cut the tape by pulling the razor blade through the slit. Do the same at the first grease mark. Remove the middle piece of tape, bring the two ends together (and they fit because they were cut on the same slant), and tape them together with a special tape called *splicing tape.* Then use the razor blade to cut off the edge of the splicing tape. Cut slightly wasp-waisted at the spliced point so the sticky stuff of the tape won't rub against parts of the tape deck. Now, when you play the tape, the un-

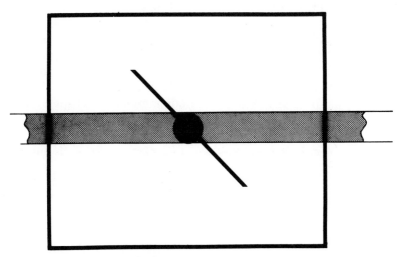

*FIGURE 2.28*   Editing block

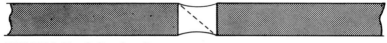

*FIGURE 2.29* Spliced audio tape

wanted part will be gone. You can get good enough at this to eliminate one sound of one letter of one word if you want. Tape editing is a real art and can be undetectable if carefully done.

Be careful with tape. Don't store it near electrical motors, because they generate electrical fields which can upset the particles. Keep it in boxes so it stays clean. Keep it cool, as heat can make it brittle. Label the boxes so you know what's on the tape. Also, if you don't play a tape very often, rewind it at least once a year. This is because the particles will influence those close either above or below them and will move them somewhat. This could produce a faint echo of sound one layer up or down. Rewinding once a year moves everything around enough to destroy such "print-through" patterns. Carts, because of their constant reuse, seldom face this problem.

You'll get a lot of tapes sent in to the station, some with commercials, some with jingles, some with just plain music. These can come in on carts, cassettes, or reel-to-reel. The reel tape is the most common. Take the case of jingles. Your station management may buy a package of jingles from a company specializing in the creation of ID's, show themes, stingers (the short music bursts used for emphasis) and any number of other specialized music needs. All these jingles arrive on one tape. You'll want to dub these over to separate carts, one for each jingle, so you can identify the particular one you want and play just it without having to search through that whole tape of jingles. The same is true with commercials. You may get a tape with four or five commercials on it. Perhaps each one is to play for a week, followed the next week by the next one on the tape. A dub of each one over to a cart makes each one instantly available to you. Some stations even transfer all the songs they play over to carts just for convenience. Besides, all this dubbing eliminates wear on the original source. Records wear out, tapes played often can get broken or creased. If you are dealing with a dub and something happens, you can always go back to the original and start all over again. Besides, the prerecorded material you get in is at all sorts of different sound levels. One tape may be very loud at a slider setting of 6, another very low. If most of your program sources sound about right at 6, dubbing the prerecorded material over to carts at the right level for you gets everything back near your standard of 6. Of course not everything will be exactly right at 6, but they can come close, and that's handy.

PATCH PANEL

Now let's get back to the board itself.

Just because the fifth slider from the left is labeled "TT2" doesn't mean it must always control turntable two. Sure it's possible to get inside the board and rewire so that suddenly tape deck one comes through there. That's a long-term change though, and there is a way to make a short-term change. It's called a *patch panel.*

Somewhere near the board you will find a series of holes. They come in pairs and there are generally two pairs for every function of the board, plus a couple more. A device called a *patch cord* will fit in a pair from either end.

Suppose you take a patch cord and put one end in the pair of holes on the top, or output, row for tape deck one and put the other end in the lower, or input, row for turntable one. Now when you flip the switch for turntable one and move the slider up, you will hear the tape deck, plus the turntable. Here's the story. A patch panel has the material from each slider going to it. By plugging into the output section, you can take the sound out of the patch panel. Then, with the other end of the

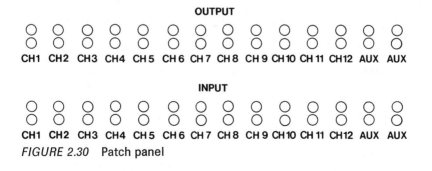

FIGURE 2.30   Patch panel

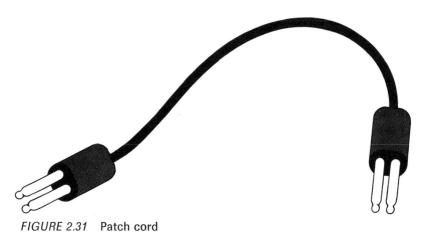

*FIGURE 2.31* Patch cord

cord, you can put the material into the panel by going into any of the input pairs. So if you have music playing on tape deck one, you can take it out of the patch panel, and hence out of the board, and put it in anywhere you want it. That includes putting it into something other than the board if you want.

Suppose you have two tapes on open reels and you want them mixed to another tape. You can take the output of tape deck one and put it into tape deck two, thus getting both sounds together. But how do you record now, since both tape decks are in use? You take the output of tape deck two, now both sounds, and put it directly into another tape deck which is not connected to the board. Most tape decks have an input jack, and that's what you plug into. Quite often, this input jack is a single, not a pair. That's OK, though, because patch cords come in a single-double form.

Or suppose you have a tape you want to play on the air but all the machines are going to be in use for the production. You can patch in an outside tape recorder by use of a single-double plug going from the output jack of the tape recorder to the input pair of whatever slider you choose.

There are other uses too. Often on a board you will have several things coming through one slider. Generally they are things you don't often need together, like a network feed line and a supplementary studio tie-in. But someday you're bound to need both simultaneously. The patch panel will have a pair for each, so take a cord and put one of the two into another slider. Say slider ten has a five-position selector switch above it, the net is position one and the other studio is posi-

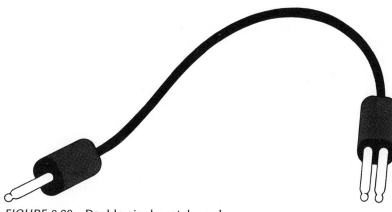

*FIGURE 2.32*   Double-single patch cord

tion two. Put a patch cord into the other studio pair on the panel and go into the input for slider nine. Set the selector switch on slider ten for one and you can now get the two things separately, as you would any other two separate sources.

Suppose, just before air time, you check one of the mikes in your studio and you get nothing. You check the mike itself and it's fine, but to check it you had to move a mike you knew was working because all your mike outlets are in use. In other words, it looks like the circuit in the board is dead, since the mike works elsewhere. Go ahead and plug it in the nonworking circuit and patch out of it to some other position on the board. You should, then, get something from the mike. If you don't, the fault is between the plug in the studio and the board, and that can't be fixed before air time, so find a way to fake it through the show. That happens rarely, though, so the patch can become an emergency first-aid measure.

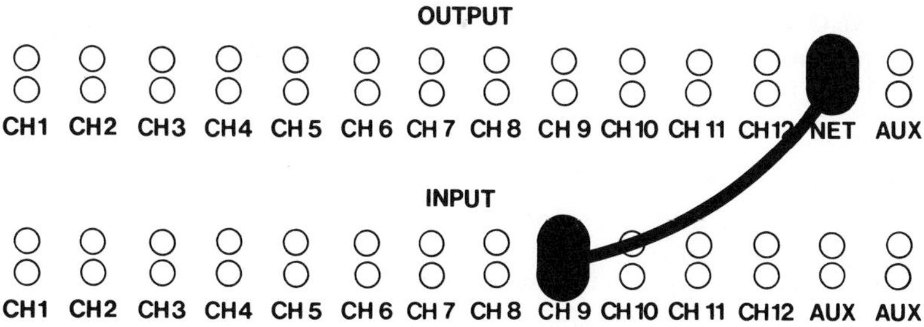

**OUTPUT**

○ ○ ○ ○ ○ ○ ○ ○ ○ ○ ○ ○ ● ○
○ ○ ○ ○ ○ ○ ○ ○ ○ ○ ○ ○ ○ ○

CH1  CH2  CH3  CH4  CH5  CH6  CH7  CH8  CH9  CH10  CH11  CH12  NET  AUX

**INPUT**

○ ○ ○ ○ ○ ○ ○ ○ ○ ○ ○ ○ ○ ○
○ ○ ○ ○ ○ ○ ○ ○ ● ○ ○ ○ ○ ○

CH1  CH2  CH3  CH4  CH5  CH6  CH7  CH8  CH9  CH10  CH11  CH12  AUX  AUX

*FIGURE 2.33*   Patched channels

You may also want to move some things around so as to get all the sliders for a particular show bunched in a row instead of strung out all down the board. A few patches can line you up in sliders 1, 2, 3, 4, and 5, which can be a blessing in a complex show.

The major problem you have to watch for is a difference of levels. Generally when you move the sound from one slider to another, it's because the slider you move to is not being used for anything else. But if you are running two sounds together on one position, remember that you can't adjust their sound levels individually. If you change one, you change both. So if one source has a high level and the other a low one, you've got problems. In that case, a patch gives you a problem instead of solving one. Figure out another way to do it.

That covers all the pieces of equipment you have to deal with. Now you need to know what you're going to be doing. Again, scripts become your guide. They are the written form of somebody's ideas on what should come out of that board you can now manipulate. So let's talk about scripts.

## RADIO SCRIPTS

The heading on a radio script should give you instant information about whether or not you've picked up the right script. If you're looking for the script for the sixty-second commercial for Sunshine Soap, you should expect to find a listing of the time and the product on top of the first page. Because the sponsor's name can be different from the product's name, you'll also see the sponsor's name there. Other information may be there as well, like the particular show the script is to be used for (if it is limited to one show), perhaps the date when it was written, and whatever else the writer, agency, or station finds relevant. So the heading might be something like this:

```
Sponsor:  Gilding Co.
Product:  Sunshine Soap
Length:   :60
Program:  I Dream of Tomorrow
Date:     30 February 1977
```

Below that, centered on the page, is the indication of who is reading. This goes in all capital letters, as does all material not to be read.

```
                        ANNCR.

Baby your skin with Sunshine . . .
```

But suppose there is to be music under the announcer's voice throughout the spot. That sort of notice goes in the body of the copy, but in all caps.

```
                        ANNCR.

(MUSIC: ET "SYMPHONY IN GREEN," SIDE 1, CUT 4.
MUSIC UNDER.)
Baby your skin with Sunshine . . . .
```

"ET" stands for electrical transcription and refers to what you normally call a record. Any directions other than the name of the reader go in the body of the copy in all caps. If, for example, the announcer is supposed to read (SINCERELY), that's the way it appears in the copy. Sound effects (WIND), sounds from unknown sources (MUFFLED LAUGHTER), and any other such information intended to create a real situation go in the body of the copy in caps. Some people use a system of single under-lines for music cues (MUSIC: ET, "SYMPHONY. . .") and double underlines for sound effects (WIND). Such signals do make the various segments stand out more clearly and can be a great help to the harrassed board engineer trying to skim through a script to see what s/he has to have ready.

At the end of our Sunshine spot, the announcer finishes and the music stops. You needn't go through naming the piece of music again. Just put (MUSIC OUT). Or if you specifically want the music to slowly disappear, put (FADE MUSIC OUT). At the bottom of the first page, the second page, and so on up to the last page, put (MORE) centered on the page so the reader knows to go on. At the top of the second and third and subsequent pages, put the title, like "Sunshine Soap" or "Murder in the Night," and the page number. When you do finally come to the end, put some symbols like -0- or # # # # # or even -30- to show there are no other pages. The -30- is most common in newspaper work, but it shows up in broadcasting too, generally from people who started out on papers.

Don't divide words at the ends of lines. Don't break in the middle of a sentence at the bottom of a page. Even if you end up with a lot of empty space at the end of a line or page, keep the units together. The reason is that people reading are often on "automatic pilot" as far as the words are concerned. Their thought is on breath control, the emotion they are putting into their voices, on maintaining an accent for their characters, or on some such other point. If a break comes, that may upset both their rhythm and concentration, thus making them sound bad. Since the air sound is your main concern, you don't want that. So keep the script direct and easy and don't break words or sentences.

Besides the script, another essential in knowing what to do and when is the station log.

## THE RADIO LOG

The only way a jock or an engineer knows what is supposed to be on the air is by looking at the log. There, all typed up, is a listing of times when programs start or spots run, numbers for which carts have which commercials, indications of whether a spot is a commercial or a public service announcement, and so on. For each day of the week, the traffic department turns out this guide to the day's programming. Certain basic things have to go on this log, so let's take a look.

First, obviously, has to be the title of what's running. This is something like the "Johnny Michaels Show," or "Music from Latvia." Next, and equally important, is the time it starts. So the log starts out looking something like this:

8:30:00  Music from Latvia

Now, we need to know if the show is being done live or if it's all on tape. So somewhere there will be a column which tells you "Live" (sometimes "Studio") or "tape #47." Within the show will be commercials and public service announcements, all of which can come at varying times; these too will be identified as live or tape.

```
8:30:00  Music from Latvia     Tape #47
         Winfield Dodge        Live
         A & M Supermarkets    Cart #39
         Latvian Club          Tape #17
```

If the station runs on a particular format, with certain events always happening at certain times, like a three-minute song followed by eight seconds of the jock talking followed by a minute commercial, it would be possible to list the exact times each of these three spots should run. Otherwise, the time column will be left blank. Speaking of time, how do you know how long each of the spots is? There will be a column headed "Length" to list just exactly that. You'll also want to know which spots are commercials and which are public service announcements; another column will tell you that.

```
8:30:00  Music from
            Latvia       Tape #47  28:37  Ent.
         Winfield Dodge  Live        :30  CA
         A & M
            Supermarkets Cart #39    :60  CA
         Latvian Club    Tape #17    :30  PSA
```

Now comes the problem of telling just when within the show (assuming you're not on the tight three-minute–eight-second–one-minute type format) the breaks will come for these spots. When the show was originally taped, the people knew they had to break first for :30, then for :60, and so on. By checking the clock, they could record how far into the show the first break came, the second break, and so forth. This listing will be provided to the jock and the engineer on a separate run-down sheet. Sometimes it is included on the log, but most often it's separate. Now what happens at the end of the show? We know it will come out at 8:58:27 because that's the time it started plus the length listed on the log. So we'll have this:

|         | Latvian Club | Tape #17 | :30 | PSA |
|---------|--------------|----------|-----|-----|
| 8:58:27 | Joan's Boutique | Cart #103 | :30 | CA |
| 8:58:57 | Lyric Theater | Live | :10 | CA |
| 8:59:07 | Beef & Bird Restaurant | Cart #88 | :30 | CA |
| 8:59:37 | Jones Insurance | Cart #114 | :20 | CA |
| 8:59:57 | ID | Live | :03 | ID |
| 9:00:00 | Johnny Michaels Show | Live | 2:58:30 | Ent. |

The "Ent." is one possible abbreviation to indicate an entertainment show; "Var." for variety is another example. But back to the station break.

We can see that once the Latvian show ends, we go to a series of commercials, an ID, and into the next show, which is a live jock doing his three-hour shift. The only other essential for the log is a space to show when items actually did get on and off. Machines and people being what they are, errors will happen and sometimes everything gets on late (rarely early). So somewhere will be two columns labelled "Time On" and "Time Off."

8:59:57  ID  Live  :03  ID  8:59:58  9:00:04

The jock was just a bit late, and said a bit more than normal going into the next show. No harm is done, of course, and probably the station got a little extra hype for the "Johnny Michaels Show."

If something screws up so badly a spot is missed altogether, the jock may run it later in his show, in his next break (if he's not on a tight format); or if it was supposed to be in a station break, the jock may run it within his show at the first break. Some stations do this as a matter of policy, some don't. Running a spot again to make up for one that was missed is called giving a *make-good*. Because some sponsors buy very specific times, make-goods aren't given as a matter of policy until they are checked out with traffic. If a sponsor is buying a general time period though (between 8 P.M. and 10 P.M., say), then a make-good given at the next break is perfectly acceptable. If a station is totally sold up and only runs a certain number of spots per break, make-goods are impossible. There is no room for them. So the missed spot gets reported on a *discrepancy report* (a daily listing of all the errors of the broadcast day), and the traffic department will, the next day, see the report and reschedule the spot in an appropriate time.

Someone is always designated as the official keeper of the log. This may be the jock on the air, the engineer on the board, or even a transmitter engineer. But for both radio and television, someone has to be responsible for checking off the events as they happen, and recording the time they run. Then, when the shift ends, s/he signs the log. This makes the log an official document which can be used to prove the spots did run and the sponsors can be billed for them, and to prove to the FCC what the station actually does with its air time.

But logs and scripts and equipment are of no use to anyone without a person to put them all to work. Somebody has to come into the control room and put everything together into a smooth, finished show. That someone can be the promotion manager or program director, or even the jock, but whoever it is, let's call that person a radio producer, because s/he actually produces the air product, be it commercial, drama, or news.

## THE RADIO PRODUCER

Radio's chief advantage over television is the human mind. As Stan Freberg once said, "Television expands your mind, but only up to 21 inches." If radio wants to move from the Taj Mahal to New York's Empire State Building, some Indian music and the right accent on the announcer can be followed by some taxis beeping and a different accent, and the move is accomplished. In television, you may have a problem as complex as flying the film crew and actors to India for a day or two, and then to New York to finish up. A radio producer, then, by being aware of the differences in sound, can create an entire world in the listener's mind.

That means that when you are sitting at the board, you can create almost any part of human existence if you use the right inputs. If you are doing something as simple as a :30 spot for a local bank, you will want different sound effects than for a :30 for the local supermarket chain. Even if the bank is trying to convey a new, fresh image, they don't want nervous, agitated music in their spots. They are selling a sense of security as well, and nervousness certainly doesn't lead to security.

Suppose you are making a spot for an airline to run during the winter in the northeastern states, and the pitch is to fiy south for a vacation on the beach during the nastiness of northern snow time. You might start out with the sound of gentle surf hitting the beach. In the dead of winter, that's a very seductive sound to a northern ear. But if you listen carefully, you realize the surf sound isn't immediately identifiable. So you throw in the call of a seagull, and you have a whole scene building up in the mind's eye. Make use of some soft announcing building to a rising tempo theme and you can tie the thoughts of sand and sun and sea to the thought of an airplane and cause a shivering stampede into the airline's offices.

Admittedly, you sometimes have to say a lot more in a radio situation to set a scene than you do in television. For example, the hero walks into a darkened room and says, "It's too dark in here. Where's the light switch? Wha. . .? (THUD. HURRIED FOOTSTEPS FADING OUT.)" He's been hit on the head by an unknown assailant and knocked out. In television, he wouldn't say anything. We can see it's too dark, and with the proper shots, we can see him get hit. But the result is the same; we still know the hero is down and the villain is getting away. Dialogue, a sound effects person punching a sandbag, and an actor rapidly walking off mike and toward a corner of the studio give us all the realism we need.

These are examples of the well-chosen sound or piece of music, but one other production advantage of radio is audio tape. Since you can cut it up, you can get the exact sound you want and stop or start at exactly the right spot. If the build of a piece of music has to hit at exactly a certain word in the script, you can record the music and the words on separate tapes, then cut them to exactly the right lengths. Start them together and the two sounds will occur at exactly the instant you want. Or you can just record the music, time it to find out where the peak comes, then figure out how long it takes to get from word one to the peak word, and just start the tape at the right number of words. If you want to end at a certain time, you can time the music tape at, say, :13 and then start the tape thirteen seconds before you're through and so come out exactly on time. Tape gives you a precision of control over the sound you want, but you still have to be sure you know what you want. Sharpening up that connection between ears and brain becomes a lifelong process for an interested radio producer.

# 3

# broadcasting electronics

Anyone working in broadcasting is surrounded by machines. Without them, the jobs would vanish. It only makes sense, then, to have an idea of how they work, what their principles are, and what they can do for you. Further, the more you know about how they work, the better able you will be to figure out if you can do something new with them that no one else has thought of. If you know enough about the machine to know your idea is physically impossible, then you can drop it. But no idea ought to be dropped till you reach that point. The most creative broadcasters know enough about the equipment to know when to push for a different approach and when to shut up. That takes knowing how things work. Also, knowing how the equipment works will help you avoid doing damage to it. Since you don't want to hurt the tools of your trade, knowing how they work becomes doubly important.

## TELEVISION CAMERAS

A magician changes one thing into another. There are many natural processes that change one thing into another, such as cold temperatures changing water into ice. And there are some machines specifically designed to change one thing into another, like the machines that change raw plastic into records. A television camera is one of those machines that change things—it changes light energy into electrical energy. The light falls on a subject and is reflected into the camera. If there is enough light to activate the camera at all, certain things will happen inside of it. That's like your eye. If there is only a dim bit of light, you may not be able to see anything. But if there is enough light reflected off of objects, you will be able to see them because of what goes on inside your head with that reflected light. Let's take this analogy a bit further. Light is reflected into your eye, where the retina at the back of your eyeball breaks it up into little bunches. Each bunch causes a particular response by a portion of the retina, and that response causes some stimulation of the optic nerve. When this nerve is stimulated, it sends a particular pattern of electrical energy to the brain, which then interprets the electricity in certain ways and causes you to see. So vision is not so much in the eye as it is in the brain.

A television camera works much the same way. The light is reflected into the camera, where it is broken down into bunches called *lines.* These lines stimulate various pieces of equipment to send out electrical signals, which travel to the cable and out of the camera to master control. In master control, these signals can be turned back into a picture. So the picture is not in the camera so much as it is in master control.

OK, let's look closer at what happens to the light as it enters the camera. This light carries colors with it (by virtue of the frequencies involved), and these colors get split up by a prism. The red colors go to a red *pick-up tube*, the blue to a blue one, and the green to a green one. All pictures of light can be broken up into those three colors, and all colors, even yellow and orange, can be made from light of those three colors. Now these pick-up tubes are like the retina of the eye in that they are sensitive to light and react in certain ways. But they can't react to a lot of light any more than the retina can. So as well as breaking the scene down into the three colors, they have to break it down into smaller units of light.

That's where the lines come in. Let's just take the green pick-up tube as an example. All the green light from the scene falls on the green tube. Inside the tube is a coating of phosphors which will glow as the light hits it. In places where a lot of green light hits it, it will glow brightly. In places where little green light hits it, it will glow very little. As it glows, a beam of electrons from the back of the tube is sent up to the front. This is a narrow little line of electrons; and it gets pushed across the coating of phosphors, but it covers only a thin little line of them. If the phosphors are glowing brightly, the electrons get very stimulated. If the glow is weak, the electrons are hardly excited at all. So the beam of electrons reacts to light exactly as it is bright or dark. Here's the kicker—a flow of electrons is an electric current. That's a definition. So we have changed the light into an electrical current by this process, and this current represents the light and dark areas. If it's bright, the electrons are really stimulated, and we can say we have a stronger flow of electricity. It's the reverse if it's dark. But this beam of electrons is small and covers only a narrow line of the phosphors. That's not the complete picture, so we have to send a beam of electrons out to a spot below where the first beam went across the phosphors. After the first beam goes across the picture, we start that beam over again, but down lower, and back to a neutral level of energy. We do that over and over again and thus break the picture down into lines. Those are the small bunches we needed for the pick-up tube to handle.

All this has to be done fast, or the picture will change out in front of the camera before we are through. Our electrical system operates on a 60-cycle-per-second basis, so we can most conveniently tie into the number 60 as a basis. Since our picture needs to be fairly clear, we want quite a few lines. If we used only 10 or 20 of those narrow lines to make a picture, we'd have no detail at all. So what our system uses is 525 lines. And we get those 525 lines every thirtieth of a second, which

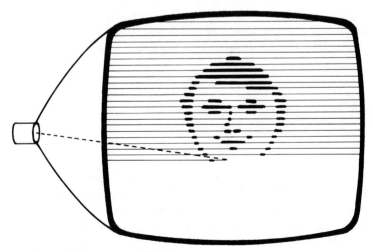

FIGURE 3.1   Picture traced by lines

is a doubling of the 60-cycle-per-second basis. In a sixtieth of a second, we get half the lines, and in the second sixtieth of a second we get the other half. There are good reasons for not doing the whole 525 lines in a sixtieth of a second.

First of all, it's easier to build the machines to operate at a lower speed. And a thirtieth of a second, even though it's fast, isn't as fast as a sixtieth. Then there are some moves which are faster than a sixtieth of a second, so the picture changes faster than we can really manage. So by showing half of how things were in the first sixtieth of a second, and how things are on the other half in the second sixtieth, we can get an average that comes pretty close to what really happens. That first half of the picture is made up of all the odd-numbered lines. Obviously, the second half is all the even-numbered lines. So in the first sixtieth of a second we get lines 1, 3, 5, 7, and so on. Next we get 2, 4, 6, 8, and so on. These half pictures are called *fields*. You have one field every sixtieth of a second. Two fields together make up a complete picture, and that is called a *frame*. Frames take two-sixtieths of a second, of course, or one-thirtieth. Therefore, you have a complete picture, or frame, every thirtieth of a second. Or said another way, you get thirty complete pictures every second. Each of these pictures has 525 lines in it.

The green picture has been broken into the smaller bits called lines, and an awful lot of them occur every second— 15,750 lines a second to be exact. That's a lot of modifying of the electrical current. However, remember we have two other pick-up tubes—the red and the blue. What happens to this mass of electrical information the cameras are putting out?

## MASTER CONTROL
## AND TELEVISION TRANSMITTING

The modified electrical currents go into a room generally referred to as master control, because so many things are controlled from there. In this room are machines which can further modify that current, make it stronger, or change it into something else, such as light. But generally these machines are used to make sure everything stays in step, that the three pick-up tubes are showing the same thing at the same time, and that the signals are amplified and transmitted out into the air.

Those lines which go across the picture are referred to as *scan lines* as well as just plain "lines" because they actually scan across the picture. Because we have to send the various signals through cables, machines, and devices, we lose a bit of the picture which is scanned by the camera. The edges get cut off by all the electronic maneuvering. Then, as we modify it and amplify it in master control, we cut off more of the scanned area. When we transmit it, more is lost. And the home receivers chop off another little bit. So the scanned area is considerably larger than what the normal viewer sees. Besides that, things happen off the edge of the scanned picture that we don't want the viewer to see.

An example is *blanking*. Suppose that line of electrons picked up information in its left-to-right sweep of the picture and carried that information back across the picture as it moved back to start over again. That would mess up the next line with an overlay of the information from the first line. So we have to blank out the information of the first line before the electron beam can go back. So after we have all the picture we want on one line, we go into what is called "blanking." It's just a return to neutral of the electron beam. All picture information is blanked out. Then as the beam returns, it won't mess up the picture. So beyond the edge of the scanned picture, we have a black area of blanking. Out in that black area, we have one other thing we also need.

That's the *sync pulse*. It stands, obviously enough, for synchronizing pulse, and it does a couple things. First of all, we must have a way to get the electron beam back to the beginning. So instead of feeding it electricity of a certain strength, we feed it electricity of an opposite strength. If it's a true opposite, instead of going left to right, the beam will now go right to left. That will bring it right back to where it started. This happens within blanking, so the picture doesn't get disturbed. This reversed signal also happens at exactly the same time for all the signals, pick-up tubes, and so on. That means everything has the same signal to use as a base and a reference point. If one element were running faster than another, it would slow down to the speed of the sync pulse.

Others might have to speed up to be in line, but all will be connected to the speed of the sync pulse every time it comes along. Hence the name "synchronizing," as everything is set by its speed. In master control, there is a way to look at things like the sync pulse and blanking, and it's called the *waveform monitor.*

This monitor takes the signals from the camera and does different things with them. You won't get a picture, you'll get a bunch of lines on a green screen that has a graph laid over it. The lines form a pattern such as that illustrated in Figure 3.2. The lines at the right and left of the blank space represent the picture you see on a normal monitor. The high peaks represent the brightest objects in the picture, and the low points represent the darkest. The long space in between represents blanking, and you can see it is well below the darkest part of the picture, so there is no information carried there. The part going below the zero line is the sync pulse. It alone goes in an opposite direction from the rest of the lines, and as we know, that oppositeness is what makes the electron beam go in an opposite direction, or back to where it started from.

Now let's take a look at those other lines. In order to get a good picture, the brightest objects in the picture mustn't make lines that go above 100 percent. The blackest shouldn't go below about 7 percent. If the brightest is too bright, the engineers

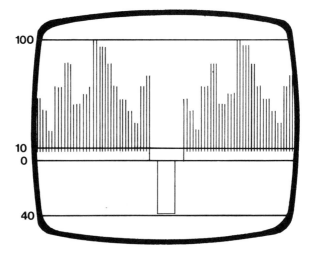

*FIGURE 3.2* Wave form monitor

will have to adjust the cameras so the line doesn't go above 100 percent. That makes other items look very dark indeed. So dark, in fact, that you can't see any detail on them. If, on the other hand, your black objects are very black, the engineers will bring the lowest point up to 7 percent so as to show some detail. However, then other objects will be so bright they become blobs of white. So to get a good picture, you need to eliminate the very bright and the very dark. That's a result of the cameras not being as sensitive as your eyes and having to be protected from extremes of light and dark.

That 7 percent level is called the *pedestal*, as it's like setting the picture up on a pedestal above the zero level. It allows you to see some detail, as otherwise something really black and with no detail would look like a hole in the picture.

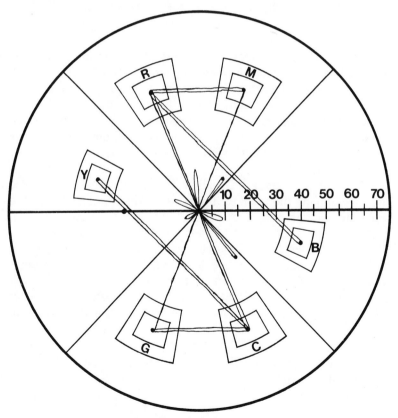

*FIGURE 3.3*   Monitor for color adjustment

There's one other screen used to adjust the picture. That's a round one called a *vectorscope* that lets you know if the various colors are in proper relation to each other. If the input of the green pick-up tube falls in the right place, as well as the red and the blue pick-up tubes, then everything looks right. However, if they start drifting out of the little boxes shown on the graph, the colors shift and people start looking purple or green.

After all these adjustments are made and the picture, the colors, the blanking, and the sync pulse are coordinated, master control can send the electrical impulses out to the transmitter. The signals are amplified, or built up in strength, then added to a carrier signal. Each station has a different frequency assigned to it, and that frequency will carry the signal along as it moves out. It's sort of like channel 2 using a Ford to carry passengers, channel 3 using a Chevrolet, channel 4 a Dodge, and so on. All the stations use roughly the same sort of thing to carry their signals, but there are some significant differences. The main difference is in how many cycles per second their carrier frequency has. Frequency is a number which tells you how many cycles per second you have, and as you go up in channel numbers, you go up in frequency as well. As the frequency goes up, you need more power to get the carrier frequency out. Some stations can use as much as a million watts of electrical energy to transmit their signal. Compare that to the hundred-watt light bulb you use!

As with anything, the farther the signal goes, the more tired it gets and the weaker it gets. At a long distance from the transmitting antenna, the signal becomes so tired you can hardly get any picture out of it at all. There's another problem besides distance. These signals travel in a straight line, so if there is an object between you and the antenna, you won't receive the signal. It hits the obstruction and stops, as it can't go around. It can, though, bounce off. Sometimes when it bounces, it hits another object, bounces again, and goes off in approximately the original direction. That happens in a big city, and the signal bounces off tall buildings. Your set may get so many of those bounces that the picture you see is a series of the same images, slightly out of line. This is what we call "getting ghosts." But just how are you picking up these signals anyway?

## TELEVISION RECEIVERS

You have an antenna on the roof of your house or on the set itself. In certain positions and with certain distances between its ends, this antenna becomes sensitive to the carrier frequencies of the various stations. It then captures the frequencies plus all those modifications which the station has put out. Like any electric current, the captured signals can be taken along wires into a receiver. Then, this receiver does what the camera did, but in reverse. It sends a beam of electrons toward a screen coated with phosphors, but it already has the varying bits of energy so it makes the screen glow bright or dark. If it is carrying information for the green part of the screen, it makes a green phosphor glow. If for red, then red glows, and so on. However, it does it a line at a time, just like the camera. The difference is that the camera splits everything into three parts for the three colors, and the home receiver uses only the one beam to activate one of the three phosphors at each point along the line. So one beam does the work of three, so to speak. This beam is controlled by the sync pulse just like everything else. It goes back and starts over when the sync pulse comes along. It makes thirty pictures a second. And it does all this on command of equipment many miles away with no more connection than the air between them!

The pictures you see come from the glowing phosphors on the front of your picture tube, so the electrical energy has been converted back into light. Your receiver, then, is another one of those machines that makes one thing into another. The whole television process is a way to convert light into electrical energy and then back into light.

We've talked a great deal about light energy; now it's time to turn to sound energy. That, of course, means radio.

Radio comes in two flavors—AM and FM. The first means "amplitude modulation" and the second "frequency modulation." By experience, we know that AM can be torn up by static and sounds less full, or dynamic, than FM. We know also that only FM stations can be stereo. In some cases, we can even hear quadraphonic sound on FM. So we need to talk about the electronics of all this and see just what's going on. Let's discuss AM first.

## AM RADIO

All sound involves the motion of molecules. You know that, and you know that's why there's no sound in outer space—it's a vacuum and has no molecules to move around. If you have one sound, one clear note, the molecules move in regular waves like very even ocean waves. When they hit your ear, you respond to that as sound, and identify it as that particular note. It's like the waves hitting the shore; that makes a sound too. As the waves are different, so is the sound different. Stormy waves hitting the shore sound different from peaceful waves. Likewise, one note of a trumpet sounds different from one note of a drum.

If you diagram a one-note wave, you get something like Figure 3.4. No doubt no sound wave ever looks like that, but we can use the diagram to represent the sound just like we use these little black marks on this page to represent the sound we make when we speak. So we can call Figure 3.4 the wave of one particular note. If we wanted a higher note, we would make the wave more condensed, like Figure 3.5. A whole bunch of notes together, then, could give us a really complex looking diagram, like Figure 3.6. However, that might represent only three or four instruments playing a very few notes. A whole musical piece could be even more complex. So rather than chance messing up that complexity in transmission, radio decided to deal with a simpler wave. It's called a *carrier wave*. Like the one-note wave, it goes along in perfect regularity, as illustrated in Figure 3.7.

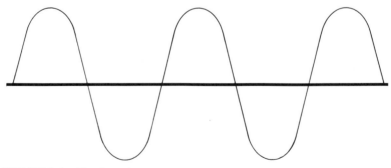

*FIGURE 3.4* Single note

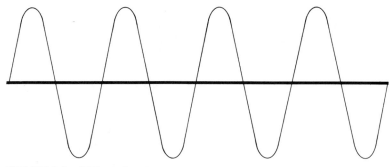

*FIGURE 3.5* Different note

How high up and how far down it goes from that center line is called its *amplitude*, which is just a big word for the height and depth of a wave. Someone discovered that if you vary the amplitude, or the height and depth, of the wave, you change the sound of this carrier wave, just like making sound waves more condensed. So if you change the amplitude of the carrier wave to match the changes of condensation or expansion of the sound waves, you'll recreate the same sound. This is shown in Figure 3.8.

If you can build a device to pick up that particular wave, you can interpret those changes in amplitude as particular notes and thus reproduce all the notes of the original sounds. That, of course, is what a radio does. It picks up the changes, or modulations, of the height and depth, or amplitude, of a wave of a particular sort and interprets the modulations as notes of sound. I'm still amazed it works.

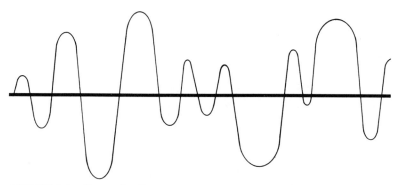

*FIGURE 3.6* Several notes

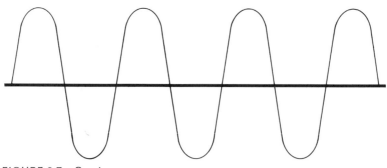

*FIGURE 3.7*   Carrier wave

That explains only one station though. The carrier wave we have talked about was stretched out a certain distance. Suppose the carrier wave were stretched a little less far, as in Figure 3.9. You could still modulate the amplitude, so you can now do the same thing, but with a different carrier wave. As the waves are crowded together or stretched out, their frequency changes. *Frequency* means how frequently the waves are going through a standard distance, such as a mile. If a lot of waves fit in the distance of a mile, you would pass waves frequently in going over that mile. So we would say the frequency is high. If the waves are more stretched out, and you meet fewer in a mile, the frequency is said to be lower. So that's how we get the different frequencies for radio stations. But they all work the same way—they vary the amplitude to get sounds.

Why, then, can't we get as good quality sound on AM as on FM? Music is a very complex pattern of waves, far more com-

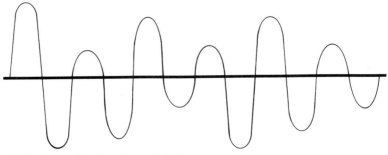

*FIGURE 3.8*   Amplitude modulation

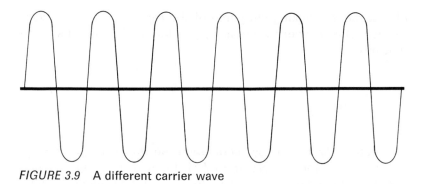

*FIGURE 3.9*   A different carrier wave

plex than that shown in Figure 3.6. Sometimes it gets so complex there simply isn't any room left when the carrier wave is squeezed down. Or sometimes the complexity is so great that we would have to go higher than our particular carrier wave can go. So the extremes are chopped off just so we will be able to broadcast anything. Thus AM radio ends up with sound limited to frequencies of music that are a good deal less than the ear is capable of hearing. For this reason, the music sounds less full, less rich. One thing that doesn't get chopped off, though, is *static*. Various things like electric motors or sometimes spark plugs in cars or lightning generate electrical waves, but in very random, senseless patterns. Music is a smooth, ordered pattern, but static can make waves such as those in Figure 3.10. No matter how random, though, they all fit within the limits of our carrier waves. So when lightning crackles, AM radio gets jumbled-up waves added to its signal, and we hear the jumble as static. It fits on the wave, so we can't get rid

*FIGURE 3.10*   Static

of it without knocking out some of the regular waves we want to save. One answer to the static problem is FM, so let's go to that next.

## FM RADIO

FM stands for frequency modulation, so you can guess right off what is different here from AM. Instead of using changes in the height and depth of a wave to represent particular sounds, FM broadcasting changes the frequency to represent different sounds. Think again about the ocean waves. If you get a whole batch of water pushed onto the shore, you have a wave coming in. If just a little water comes in, you have the trough between waves. Likewise, in FM broadcasting you can have a lot of stuff coming at you at one moment and less at another. This difference can represent the different sounds, just like a wave and a trough are different.

Let's look at Figure 3.11, again of a carrier wave. That's one sound. Now suppose we bunch some of those waves together so as to get more stuff at one spot than at another, such as in Figure 3.12. We can represent two notes this way. But because we have more cycles going through a standard distance, like the mile I mentioned earlier, we can say we have varied the frequency. So we call this frequency modulation. But how does this approach get better sound and no static?

Think of the call numbers you associate with various radio stations. An AM station might have something like 1300, which means 1300 kilohertz, or thousands of cycles. FM might be 102.5

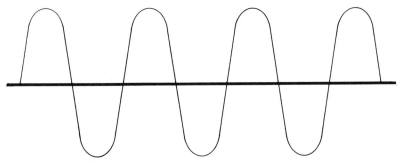

FIGURE 3.11 Carrier wave

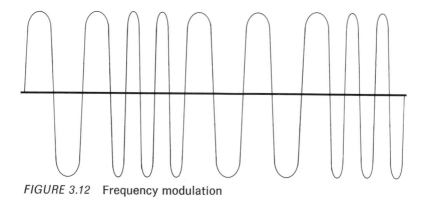

*FIGURE 3.12* Frequency modulation

megahertz, or millions of cycles. AM obviously has a lot fewer cycles to play with. To get as much sound as possible included, you can't afford to chop out any of the thousands of cycles. The thousands is so limited an amount already that the top frequencies of music have to be left out. But when you get to the millions of cycles of FM, you can chop out a lot and still have plenty of room left. So you can suppress the frequencies where static happens and still have room enough to include all the frequencies music makes.

## RADIO TRANSMISSION

However, nothing comes for free. FM gets some advantages from its millions of cycles, but it pays the price by losing in the amount of territory it can cover. It also takes a lot more power to cover an area than does AM. All of us have heard radio stations from hundreds of miles away, particularly at night. Think of it this way: an AM wave is more stretched out and so covers more territory. Given enough power, like a 50,000 watt clear channel station, AM will cover thousands and thousands of square miles. FM simply can't. Even with a lot of power, the waves are just too close together to go very far. A hundred miles from the station is about the absolute maximum distance you can expect FM radio waves to travel under the best of conditions. To accomplish that, a station may need a million watts instead of the 50,000. The FM signal may be better in quality, but it doesn't have AM's distance ability.

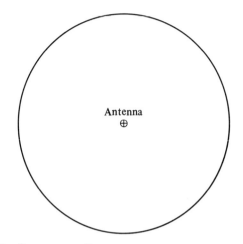

*FIGURE 3.13*    Coverage pattern

A number of things affect the distance radio waves can travel, so let's talk of what happens to them once they leave the transmitter. Each station, of course, has a lot of electronic gear which takes the sounds from the studios and converts them into the right types of electronic waves. Then somewhere, generally near the station, there is a transmitter and an antenna. The transmitter sends the waves up the tower which then radiates them out into the air. Sophisticated antenna design can even determine what pattern these radiated waves take. You might assume the pattern would have to be a circle around the antenna, as illustrated in Figure 3.13. But that's not necessarily so. The pattern can be something like Figure 3.14, if

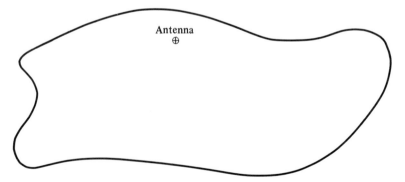

*FIGURE 3.14*    Controlled coverage pattern

*FIGURE 3.15*    The earth dropping away

necessary. But once the waves leave the antenna, what happens to them? The earth drops out from under them. Really.
Those waves travel out from the antenna in a straight line, but
the surface of the earth curves down and away. So the waves
end up travelling right off the planet, as shown in Figure 3.15.

That's why, when you get a certain distance away from a
station, you can't hear it any longer. The waves are way up
above you, heading out into space. However, that's not the
whole story. The waves that do that are called *ground waves*
because they travel along the ground, or close to it, before
they become unreachable. But some waves leaving the antenna,
also travelling in straight lines, hit that layer in the upper
atmosphere called the *ionosphere* and bounce off it back toward
the earth. Most of the waves go on through, but some don't.
Particularly at night some will bounce back to earth. The
ionosphere gets closer to the earth and a bit more dense and
hence throws a few more waves back. Those waves seem like
they are coming out of the sky, and so they are called *sky
waves*. Sky waves look something like Figure 3.16. Figure 3.17

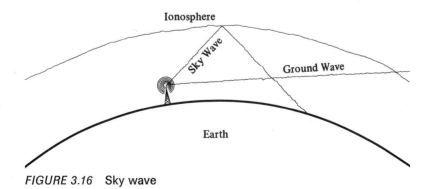

*FIGURE 3.16*    Sky wave

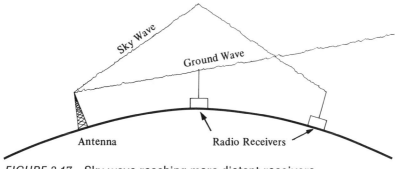

*FIGURE 3.17* Sky wave reaching more distant receivers

shows what we get when we put these two waves together. A sky wave covers a bigger area than a ground wave. Since sky waves work best at night, we are able to get many distant stations after the sun goes down.

## RADIO RECEPTION

Because sky waves work best at night is also why you get two different types of coverage patterns for a station. That radiated pattern around the antenna is generally the pattern of the ground wave. The signal in there is fairly constant and fairly clear. Rain storms, tall buildings, and the like can cause some variations in the pattern, but it stays pretty much the same. It's this pattern the FCC has worked with for determining the frequency for a particular station. The Commission makes sure no other station on the same frequency exists within that pattern. That way, interference is minimized. But the sky waves give another, larger pattern in which that station can quite often be heard. The first pattern is called the *primary coverage pattern*, and the one from the sky waves is called the *secondary coverage pattern*. The two are illustrated in Figure 3.18.

The town of Medway is not in the primary coverage pattern of the station in Oak Bluff, but it is able to pick up the station most of the time. At night, the secondary pattern gets even bigger and includes Fairfield, which otherwise never hears the station.

But what about a station on the same frequency in Dewey? The primary pattern never touches Oak Bluff, so the stations

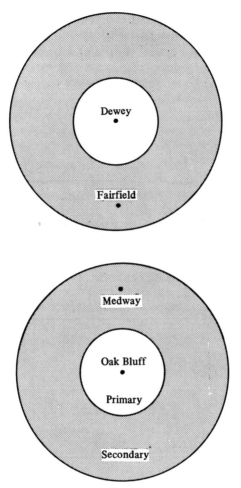

*FIGURE 3.18* Coverage patterns from two separate towns

don't interfere with one another. At night, though, the secondary patterns overlap in both Medway and Fairfield. People in those two towns get both stations at once, and the interference is so great they can't listen to either one. The FCC has tried to arrange frequency allocations so that happens as seldom as possible, but we all know there is a good deal of interference in AM. The Commission has even insisted there be at least 10,000 cycles between frequencies in an area. That is, a station broadcasting at 860 khz (kilohertz) will not have neighboring

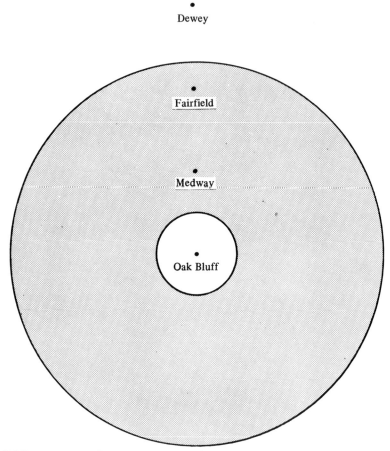

*FIGURE 3.19* Night coverage from Oak Bluff

stations any closer than 850 and 870. However, stations still cross each other. Nothing's perfect.

The FCC has even set up a classification of stations in an attempt to keep the interference down. The classification works pretty well, if not perfectly. It runs like this. Class I stations can use from 10,000 to 50,000 watts of power and are on clear channels. That means very few other stations anywhere in the U.S. use the same frequency, and those that do are separated by hundreds and hundreds of miles. One is totally alone: WLW-AM in Cincinnati. It's the only station in the country on 700 khz. Class II stations have power from 250 to 5,000 watts and are

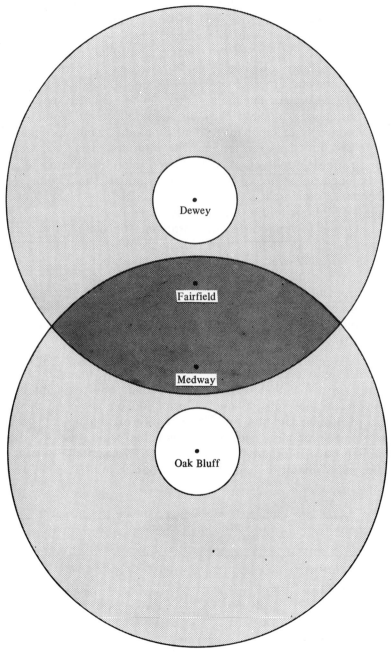

*FIGURE 3.20* **Night interference**

also on clear channels. Very few others in the country share their frequencies. But they may have to be controlled in various ways so they don't interfere with Class I stations. Some go off at sunset and some have closely controlled radiation patterns from their antennas. Class III stations have from 500 to 5,000 watts and are regional stations controlled so as not to interfere with clear channels. Others in the country may have their frequency too, but they are generally quite a distance away and only at night may some problems come up. Finally, there are the Class IV stations with no more than 1,000 watts during the day and 250 at night. Some even have to go off at night because so many surrounding stations share their frequencies. Interference is most common in this class. About half the stations in the U.S. fall into Class IV.

FM has fewer interference problems because the signals just don't go out as far. There simply are no equivalents to the Class I 50,000 watt clear channel AM stations. So all FM stations are licensed to operate twenty-four hours a day and at full power for the entire time. That's not to say there is no concern over interference. Obviously, two stations on the same frequency still can't operate close to one another, but it's easier to keep them separated in FM than in AM.

There's another aspect of FM broadcasting that's important to both stations and listeners. That's stereo, and in some cases, quad. You know that to get stereo sound from a record, you must have the right channel information on one side of the record groove and the left channel information on the other side. In FM broadcasting, you can get this same type of sides-of-the-groove information by sending out your signal in a certain way. Think of the signal as going out all in one plane, as if

TABLE 3.1    Station classifications and their power ranges and characteristics.

| Class | Power (Watts) | Characteristics |
|---|---|---|
| I | 10,000-50,000 | clear channel |
| II | 250-5,000 | clear channel |
| III | 500-5,000 | regional |
| IV | 1000 maximum day, 250 maximum night | local |

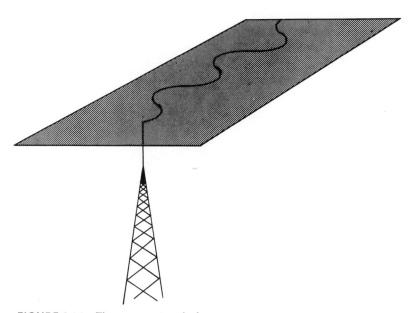

*FIGURE 3.21* The mono signal plane

all the bumps and changes and modulations of the waves were written on a flat sheet coming out from the antenna. That's like one side of a groove. Send out another batch of modified waves on a flat sheet that's perpendicular to the first, and you suddenly have two paths for information.

Your receiver at home can distinguish between these two sheets and so can send the right information to the right speaker, and the left to the left. Clever people, these engineers. Next comes quad. Can you just add a couple more sheets? So far, no. The FCC hasn't approved that sort of thing because no one knows for sure what that sort of modification might do to coverage patterns, intereference patterns, or frequency separations, and so on. So for radio, a quad set-up has been devised that superimposes two signals on one sheet and two on the other. Then, with the right gear at home, a listener can get the normal two sheets of information but break each sheet in two and thus get the four channels needed for quadraphonic sound. The separation may not be as good as with four distinct, or discrete, channels, but it's good now and is getting better. This process is referred to as a *matrix*, or matrixed sound, because a matrix is a supporting structure giving form to something

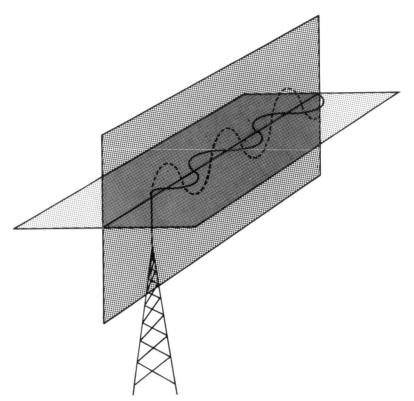

*FIGURE 3.22* The stereo signal planes

else. The final signal supports music in the form of quadra-phonic sound.

The next time you listen to a stereo FM broadcast or a favorite AM station, think about that little box you call a radio. It's picking up signals which pass right through solid walls and through you, for that matter. From all the signals around, it singles out the one you want and converts it into music or a human voice. Amazing!

# PART 2

# STATION TIME

# 4
# broadcasting's
## past

We've all seen those commercials on television that show the multiple images left by people or objects moving across the screen, so we see a continuous record of all the movements the person or object goes through. This multi-image scene gives us a record, or trail, back through a portion of time to all the changes that have happened. If your eyes worked like the film camera making those spots, you would see a time-trail going back over all the events of your life. You can expand this time-trail idea to include things as well as people.

In a historic city like Boston, you'll find buildings that go back to the time of the Revolution. If you visit Paul Revere's house, you can imagine a long time-trail going back to that one dark night when he set out on his ride. Besides people and objects like houses, you can imagine a time-trail for something a bit more intangible. How about the local car agency that now covers a square block but started out twenty years ago across town in one small building? Here's a business which has been housed in different places and been different sizes, but it's been the same business all along. And that, of course, brings me to the point.

Broadcasting has a time-trail that stretches a long way back. Right now you may see only your part of it, perhaps only a studio with a batch of machines you know you can run successfully. But what of all the other departments of the station? How did the news department get separated from the production department? Who first had the idea of selling something as intangible as time? Where did all the machines come from? If we follow broadcasting's time-trail back about a century, we can get some ideas of how it got in the position it's in now.

We'll find there are two distinct aspects to this trail, though. One is the technical side, the development of the tools and gadgets and machines that give us sounds and pictures. The other side is how the technical materials were used—how stations were set up, how they were organized, how broadcast content was determined, how controls were set up, and so on. But let's go back to the beginning of the trail and follow on up to the present day.

## THE THEORIES
### AND THEIR EARLY USE

We can start with just one man—James Clerk Maxwell. He knew about electricity, knew that messages could be transmitted across wires by Morse code, and knew still pictures could be sent over wire. With that knowledge, plus the knowledge of how light waves behave, he began thinking about how waves from the rest of the electromagnetic spectrum must behave. So in many senses, we can say the beginning of the broadcasting trail starts in 1873 with his publication of a paper describing the nature of radio waves. Until he explained what these wave *ought* to be, no one could do any experiments to see if they *were* this way. But once the paper was out, a man named Heinrich Hertz started experiments to test Clerk Maxwell's theories. In 1888, Hertz published his results and verified the predictions. The trail grew wider as more people started trying different things with radio waves. An Italian named Guglielmo Marconi developed radio as a medium to send messages. All through the early 1900s, he built transmission stations and receivers and set up companies. The First World War slowed all this and changed the ownership situation so that it wasn't until 1920 that we can say radio broadcasting really began in this country. True, in 1909, Dr. Charles David Herrold of San Jose, California reportedly distributed crystal sets to friends in his neighborhood and kept them entertained with music and news, but organized broadcasting came after the war.

KDKA, Pittsburgh, is most frequently recognized as the pioneer broadcast station. The station, operated by the Westinghouse Electric and Manufacturing Company, began its operation on 2 November 1920, with coverage of the Harding-Cox presidential election returns. However, at least one station in Detroit went on the air prior to KDKA's first broadcast. A newspaper, the Detroit *News*, chose the occasion of the Michigan primary elections on 31 August 1920 to begin operation of station 8MK.

Another Westinghouse station, WBZ, Springfield, Massachusetts, did in fact receive the first commercial broadcasting station license authorized by the Department of Commerce and Labor under the Radio Act of 1912 on 15 September 1921. The license for station WBZ has since been moved to Boston. KDKA was licensed on 7 November 1921. Station 8MK was later licensed under the call letters WWJ.

All three are still on the air today, and that is no small accomplishment when compared with the fate of many of the early stations. Until the Radio Act of 1927, there was little control exerted over who could build a station and at what power and frequency a station could operate. Consequently, a great many people built "radio stations." By late 1922, there were no less than 600 stations on the air and almost one million receiving sets in American homes. Many of the stations were poorly equipped and mismanaged and suffered the life span of a butterfly. But in the following year, the first step was taken in developing something which was to prove more deadly to radio than all the poor equipment and bad managers around.

## TELEVISION ARRIVES, RADIO GROWS

In 1923, Vladimir Zworykin patented something called the *iconoscope*. That was the first essential step in the development of television. Up until then, people had been trying to devise a mechanical way to send out moving pictures. Their efforts had concentrated on whirling discs with holes in them, so only a small portion of a picture would be visible at any one time. To see the whole picture, the disc had to go very fast and the picture had to be fairly small. Zworykin got away from the discs by breaking down a picture electrically instead of mechanically. He used something very small, smaller than any hole in a disc, to scan the picture—individual electrons. These electrons moved faster than any disc, as fast as the speed of light. So his iconoscope was a way to see a picture in bits no bigger than an electron and to see it very rapidly. Thus television got its first start.

However, the American audience knew nothing of this. They were just beginning to react to radio and by 1923 had only been listening for about three years. Already, though, they were becoming sophisticated and discriminating listeners. They were no longer intrigued with the magical talking box in their living rooms. No longer were they satisfied to turn on their receivers and listen to just anything. There was a clamor for higher-quality reception, and better and more regular programming. Most stations were not broadcasting regularly or for extended periods of time, had little power, and suffered from a high degree of interference.

The outcry for better programs was satisfied in 1926 and 1927 with the birth of the networks. Prior to 1926, radio had been something less than a huge financial success for station owners. In fact, no station had finished a year in the black. It takes money, a great deal of money, to provide regular, high-quality programming. Without money, the normal program diet consisted mostly of lengthy interviews, lectures and discussions, plus some amateur musical talent. Virtually all station income was derived from advertising time sold to small local store owners. This started out as ads to come in and buy radios and only slowly expanded to other products. The large and wealthy national advertisers were not interested in expending their advertising dollars in small-time radio.

The Radio Corporation of America (RCA) began operation of its National Broadcasting Company (NBC) on 15 November 1926 with a twenty-five-station network extending from New York to as far west as Kansas City. On 1 January 1927, NBC established a second network. The two networks were designated NBC Red and NBC Blue so that telephone engineers could distinguish between them on routing maps. A third network, Columbia Broadcasting System (CBS), began operation 18 September 1927. The first coast-to-coast network service was inaugurated by the original network, NBC Red, in December of 1928. A fourth network, Mutual Broadcasting System, initiated programming in 1934.

Because these networks were formed, radio could now offer the major advertisers the potential of reaching large national audiences. For the first time in history, a person's voice could be pitched the length and breadth of the nation. Advertisers decided it might as well be a sales pitch. Radio's total advertising revenue in 1927 was $4.82 million. In 1929, the total had risen to $26.8 million. This economic stability provided the base for a new level of quality programming.

In the late twenties and early thirties, the lectures disappeared; and quiz shows, dramas, variety shows, and situation comedies appeared. Edgar Bergen and Charlie McCarthy, Eddie Cantor, Al Jolson, Will Rogers, Ed Wynn, and Fred Allen were household radio personalities. One program, "Amos 'n Andy," was so popular in the early thirties that it has been estimated it was heard in more than one-half of all radio homes —a total exceeding ten million. Soap operas became the backbone of daytime radio. At their peak in 1940, fifty-seven different soaps were on the air.

The other problem mentioned was interference. By 1926, stations were interfering with one another's transmissions to such a degree that in some areas, the audience could not tune their receivers to some frequencies without receiving interference from competing stations. The situation was so bad the broadcasters themselves asked the government to step in and set up some rules to control transmission. So in 1927, Congress passed the Federal Radio Act. Under its guidelines, the Federal Radio Commission (FRC) was formed to license broadcasters and regulate the assignment of broadcast frequencies and the power of station transmitters. It was this act which stopped the broadcasters from choosing for themselves the location from which they would broadcast, the power they would use, and even the spot on the dial where they would be heard. This act was modified in 1934 to establish a few more rules and a seven-man board called the Federal Communications Commission. It's this body which still presides over radio and television today.

## TELEVISION ADVANCES

Some of radio's big problems were solved, but what of television? Some people still thought that spinning disc was the big problem and went on working on it. As a matter of fact, a man named Chester Jenkins worked hard on it, eliminated a lot of the bugs and came up with a model he tried to sell in 1925. But clever as he was, that approach was a dead end.

The more productive research was electronic, using Zworykin's approaches. At the telephone company in 1927, a man named H. E. Ives demonstrated how to get a moving picture from Washington to New York. He used the iconoscope to get the picture but, because he worked for the phone company, he used wires to send the picture up the coast.

But others were going a bit further—they were getting rid of the wires altogether. During the twenties, using the iconoscope, groups working for RCA, Westinghouse, and General Electric refined the pictures they could get from a crude 60 lines upwards into the hundreds. They also broadcast these pictures from one point to another without wires.

Ives didn't give up trying though, and in 1929, he showed something no one else could come close to matching. He sent pictures in color! He was still a phone man at heart though, because he was still using wires to send out the pictures. That, however, wasn't the path television transmissions were to follow.

Throughout the thirties, research centered on wireless electronic transmission. In the early part of the decade, a man named Allen B. Dumont started making tubes very like the picture tubes we find in home sets but used then as basic tools in research. That research led from a two-inch, 60-line screen to a nine-inch screen with increased brightness and 441 lines. With all these improvements, the man who started the decade just making tubes ended it in 1939 by marketing the first home set. That's also the year David Sarnoff started regularly scheduled television broadcasting with a speech from the New York World's Fair. Lots of events had been televised before then, things like dramas in 1928 and President Roosevelt's inaguration in 1933, but nothing was done on a regular basis. Besides, these earlier events went mostly to receivers in laboratories or to the houses of some electronics fans who built their own sets. But with this broadcast by Mr. Sarnoff, the president of RCA, regular broadcasting to a home audience began.

All this left the FCC with a problem. They knew Britain had authorized television broadcasting in 1936 but at only 405 lines. That's as good a picture as they could get then, but it wasn't too clear, and by 1939 they felt stuck with it. The FCC didn't want to freeze development at too low a point the way the British did. They decided to allow *limited* commercial operation at 441 lines so development could continue without locking everyone into one form.

RCA, however, had put millions of dollars into the development of television and badly needed to get some of its investment back. So it decided to go all-out to sell sets on the 441-line standard. If enough receivers were out, the audience size for programs would be large enough so that RCA could charge sponsors for putting their messages on the air.

The FCC then decided to take back their authorization, because they were getting exactly what they didn't want—a lot of home receivers built to one particular standard, in this case, 441 lines. It took until May of 1941 before they issued standards for full, not limited, commercial operation. The line standard was up to 525, the sound was to be FM and not AM, and there were to be 18 VHF channels.

Then came the Second World War. Development in both radio and television came to a halt. No new station licenses were granted, no new receivers were built, no station equipment or even replacement parts were built. The six television stations went on broadcasting a few hours a week to about ten thousand sets. In contrast, radio was already well established and the long-range effects of the war were actually minimal. In fact, one great plus which emerged from this period was the rapid development of radio as a major news medium. Only thirteen hours a week were devoted to news by the four networks in 1941. At war's end, in 1945, the total weekly news output had grown to thirty-four hours per week.

One change occurred during the war, although it was not caused by the war. NBC was ordered by the courts to sell one of its networks. In 1942 they sold the Blue network and in June 1945, it was named the American Broadcasting Company (ABC). At this point, of course, it was strictly a radio network.

## POSTWAR BROADCASTING

At the end of the war, radio was the primary entertainment medium, but television was coming up fast. CBS started arguing the case for color broadcasting. They had a system which gave good, full-color pictures but wasn't compatible with the then-current black-and-white standards. That is, the receivers people already had couldn't pick up a CBS color show. However, since so few sets were working at the end of the war, it seemed a good time to change to color. The FCC pondered, but didn't think the system was ready yet and so gave the go-ahead to the black-and-white system.

The CBS color system depended on a spinning wheel. No, we aren't back in the 1920s, but the problems are similar. The spinning wheel was mechanical and therefore a bit slow. The color looked good but seemed to waver almost as if heat were rising in front of it. The disc was in three primary colors, and a different scene appeared as each color came up. If the disc went fast enough, the colors appeared to blend. But sometimes the actors moved rapidly and seemed to leave a trail of pure color behind them. Nobody, not even CBS, found all the answers to the spinning disc problems.

So at the end of the forties, the sets were still black-and-white and were tuned to shows starring Milton Berle, roller derby stars, live drama, or variety with Ed Sullivan. The formats made popular by radio were adopted by television, plus several more. During the year 1948, stations more than doubled in number, cities with stations increased from eight to twenty-three, and set sales went up five times over the preceding year. But the audience increased by 4,000 percent! Once again the FCC got worried.

There was interference on the channels. There weren't enough channels to accommodate the demand for stations. Color was still a problem. What to do? They decided to freeze all applications for the construction of new stations while they figured things out. And that would take some time.

Meanwhile, back at the stations, things were going great. More and more sets were being sold, more advertisers were switching from radio to television, and more and more stations were making back a bit of the money they had invested in this new medium. The station owners didn't have to flounder around wondering how to organize themselves or whether or not they could sell anything to an advertiser. Those problems had been solved in the early days of radio, and now television just moved in.

Obviously, if advertisers were moving from radio to television, things weren't going quite so well at the radio stations.

The amount of programming provided affiliates by the networks began to decrease. Affiliates found themselves with more and more time to fill locally. It should be pointed out, however, that even at radio's peak, the networks provided less than half of their affiliates' programming. The remainder of the time was filled locally. Recorded music was the most common filler. Also, at no time were more than half the existing stations affiliated with the networks. The majority of stations were independents responsible for programming all of their broadcast time. Recorded music had long been their major programming source.

Radio's new face developed by taking advantage of television's weakness. Because of the great expense involved in building and operating a television station, stations were clustered in and around metropolitan areas. Programming was either originated by the network or, if local, concerned itself almost entirely with issues of interest to the metropolitan audience. Large segments of America had little personal contact with television fare.

Radio localized. It personalized. Local news, local talk, and local people: radio became the voice of its community. It gave up the prime-time hours of the evening to network television. Programmers defined the radio audience as being most available in the mornings when people first get up and in the afternoon when those same people first leave their jobs. The late morning and early afternoon hours belonged to the housewife. The age of the disc jockey ensued.

Recorded music interspersed with commercial announcements read by a local announcer had been a major programming form at many stations since the early forties. The networks had provided the forerunner for Top 40 radio way back in 1935 when they first aired "Your Hit Parade." Disc jockeys had appeared on the networks in the 1947–1948 season. By the mid-fifties, most stations were staffed almost totally by disc jockeys who provided virtually round-the-clock Top 40 music.

## AFTER THE FREEZE

About this same time, the FCC decided to lift its freeze on new station construction. This was in 1952, and they also decided on a new allocation pattern so television stations wouldn't interfere with each other, on putting UHF on the list of channels on which stations could operate, and in favor of the CBS color wheel. RCA, then building a system based totally on electronics, didn't like that and took them to court. CBS won, but the Korean War put a stop to building any color system. By the time that was over, RCA had perfected their electronic system to the point even CBS was glad to abandon the color wheel. So in December of 1953, the FCC adopted new rules for color television, this time based on the RCA system.

But most sets kept shining with a blue-white light. Color didn't catch on for quite some time. NBC, the company owned by RCA, broadcast color programs every so often from the very first, but the sets were expensive and most people didn't go for them. It wasn't until Walt Disney presented a show called the "Wonderful World of Color" that people really started wanting to buy a color set. Color sales started going up in 1968, a full fifteen years after the adoption of color standards.

What was coming through on these sets? A lot of live presentations were shown in 1953 because there was no way yet to record television programs, and the big movie companies weren't turning loose of any of their films. Television was hurting attendance at the movie theaters, and they didn't want to make things worse by giving the films to an industry which was becoming their biggest competitor. With all these live presentations, how could the shows be seen out in the midwest where the phone company still didn't have the cables to hook up all the town for simultaneous showing? Someone finally hit upon filming the picture off a picture tube, and the *kinescope* was born. The quality wasn't too good, but at least it was a way to get shows to those towns still off the cable line.

The shows going on these kinescopes, as well as many others, were the creations of the sponsors and their ad agencies. Television was still cheap enough that one sponsor could buy a whole show. Therefore, s/he often "packaged" it. That is, s/he approved the script, hired the actors and director, provided the sets, and presented the entire show to a television network as a package. As audiences grew larger and operating expenses got bigger, sponsors found they couldn't so easily pay for an entire show. As they started to pay for just half, or a quarter, or even just for commercials within a show, their control over the content slipped away. More and more, the networks started producing shows, creating new series, and planning more specials. Finally, by the late sixties, sponsor control of program content had almost totally vanished.

One reason for the increased prices, and hence the loss of

control by sponsors, was an increased audience. The phone company did get the cables in to all the towns, and everyone was finally able to see programs at the same time. With more people watching, the networks were able to charge more money for commercials. It makes sense that if a commercial going to five people costs a dollar, a commercial going to ten people should cost two dollars. That's the way the networks figured it, and so their rates went up. Another reason was increased production costs. As the various unions got higher and higher wages for technicians, actors, directors, and so on, the costs of making a show went up.

There's also another reason why the sponsors lost control over shows. In 1955, a game show called "The $64,000 Question" went on the air, packaged and sponsored by Revlon, Inc. It was hugely popular and soon several big money quiz shows were on. But in 1959, former contestants had been talking to everyone in sight and saying the whole thing was rigged. And it was. The contestants who were to win were given the answers in advance. The public felt cheated and was outraged at being made suckers by believing the programs. So the networks were forced to stop allowing the sponsors to have such total control, and they began to take some part in program production.

## CHANGES: FORMATS, AUDIENCES,
##     EQUIPMENT

By the time the sixties began, both radio and television faced some major technical changes. For television, this was videotape. Finally there was a way to record television programs with no loss of picture quality. Tape became responsible for a great decline in live programming, but it also is responsible for a great number of events we can see on short notice. For example, a nonbroadcast presidential announcement at 11:30 A.M. can be seen on the noon news. Video recording is also responsible for the instant replay of that last touchdown. Other than filmed shows from Hollywood and live shows like news, practically all other presentations end up on tape.

The technical change for radio was the advent of FM and stereo. FM wasn't a new thing, but the development of it was. More and more people started buying FM tuners because the quality of the sound was so much better. Then stereo was added, and FM really took off. The FM stations didn't try to attract every listener available but instead appealed to those particularly interested in the sound they were putting out. This became as great a change for radio as the introduction of stereo.

This change in radio formats has placed a growing reliance on demographics and the desire to reach a segmented audience. *Demography* is defined as the study of the characteristics of human population. In the fifties, stations were interested in reaching the largest possible audience. This helped breed a rather stereotyped sound. Stations all seemed to have similar-sounding announcers playing similar-sounding music. Today's station managers are no longer as interested in reaching the largest possible audience as they are in reaching the largest possible *marketable* audience; the listener with the dollars in the pocket. The potential audience is divided up into smaller audiences distinguished by characteristics such as age, sex, and income. Advertisers want to reach the listener with the cash in hand, and they spend their advertising dollars with those stations that reach that audience. Since most of the money is in the hands of adults between the ages of twenty-five and fifty-five, those stations reaching that age group are often among the most financially successful in their areas. Their format may be middle-of-the-road (MOR) or "beautiful" music or talk or all news. Whichever it is, it has been chosen in order to reach the buyers.

Other station programmers have been successful with formats geared to reach a youth audience (Top 40 or Progressive Rock) or some other cross-section of America with a Country & Western, Ethnic, or Classical format. While each can be successful, you will probably find the leading station in terms of income in a multiple-station market will be one whose programming is tailored to roughly a twenty-five to fifty-five age audience.

There are many stations today making a relatively small profit. Many are making no profit. Salaries are one rather good indicator of station security. While many announcers in major markets are well up in five figures, even today, in the face of the shrinking dollar, many small market announcers are working for $125 a week or less.

Still, it appears radio has weathered the dawning of television rather well. The number of radio stations has more than doubled since 1952. There were 2,331 AM stations and more than 800 FM stations on the air in January of 1952. Today, there are more than 4,300 AM and 2,700 FM stations broadcasting.

Television too has grown, although the stations number around 1,000 instead of several thousands. They have not gone after certain segments of the audience as has radio, so they are still trying to get mass audiences with shows of mass appeal. Only rarely do they go into special presentations, generally news documentaries covering urban riots or foreign affairs, which draw small, select audiences. When they do, it's usually at the prompting of some government official who attacks television in a speech. Newton Minnow, a commissioner of the FCC, caused just such a reaction when he characterized television as a "vast wasteland." And yet, the two biggest events of the decade of the sixties, and perhaps of the century, were made more real to all Americans because of the coverage of television—the assassination of President Kennedy and the landing of a man on the moon.

But in general, we can say the stations themselves have not tried to create specialized programs for small audiences. Instead, the moves in that direction have come from Congress. We cannot yet say television programming has been made to provide better programs for everyone, but that's been the intent of a couple of changes. The first was a law requiring all television sets made after 1963 to be able to pick up UHF stations as well as the regular VHF ones. That meant eventually everyone would be able to tune to eighty-three channels, so a lot more stations could be put in each city. That would produce a lot more competition and hopefully that will result in better shows. The second was the Public Broadcasting Act of 1967. That set up a program of federal funding for use by the noncommercial stations. The intent is to upgrade the quality of their shows, which are generally a little more adventurous and a little more specialized than those of commercial stations. The funding wasn't long-term, so it wasn't free of political maneuvering and attempts at control, but it was a start.

In both areas of broadcasting, we find the changes are now centered on programming rather than on technology. Color, FM stereo, videotape, miniaturized electronics, and so on have had great impact on broadcasting; and the technological changes and improvements of the future will continue to have great impact. But broadcasting of the seventies is a story of changing programming. The most immediately apparent aspect of that is the reasoning behind the prime-time access rule for television. In 1972, the national networks were restricted to providing three hours of programming to their affiliates in the top 100 markets (hence everywhere) during the evening hours. The hope was that more independent production companies would spring up, offering a greater diversity of programming to stations, and that stations themselves would produce more of their own shows. Technology had nothing to do with this ruling. The result, by and large, was that stations bought more of the game shows and reruns which had been available all along. So, as you would expect, arguments were soon heard to go back to things the way they had been, since increased programming of higher quality and greater diversity had not occurred.

But in one area, stations did start doing more of their own shows and generally of a greater quality than many of those game shows and reruns. Many stations started expanding their news operations. An hour or hour and a half of local news in the early evening began to be, if not common, at least widespread. The Vietnamese war and the Watergate scandal were partly responsible, in all likelihood. Regardless of whether we agreed or disagreed with what was going on, we wanted to know what was happening. In spite of the feeling many expressed of being isolated from power and being unable to affect events in our government, we needed news broadcasts to tell us what we were isolated from. Those who didn't feel isolated needed the same news so as to know what had occurred that they were going to support or attack. From either point of view, we were participating in the news, and it was broadcasting that brought us that news. The proof that we took broadcasting's actions very seriously came with all the arguments about bias and unfair reporting. Having an opinion of the fairness of news coverage came to be an expected part of the intellectual equipment of every citizen.

Radio, of course, participated in this expansion of news coverage but with one unexpected side effect. It has been suggested that listeners found they got a great sense of reality from radio news. The descriptions and sounds of on-the-scene reporting created reality in their imaginations, and that was the same process radio drama had used years ago for its listeners. The result, therefore, was a newfound audience willing to listen to radio drama once more, whether it be replays of old "Green Hornet" shows or new presentations of plays written just for radio. The audience wasn't big, but for twenty years it hadn't existed at all.

So what is done came to be more important than how it's done. The use of equipment became more important than the technical improvements of that equipment. And with that emphasis, we began teaching children how to read instead of how to go on a hunger strike if Mommy didn't buy Crispy-Toasties for breakfast. We began to consider the news reporter's impact at the news scene instead of assuming "the neutral observer" completely described the reporter's status. And more of us began to think more often about just what we want broadcasting to do for us. These are concerns of the present and the future, not the past. Since you have an idea now of what's gone into that past, you may be able to make better guesses about what will go into the future. Into that future, after all, is where the history of broadcasting is going.

# 5

## STATION
## ORGANIZATION

Before we even start to talk about the various people at the station, I want to discuss a subject that lurks in the backs of all their minds—ratings. The amount of profit the station can make, the shows that live or die, the programming decisions that are made, and the people who keep or lose jobs can all depend on the ratings. They arrive in a book filled with numbers, provided by a rating service. They are both eagerly awaited and slightly feared by the majority of people I will discuss later, so in order to see just what it is that has such an impact on the station, its people, and its operation, let's take a look at the rating services.

## RATING SERVICES

Ratings are percentages. We've all heard of programs getting ratings of 18 or 22 or 3. Those numbers mean that 18 percent or 22 percent or 3 percent of the total number of people in the broadcast area were tuned in to that particular show. How do the rating companies get those numbers? They randomly pick about a thousand people and ask them to keep a record of what they watch or listen to for a week. Generally they do this with four groups of a thousand each for each of four consecutive weeks. Then they compile the four thousand records, figure out the percentages, and give them out to the stations. Since this is a lot of work, the stations have to buy these figures from the companies. The major companies are Hooper and Pulse for radio and American Research Bureau (ARB) and Nielsen for television. Depending on the size of the area, this is done three times a year for a relatively unpopulated area, five, six, or seven times a year for a metropolitan area, and in the case of really big cities like New York and Los Angeles, it is done almost every week of the year.

There are several ways these companies have people keep records of what they listen to or watch. The most common method is a *diary*, a simple listing written out by the person showing what programs were watched or listened to, and at what times. Another way is to call people on the phone and ask them what they are watching at the moment. That's called a *phone coincidental*, because it's coincidental with the time the show is on. Sometimes companies also call and ask what was watched or listened to the day before. That's called a *phone recall survey*. This same sort of thing can be done by having a person actually go out to homes and interview people, but this interview method isn't used too often because it's so much more expensive than phoning. A fourth method used in some larger cities is to attach a box to a set which automatically records when the set is on and what channel it is tuned to. Obviously, this only works for television. But whatever method is used, ratings are not the only pieces of information the services provide.

They break the audience into groups like men eighteen to thirty-four, women eighteen to forty-nine, teens, children two to eleven, and so on. They give a percentage figure for each of these groups, so that rating of 22 gets broken into 2 for men eighteen to thirty-four, 7 for women eighteen to thirty-four, and so on. This is referred to as the *demographic breakdown* because *demographics* refers to the statistical characteristics of portions of the population, in this case, a statistic of how many were listeners or viewers for a particular program. You may think you have a show for men in their twenties, but if several rating books show the audience to be mostly teenagers, you might want to attempt to find an acne cream sponsor instead of the singles-cruise ship line.

There's another statistic provided by the books, and it's often more useful for stations. That's *share*, a percentage of all the people who are listening to or watching any station at all in the area. You might have a rating of 22, which means that 22 percent of everybody around, and a share of 48. That means that of all the people who has sets turned on, 48 percent were tuned to your station. Suppose the area has a population of 100,000. With a rating of 22, you have 22,000 in your audience. Suppose that out of that 100,000, only 46,000 were listening to or watching anything, your station or anyone else's. Your 22,000 is 48 percent of that 46,000, so you have a share of 48. Share, then, tells you how you are doing in terms of the competition. That's very useful. Suppose you have just put on a different sort of late-night show, and the rating book shows a low number of 3. That sounds terrible. But look at the share and you may see something like 65! That means that almost everybody around is asleep and, of course, not listening to or watching anything. But of those 3 percent still up, you are getting 65 percent. Your show is very successful. However, you still can't charge the sponsor much because the total audience size isn't big, but if s/he wants the night owls, you're the station to come to. So the share can tell you if your programming decision is working.

Those are the major pieces of information which rating books will give you. As with any statistical work, there are a lot of other things that get listed, and there are a lot of other uses for the books. One quick example. The sales department will look in the book to see how many thousands of people were in the audience for a particular show. Then they will take the cost of one spot in that show, divide it by the number of thousands, and get a figure called the *cost-per-thousand*, or CPM. They want low CPMs so they can pitch those spots to sponsors as better buys than the competition (hopefully with higher CPMs) can offer. But this gives you an idea of what the books provide, and you can see why so many people around the station use them. You can guess how a show is doing, but the books will give you far more exact information. That exactness is important for many decisions made by a number of people. Now, let's move on to those people and see just what they do.

## STATION PEOPLE—THE GENERAL MANAGER

Every organization has its leader. In a station, it's the general manager. S/he is the big boss, the person everyone answers to. Now, s/he may have to answer to someone higher up, such as a corporate vice-president or stockholders, but in general s/he is the person everyone at the station looks to as the boss. So the general manager's responsibilities include everything. S/he has to be sure the station makes money, gets good shows on the air, produces local shows smoothly, satisfies local needs, covers the news fairly and completely, adds new members to the audience and keeps the old ones, and generally makes everyone happy to work there. Of course s/he can't do all this alone. S/he delegates responsibilities to department heads and expects them to be experts in their particular areas. S/he has to know enough about each of their jobs to be able to judge their competence, but s/he doesn't have to be able to do each job as well as they can. The general manager's expertise has to be in getting all these people to work well together. If the production manager and the program director are bitter enemies, the shows done locally will suffer, and the station will come off looking bad. So the general manager has to be able to make them work together and like it. When one department starts on a particular approach, s/he has to make sure the other departments know about it so they will be able to work with, instead of against, the new effort. Suppose a TV news department discovers a documentary on the history of the city is very well received. The program department may need to put a director on such a series to work with a producer in building several shows. The promotion department will want to get out ads to let people know more such shows are coming. The sales department may need to know so the salespeople can talk to sponsors about paying for shows as popular as these will be. The general manager is not, however, a glorified gossip center, telling all the departments about the new shows. S/he has the ultimate responsibility to decide to go ahead with such a series, and s/he then tells the others of the future programming and asks their support for the venture.

We can say, then, that the general manager is responsible for the direction the station takes. In TV, if s/he feels the sponsors will pay for more situation comedies, s/he talks to distributors about buying such shows to run on the station. In radio, if s/he feels a change of format to Golden Oldies will up the audience, hence the revenue, s/he starts the changeover. If s/he is interested in a prestige image, s/he may decide to use the station to back a community effort to build a new auditorium for the symphony. If s/he thinks the news department will be the most effective means of building a good image with the audience, s/he will emphasize support for news. It's the general manager's concept of what the station should be that determines how the rest of the station acts.

Yet, it's unfair to say s/he does this arbitrarily. In most cases, s/he talks to the department heads and gets their ideas. S/he will discuss various approaches with them and will consider their ideas. S/he will listen to the changes they suggest, and their reasons why those changes should be made. S/he and the department heads will also consult the rating books to find out what they reveal about the makeup and size of their audience at various times. The rating books have become one of the most basic tools used at a station by the general manager, the program director, the sales manager, the promotion manager, and the news director. Others use the books as well, but these people are guided by them almost daily. These books are one more factor taken into account in this decision-making process we're into now. Whatever the final decision is, it will generally be a combination of ideas about the station based on ratings statistics and reflecting several attitudes about what the station ought to do. Tyrants still exist in the world, but general managers are seldom included in that category.

The general manager's overriding concern, of course, is that the station show a profit. Without that, the station cannot stay on the air. So the bulk of what the station airs has to have sponsors who pay enough to cover all expenses and leave a little left over. The manager has to worry about the tape recorders blinking out or the cameras breaking down and needing repair, the salaries going up, the next union contract negotiations, and a million other financial details while at the same time trying to figure out just what to do to get more money from more sponsors. S/he wants to give the public the programs they want, the sponsors the low cost per listener or viewer that they want, and the profits necessary to meet expenses. So quite often, the general manager advances by way of the sales department. S/he may have been national sales manager before becoming general manager, so s/he understands the problems with money.

So here is a person concerned with finances, station appearance, the performance of everyone at the station, and who needs the diplomacy to make everything run smoothly. What training does s/he have to get to this position? Primarily, s/he's

worked at stations for quite a while. S/he's proved some expertise in a particular position, such as sales manager or
program director, and has demonstrated an ability to work
with and manage people. Beyond knowing financial matters or
having production skills, s/he must understand psychology.
S/he knows the theories of what makes people tick, and s/he's
kept his or her eyes open to see how various situations
actually work out. S/he knows something of management
theory and how to organize people effectively. S/he knows
something of sociology, too, because that also deals with how
people function together. And, believe it or not, s/he knows
quite a bit about the use of the English language. S/he knows
deep inside that s/he has to be very careful about what s/he
says or writes because s/he's involved daily in convincing
people to do or not do something. Since language is the major
propaganda weapon to do that convincing, s/he pays a lot of
attention to his or her English.

So this person has a variety of skills broader in scope than
the specific ones demanded of the people at lower levels. We
need to look at these other people, their responsibilities, and
their departments. First, let's look at Figure 5.1, an organizational chart, so you can see who answers to whom. Then we'll
go on to some details about the responsibilities of all the people
at a station.

## STATION PEOPLE—
### THE PROGRAM DIRECTOR

Other than the general manager, the program director covers
more areas than any other person at the station. As the title
suggests, s/he is concerned about the programs the station
airs. S/he spends a great deal of time determining what programs will run, when they will run, and in what order. S/he
talks to the research director, the sales manager, the production manager, and in TV, the film director to get information
about programs. S/he discusses public affairs programming
with the news director and the public affairs director. S/he
surveys the population of the region the station covers to
discover what they want to see or hear. S/he studies the ratings
books to see what the population actually did watch or listen

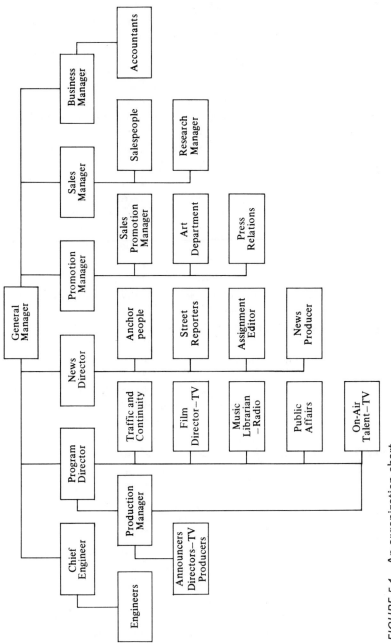

FIGURE 5.1   An organization chart

to. Then s/he takes all this information, passes it around to the general manager and all others who may be in on the decision process and makes recommendations as to what programs should go on the air. Let's see if we can get a clearer idea of what s/he does by looking first at a television program director and seeing how s/he would handle three different types of shows, then we'll consider a radio program director and examine what s/he would do with a format change.

Suppose it's the month of April and the TV program director is trying to choose new shows to run on the station next fall. First, a movie distributor has a package of twenty-six different movies, only ten of which are really very good, but the price is low. Next, a local group has submitted a proposal to the program director for a half-hour show discussing the problems of the large Siwanese population of the area, which is to be videotaped in the studios. Finally, a syndicator has given an option to buy a brand-new, hour-long variety show, formated like the "Tonight Show," available on videotape. What will s/he decide to do?

Let's take the movie package first. S/he would talk to the film director to see if any of these films have been run in the area recently, if they are available in better packages, and if they were well or poorly received when they came out in movie theaters. If some of the movies have run in other markets, s/he will check with the research director to see how well they did, whether or not they had a large audience, whether they appealed to a special group like children or women over fifty or whatever, and if the best ten are new enough to pull good ratings during the ratings periods. S/he would look over a synopsis of the plots to see if any are unacceptable to the station. S/he would talk to the sales manager to see whether s/he thinks it would be difficult to sell these movies to sponsors, because if it is, that ends the matter right there.

S/he knows s/he will run the best movies during selected times, generally during the four weeks of a rating period. S/he knows s/he has three major rating periods in which s/he must run the strongest material so as to get the best audience possible. These periods are November, the end of February and the first of March, and the month of May. That's twelve weeks, and s/he only gets ten strong movies in the package so s/he has to decide what ones to repeat, and whether the package is worth what s/he will pay when there may be other good packages that offer twelve strong movies. Finally, s/he simply has to sit down and decide whether or not to buy the package.

If the film director says the movies have done well, especially the ten strong ones, the research director says they get big audiences, and the sales manager says s/he can sell all twenty-six tomorrow, then the program director has no problem except to decide in what order to run them. However, things are seldom so easy, and s/he makes tough decisions on almost every movie package. But once s/he decides to take it, s/he goes back over the synopses of plots, the lists of stars, and the ratings the movies got before and figures out when each one will run. Very likely, s/he would pick a strong movie or two for the first two weeks of the new season. Then s/he might run four medium-strength ones before the rating months of November. That's when s/he will run four strong films. Next s/he throws in the complete losers, saving four more strong ones for the February–March period. By the end of that, s/he used up twenty-four of the twenty-six movies and has shown all ten of the strong ones. S/he might go back to the medium ones and show those four again, then the two new films, then go into the May rating period with repeats of the September and early November strong films. That is also part of the decision process. Will scheduling like that work out? If it won't, s/he may finally decide against buying the package. Sometimes s/he may want just to flip a coin.

Now, what about that local show? First of all, s/he needs to know the community well enough to know if there really is a large enough Siwanese population who will care about a show on their problems. S/he will talk to both the news director and the public affairs director to get their opinions of the position of the Siwanese in the community. If s/he finds this group does indeed exist and care about such a show, s/he will want to talk with Siwanese leaders to find out what they think the major problems are. If there are no hot issues, perhaps there is no need to do a show. If there is sentiment against "outsiders" trying to poke their noses into Siwanese problems, the station would be better off dropping the whole project. But if there is concern over problems of the Siwanese group, perhaps the station can render a public service by creating a series to discuss them. The next step, then, would be to find a Siwanese capable and willing to function as the producer of the show. This producer will have to arrange for guests, organize topics for discussion, and work with station personnel to create an interesting and well-done show. Let us suppose there is such a producer. Next, the program director must talk with the production manager and members of the production department to see who can work with the producer to direct this show. Also, s/he will discuss with the production department the various ways the show can be presented. Will it be a talk-interview show? Will it be dramatizations of various problems? Will it be largely shot on film on location and narrated by someone from the studio? Once these topics are decided, generally with the producer's advice and always within the limitations of the station's capabilities in both money and facilities, the program director will meet with the producer, the director, and the staff they collect to make sure the first few shows are going smoothly. S/he will also meet with the production director to see if the studio time and facilities which can be made available are adequate to do a good show. Then the only remaining problem is deciding when the show can run. S/he needs to schedule it at a time when the Siwanese can watch. Yet they are probably just as interested in seeing their favorite shows at regular times as the rest of the population, so s/he doesn't want to run it in place of the most popular situation comedy the station carries. S/he pores over the schedule and eventually finds a place. Too often it is at 6:30 Saturday evening or at 10:30 Sunday morning. But s/he does eventually find a place and then turns to consider the syndicated talk-variety show.

Here is a show s/he can look at, check out what the star has done before, and what other shows the producers have had. If they all have good "track records," that's one step in the show's favor. S/he can't check what the show has done in other markets because it's brand new, but s/he can check on how similar shows have done before in this market, and that can be very helpful information. Maybe the community turns away in droves from this sort of show. That would settle it; s/he wouldn't touch the show. Maybe there are millions yearning to see something like this. In that case, s/he buys it. Mostly, however, s/he will encounter a middle ground where some similar shows did well and some didn't. So s/he looks around at the schedules of the other stations. If they are each running shows like this, s/he will decide not to chance another one. But if none has such shows, it might be a good bet. Also, as with the movie package, s/he will check to see how easily the sales manager thinks s/he can sell the show. For the public affairs show s/he didn't care, but from this, s/he is trying to make a profit. Then s/he will decide whether s/he thinks it is a good show. That doesn't mean she wants to watch it, but that s/he thinks most people will want to. That's an educated guess, and it's the good program directors who guess right most of the time. If s/he does decide to buy it, s/he faces the same problem of deciding when to run it. Perhaps s/he wants to get the housewives to watch, so s/he shows it from noon to one. Maybe s/he wants to build the late afternoon audience, so s/he puts it in from 4:30 to 5:30. Maybe s/he wants a late night show and so puts it on after the late news. In any case, it runs five days a week, and is referred to as *strip programming.* The show is stripped in every weekday at the same time.

Now, let's turn to the radio program director. Generally, s/he has fewer programs to deal with than his or her television counterpart. Most radio stations have a particular format that runs all day long and doesn't change—it's Top 40, Country & Western, Beautiful Music, or all talk, etc. That means most of the programming is done with a DJ and a stack of records. But "most" isn't "all." At various times, the station will still run special programs for special interests. The most obvious break in the routine is news. Generally every hour the station will have some sort of news report. These are quite often simply a matter of the DJ reading the copy that has come in over the news wire machines. But once in a while, perhaps during evening drive time, the station will provide something a bit more complete. This may be a ten- or fifteen-minute report of local, national, and international news, plus some sports, plus a weather report. Perhaps the station may even have a couple of reporters out around town who have gotten interviews on tape during the day, and these will run in this newscast. The timing and complexity of this newscast are partly the product of the program director. Although the news director is responsible for the daily production of this newscast, it's the program director who decided in the first place that the whole thing was a good idea, and fit its particular time slot. Besides news, the program director may arrange for other specialty programming. A church service heard every Sunday morning is an example, as is a half hour every Saturday night devoted to the local garden club. Every group or special interest in the community may be the source for a special program which the program director may decide to use. Part of the job is to decide which groups deserve air time and then to find a place for them on the schedule. S/he'll leave it up to the news and public affairs director to contact the group, organize the program, and oversee the weekly production.

But suppose the station decides to change its format. Suppose the station has been running Golden Oldies and finds the audience shrinking away to nothing. It's time to switch to a more popular music style. The program director takes a good, hard look at the market and at what the other stations are running. S/he checks the ratings books to see how well they are doing. S/he sees what styles are popular and are working. S/he checks to see if there is room for another station to get on the bandwagon or if the audience is already so split up that s/he would be better off going for the second most popular format, or even the third. S/he checks to see if some formats draw only old people or young children. Neither have much money to spend and are thus hard to sell to sponsors. Once s/he settles on a popular format that draws the sort of audience s/he wants, s/he starts figuring out what the station needs. New records, new jingles, new intros and closes, new approaches by the jocks. S/he talks to the promotion manager about how to let everyone in town know something new is coming on the scene. It's almost like deciding to become a different person; all the major aspects and little details become different, and feel strange for a while. Eventually, though, the day comes, and the station goes on with a different sound. Then all the program director has to do is sweat until the rating books show whether or not the audience likes the change. If they don't, it's time to try something else.

These are some of the things program directors go through in deciding on programming for the stations. What does s/he need to know for this job?

The program director should, like the general manager, have a working knowledge of psychology. S/he has to deal with people both inside and out of the station and get them to work together to produce programs s/he can air. S/he has to know what sorts of programs appeal to the interests and desires of the audience. All of this takes a knowledge of people. S/he also needs to know economics. If, in television, s/he buys a film package, s/he knows how much that costs. S/he also knows how much the rate card says the sponsors will pay to include their messages in a showing of the films. But s/he needs to know enough economics to figure out the hidden costs of running such a film and thus to figure out whether or not the rate from the rate card is high enough to cover expenses, plus make a little profit. If there's no profit, or perhaps even a loss, s/he'll need to buy a cheaper film package. S/he also needs to know enough about mathematics to be able to work with the statistics of the ratings books. A change of a rating from 12 to 13 means a lot more if that one point represents 100,000 people. S/he's got to be able to figure some CPMs, plus a few dozen other simple mathematical maneuvers —simple, but important. Then s/he needs to know the skills required in production. How can s/he develop a new show if s/he has no idea of whether or not the studios can handle the program's demands? S/he may not be a super-whiz-wonderful producer, but s/he needs to know the limitations imposed by mike placement or chroma key.

Now that we've seen what the program director does, a little of what s/he knows, and who the people are s/he works with, let's take a closer look at the sections of the department s/he works and consults with. Because of the responsibilities of this department, the following people will generally be under the program director: production manager, public affairs director (who in radio is generally also the news director), in television the film director, and in radio the music librarian.

## the traffic department

One other segment under the program director is the traffic department. After all the decisions have been made as to what shows will run and at what time, someone has to make up a chart every day of what runs at what times. This chart, as we have already discussed, is called the station log; and it lists every program, every commercial, every ID, and every other program element that goes on during the broadcast day. The people who make up this lengthy and exhaustive log are in the traffic department, presided over by the traffic manager. Ultimately, every program element has to pass through the traffic department, even if only in the form of a title on the log.

## the music librarian

Another person from our list is the music librarian. This position varies in importance and even in organizational position from station to station. Sometimes the music librarian is under the production manager and is responsible for what are essentially the functions of a file clerk—keeping the records cataloged so they can be found and keeping them in good condition so they sound right on the air. New records coming in go to the librarian to be filed, and old records that have been played go back for refiling. In other stations, this person is part of the team that listens to every record and evaluates each one to determine what will or will not be played on the air. For example, a station running a Beautiful Music format might get an album from a major singer but decide that cuts 2 and 4 on side one and 3 and 5 on side two are just too upbeat for the soft sound they want to broadcast. The station team that makes that decision might include the program director, the jocks, and sometimes the music librarian. This decision of play or no-play by the major stations in major markets, primarily in Top 40 formats, is of vital importance to record companies. If a station decides to play a cut, or single, the sales of the record may go way up. A no-play decision, however, may keep sales in the cellar. So being part of that decision-making team can be a very important position at a station.

## the film director

One further step back on our list brings us to the film director. Obviously, the feature films which the station runs will go through this department. S/he will be responsible for the ordering, receiving, checking, and shipping out of these films, plus the cataloguing and storing of films which the station owns outright. It is the people under the film director who decide where the breaks can be made in the films for the insertion of commercials. They are the ones who cut, splice, and edit the films at the places they have chosen for such commercial insertions. But there are many other films which come to a station which must be handled by this department. Many commercials are sent out by advertising agencies on 16-mm film. They must be stored and catalogued so they can be found readily for repeated showings. Finally, they must be returned or disposed of when their usefulness ends. But besides film, programs or commercials that are on videotape are handled by this department. The processing is much the same, but the material they work with is videotape instead of film. The film department handles a video cassette instead of a film reel. That's the only difference.

As well as handling the flow of films and videotapes, the film director quite often views programs to form an opinion of their acceptability for airing by the station. If s/he finds the content offensive, s/he will suggest to the program director that the program be excluded from possible scheduling. S/he also maintains contacts with various film distributors and keeps abreast of current offerings of film packages. S/he maintains books and catalogues which show what is available and describe the films in terms of stars, critical reception, and plot outlines. S/he tries to know as much as possible about films available for television.

## the public affairs director

Next, let's discuss the public affairs director. As all stations are required to operate in the public interest, convenience, and necessity, it is mandatory that a station pay attention to the particular demands of its audience. It's the public affairs director who keeps tabs on those demands. S/he finds out what people in the community are concerned about, what approaches they are taking to solve their problems, and who the leaders are for the various groups. S/he establishes lines of communication with these leaders and works with them to further their aims by appropriate use of the station's facilities. The public affairs director has a very delicate position because there is often a good deal of controversy surrounding some groups, and s/he wants to be perfectly fair to all factions. S/he can't, therefore, take sides or exclude any one group. S/he has to be quite a diplomat as well as being a responsible broadcaster. S/he works closely with the news department of the station, because many public affairs activities come from the forefront of community actions. And s/he often is the one who initiates program ideas by locating a problem, figuring out a program format to handle the community needs, and going to the program director to discuss the ideas.

## the production manager

Finally, let us discuss the production manager and the production department. The production manager schedules all studio time, all crews, in TV assigns all directors, and in radio schedules the shifts for the jocks. S/he makes sure each program done by the station personnel has adequate studio time and as much rehearsal time and post-production time as possible. In TV, s/he judges the capabilities of the directors and assigns them to shows which best utilize their talents. S/he tries to build good crews for the directors to work with by recognizing the strengths and weaknesses of each member of the crews. S/he expects the tensions of production to produce friction, and s/he tries to sooth ruffled feelings. S/he, like the public affairs director, is in great part a diplomat. But among the more formal duties is the final say on the technical quality of the station's productions. S/he is also, in many ways, responsible for on-air talent. S/he may schedule the shifts for the booth announcer and handle details like vacation schedules and replacements for the host of the afternoon movie. But s/he doesn't do this alone. The performers have a large impact on the quality of programming, so the program director makes some major decisions here. S/he may decide a woman's voice works best for late afternoon and early evening announcing from the booth. S/he'll tell the production manager, who then does the specific scheduling. Likewise, the selection of a host for a movie is a programming decision carried out by the production manager but not made by the program director. Of course, the production manager works closely with these people and makes sure they keep their work up to high standards so the program director gets what s/he planned on. The production manager also keeps a sharp eye out for sloppy production and insists it be corrected. In radio, s/he judges the best voices and best styles for various times of the day. S/he works with the station's producers to get clean, polished shows. If outsiders are chosen by the program director as producers, s/he works closely with them for the same reason. S/he can put more pressure on the station's own producers to do things right, but outside producers are often chosen by the program director because they represent a group s/he wants on the air (as for a public service show) rather than because they are knowledgeable about radio. So it's up to the production manager to keep their shows up to the station's standards.

S/he advises the program director on the availability of studio time and personnel to handle new program ideas. S/he needs to know how to handle an infinitude of production situations so as to create a good show. S/he needs to be creative and imaginative so as to impart a sparkle and incisiveness to the station's productions. Because s/he is so directly involved in the look or sound the station presents to the public, s/he is quite generally consulted in the decision-making process of programming.

These, then, are the people who work with the program director in determining what goes on the air and what represents the station in the public's mind.

STATION PEOPLE—THE SALES MANAGER

The sales department generally has a national sales manager, a local sales manager, and several salespeople. As the station gets smaller, some of these positions may be combined in one person, as in the common situation where the general manager of the station is also the national sales manager. But suppose we walk into a fairly large station with an appointment to see the national sales manager (who is not the general manager) to ask him a few questions.

*Secretary:*    May I help you?

*Us:*    Yes, we have an appointment with Mr. Nat Sales at ten o'clock.

*Sec.:*    Mr. Sales is still in a staff meeting, but he should be here shortly. Would you care to wait?

*Us:*    Yes, thank you.

.  .  .

*Sec.:*    Mr. Sales will see you now. Follow me please.

.  .  .

*Us:*    How do you do Mr. Sales. We're here to ask you a few questions about your department.

*N.S.:*   Fine, that's fine. Just sit right down and I'll see if I can fill you in. We have a fine group of boys here who really know their business, and I'm always glad to talk about them. Would you like some coffee?

*Us:*   No, thanks.

*N.S.:*   You're sure now? Mary, bring me a cup please. How about a Coke? Tea?

*Us:*   No, thank you.

*N.S.:*   Well, what's first?

*Us:*   Can you tell us what your position is in the organizational chain here at the station? Who's over you and who's under you?

*N.S.:*   First, of course, is the general manager. He's over me just as he's over all the departments. So I'm on a par with the program director, the promotion manager, and the news director. Oh yes, the chief engineer and the head accountant are also department heads, but they are service departments rather than being involved in our programs, so they tend to slip my mind occasionally. They're both fine people, you understand, but I just tend to think in terms of the programs and the schedule and things like that, so I forget areas outside of that.

    Now as to those under me, I have a local sales manager and four salesmen, plus the secretaries and clerks. Speaking of clerks, let me include the research director. He works with the ratings books and does a lot of number work, so I guess you could call him a sort of clerk. And that's my staff.

*Us:*   Let's take those people one at a time. How about the research director? What does he do for you?

*N.S.:*   Well, when the ratings book first come in, he sees how we stand in relation to the competition. Then he figures our CPMs for the local shows. You know, the cost of a spot divided by the number of thousands of people who were in our audience at the time the spot ran. There's a lot of information in a rating book. Women, men, teens, children, people over fifty, you name it. He figures out the CPMs for each group. It's a lot of numbers work, but it tells us if we can sell a spot that's more effective than our competition. Even if our rate is higher, so long as the spot gets to more people, it's cheaper per person. That's what the CPM will show.

    He'll also figure out some packages for us. For example, in TV that's a combination of several programs we want

to sell, usually with at least one dog of a show we have
trouble selling by itself. If he ties it up with three or four
shows we can sell easily, then we get some spots for it as
well. The problem is to take a dog show, which of course
won't have much of an audience, and find other shows with
high enough audience sizes so the overall CPM is still good.

Other than just numbers, he'll take a good look at the
audience compositions and tell us if we have a strong
children's show followed by something for the senior
citizens. That's what we call bad audience flow. The first
show doesn't deliver any viewers for the second show. So
our research director will suggest we either follow with
a show for people in their late teens or early twenties, or
replace the children's show with one for regular adults.
But that gets into programming, and not sales.

*Us:*    Does sales get into programming?

*N.S.:*    You bet it does! I'll scream bloody blue murder if they
try to put in some complete loser. They may think it's a
great show, on a par with Shakespeare, but if I can't get a
sponsor for it, they better junk it or think of becoming a
nonprofit organization. Sure, I like a cultural show as much
as the next guy, but I make my living out of the popular
shows.

*Us:*    Are you saying cultural shows aren't popular?

*N.S.:*    All I'm saying is the heavy dramas and documentaries
and symphonies draw very small audiences and can't be
sold for very much money. And without the money, this
station or any other, will go out of business. Sure, we
will run an occasional drama or ballet or documentary,
but the bulk of our schedule has to have big audiences.

*Us:*    So you do argue against such shows at programming
meetings.

*N.S.:*    As regular parts of the schedule, yes.

*Us:*    Perhaps it would help if you would explain just what the
arrangements are by which you take in money.

*N.S.:*    Well, first of all, we get money for the commercials we
run. They can run either in station breaks or during the
shows we put on. For our radio station, that accounts for
practically all of our revenue. We do take a news feed from
a network every hour, and the network pays us to run their
material, including their commercials for people like Colgate
or Plymouth, but most of our income is from our local
spots. Now in television, the network is a different story
because they provide us with shows through most of the

day. We carry programs from them in the morning up till noon, from 1:00 to 4:00, and then from 8:00 till 11:00, plus the network news at 6:30. All the other times are ours. We cut out a few network shows because we can run our own shows in the time periods instead, and that makes more money for us. And just like in radio, when you carry a network show and its commercials, the network pays you for each commercial you carry, but at only about 15 percent of your normal rate. So if you put your own show in there and put in spots for some local advertiser, you get 100 percent of your spot rate. Of course, out of that you have to pay for the production costs of the show you run, and if the show isn't popular, you can't charge much money, and so it sometimes isn't worth doing. But generally you can make more money that way. The networks expect you to do this a bit, but if you start preempting everything, they really get upset with you and give you a hard time.

So in brief, you can say we get money for the spots the station runs, and they're paid for by the particular advertisers; and we get money from the spots the network runs, and they're paid for by the networks. The networks, of course, get paid by the sponsors or they wouldn't be able to afford to pay us.

*Us:*   Now how about the other members of the staff you mentioned?

*N.S.:*   Let's see, I mentioned the local sales manager and the salesmen, I think.

*Us:*   Right.

*N.S.:*   The local sales manager handles a great deal of the advertising this station runs, but not all of it. Of course, he doesn't handle relations with the networks about the spots they run. I do that. But there is another part of the station advertising he doesn't handle and that's the national sales. What he handles, see, are the local boys, the car dealers and the department stores and the furniture stores right here in town. When we make a deal with a national company like Coke or Ford or Ivory Soap, I'm the one who handles that. Those companies buy some of our time directly, instead of getting it indirectly by buying through the network. Sometimes it's because they want time periods the networks can't offer. Sometimes it's because they don't want to buy all the stations the network represents so they deal with just a few individually. In any case, I'm the guy who works out those deals. The local sales manager just sticks to the local market. And after all, that makes up the bulk of our particular station's advertising. He and the salesmen maintain contacts with all the owners of the stores and businesses, figure out what sort of schedule of spots will offer the best deal, try to undercut the competition, and so on. They really know the local market conditions, who's doing pretty well, who pays his bills, and so on.

*Us:* You keep referring to the men on you sales staff. Are there any women?

*N.S.:* No, there aren't.

*Us:* Why not?

*N.S.:* Well, there aren't any who have applied who are qualified.

*Us:* But don't you hire and train any people?

*N.S.:* Well, yeah, and I guess we're going to hire some women as salesmen, I mean salespeople, sometime soon.

*Us:* Do you think they will do pretty well?

*N.S.:* I don't know. I guess so. A couple of our competitors have women on their sales staffs and they seem to be working out pretty well.

*Us:* How do you determine how much your spots will cost?

*N.S.:* That's sort of an educated guess. We all get together and decide how much we think the market will bear. We work on the basis of the cost of a thirty-second spot and the various times of day. In television, if it's early morning, the spot will cost less than at 8:00 at night. In radio, drive time costs more than 2:00 in the afternoon. A longer spot costs more and a shorter one less, of course. And if a sponsor buys a lot of spots, we give him what we call a "frequency discount." The more he buys, the cheaper each one is. But it all boils down to a guess as to how much we can get people to pay. If the audience of a show goes up, we can get more money for it. But if it goes down . . . We have some other charges too, like production charges, and we set their rates the same way.

*Us:* Production charges?

*N.S.:* Yes, if we make the commercial here at the station, we charge for that. If the sponsor gives us the commercial on film or videotape or audio tape, we don't have the hassle of making the things ourselves so there is no production charge. But if you have to call in a director and a crew or a jock and an engineer to make a spot, the sponsor will have to pay for it.

*Us:*   Suppose a sponsor isn't watching or listening at the time his spot runs. How does he know it really got on the air?

*N.S.:*   Here at our station, we have the announcer on duty keep a record on the log as to whether or not the spot ran. If it runs, he writes in the time when it started and the time it ended. The sponsor just has to take our word, or really the announcer's word, that his spot did run.

*Us:*   What happens if, for some reason, the spot doesn't run?

*N.S.:*   Then we give what's called a "make-good." We will run the spot some other day during a comparable time period and, of course, will not charge him anything extra.

*Us:*   Did you have any special training for your position?

*N.S.:*   Well, I worked as a salesman for quite a while, and that's certainly a place to learn a lot. I learned how people react to various things, what makes them respond well to some approaches and poorly to others. You could fairly call that psychology, I think. Then I also learned about economics. After all, that's what I'm dealing with. I need to understand the business conditions so I can tell when to try for a sale with a car dealer and when to approach a department store. And believe it or not, I've needed to be fairly capable with some simple math so I can deal with some of the statistics of a rating book. I've talked about having 28 percent more women eighteen to thirty-four in our audience and have convinced people to buy spots because of those statistics. That's simple math, but useful. But the main thing is what I mentioned first—learning how people react. I started out in a small station in a small market and called on every prospect I could think of. I met all types and tried every approach I could think of. That was probably the most valuable education I ever got.

*Us:*   Mr. Sales, we can't think of anything else we would like to know about your department. Thanks for spending this time with us.

*N.S.:*   It was my pleasure. Be sure to come back if you think of anything else you'd like to know.

STATION PEOPLE—
THE PROMOTION DIRECTOR

Would you buy a triplex cam spanner? Maybe you would if you knew what it was. How do you find out about it? Most of us get the bulk of our information about products from advertising.

You see a spot on television which shows the product, what it does, where it's used, and what its good features are. That way you know whether or not you have a need for the product and whether or not you like that particular brand. The advertising process in broadcasting is the same to get you to watch a new television show or listen to a new radio show. You have to be made aware of what the show is so you can decide if, for instance, you want to watch a medical show and if so, whether or not you want to watch that particular one (Dr. A instead of Dr. B). Making you aware of shows is the job of the promotion department.

And as with other products, the promotion department will advertise on the air. That, after all, doesn't cost the station anything as it's their own air time. So the promotion department will come up with short spots, very much like commercials, which use a funny or dramatic or interesting section of a show, then announce when the show will be on and then ask you to watch or listen to it. Also, on television, the ID's may be used to show a title and a time for a particular program. Or you may just hear the announcer's voice over the ending credits as he asks you to tune in to a particular show at a particular time. All these spots are created by the promotion department and fall in the category of on-air promotion. They will be written and created by the promotion staff, then produced by the production department of the station.

You may also hear announcements on radio asking you to watch a particular show, or see spots, or "promos," on television asking you to listen to a particular station. This *cross-plugging* happens particularly if one company owns the television, FM, and AM stations as a combination. These cross-plugs, believe it or not, are not for free. However, since all three are owned by the same company, a pretty easy arrangement is made for trading time for time, and no money changes hands. Mostly, just bookkeeping details are involved. But if a television station has no radio station as part of the group, it will have to lay out hard cash to a local radio station to carry the announcements, just as the used car dealers and departments stores do. In any case, it's the promotion department that makes the deals and writes the spots and sees that they get produced.

But there are other advertising media, and promotion uses them all. The newspapers are a prime source. Not only will newspapers carry ads which the promotion department places with them, they will often have a radio-television columnist. So in order to be mentioned (and favorably) by this columnist, the promotion department has to keep on good relations with him or her. That may include remembering birthdays and sending Christmas cards or presents, but more important, it involves being sure the columnist has the information s/he needs when s/he needs it. Schedules go out once a week showing what will be aired in about two or three weeks. Changes are announced as soon as possible. Specials are discussed and explained early enough for the columnist to write about what's going to happen. Sometimes, in television, advance showings are arranged so s/he can see a show before it's aired, and can thus write about it. Generally, though, columnists hold comments until after air time. That saves the station getting a bad review before anyone else has a chance to see the show. If that's the case, the advance showings are just for the convenience of the columnist, and that's another way to stay on good terms.

The paperwork that goes with advance schedules; changes; or information on specials, stars, or new shows is all handled by promotion. Most of it is written in the department. Television networks send out information on the content of every prime-time show, every episode, and it's the promotion department that takes this, boils it down, and provides a summary to newspapers. Then with a change in the schedule, promotion prepares extensive information on the format of the new show, the stars and what they have done before, the producers, the director, and just about anything else they think might be interesting to a columnist. For radio, the promotion department is totally responsible for writing up all the information. If a new DJ comes on, promotion writes up a biography for the press. If a contest starts, promotion writes descriptions of it. Since networks are such a small part of radio station activities, the promotion department carries a far heavier burden.

The ads which newspapers run for the station may be designed in the promotion department, or they may be handled by the promotion department after being received from the network. In either case, it's up to promotion to get the ads to the papers with the proper identification as to when the ad runs and how often. The promotion department will also handle the bills which the newspapers send out for having run the ads. If the ads were totally a creation of the particular station, the cost comes from the promotion department budget. But if the ads are for network shows, as is often the case at the beginning of a season, the cost will partly be paid for by the network, and that contract is negotiated by the promotion department, generally on a half-and-half basis.

Besides newspaper ads, there are other media which can be used. Billboards may carry advertising for a particular show. Cards on the tops of taxis can be used, as can cards inside and along the sides of buses and subways. Magazine ads are sometimes used. For some shows, the programs of musical events or plays may carry station ads. A show for a young audience might be advertised in a program of the performance of a popular music group. A show after an older musical audience might be advertised in the program of the symphony. In some cases, direct mail might be the answer, with the advertising piece mailed directly to the "boxholder" or "occupant." You might even find a sheet of paper stuck in a bag of groceries by the sacker, especially if the station is promoting a show sponsored by that grocer. Almost all ways to get the public's eye—sky writing, men on stilts carrying sandwich boards, blimps, handouts on street corners—have been used at some time or another by a promotion department. The point is to make people remember a show, a time, and a station. A good promotion department comes up with clever ways to make people remember. If people remember, more will listen to or watch the show than would otherwise. And if more listen or watch, the ratings will be higher and the station can charge more money for a spot within that show. That justifies the money spent by promotion.

Speaking of money, let's see how the promotion department functions in relation to the financial hub of the station—the sales department. Obviously, the salespeople are out talking to sponsors trying to get them to buy spots in shows. But how do they present the shows? How do they get the sponsor to remember when the show runs? They take with them a schedule of all the shows and a program sheet which describes the show, the stars, the producer, the ratings, or whatever is felt to be important. These two items, the schedule and the sheet, are prepared by the promotion department. The schedule is designed and printed according to promotion plans to look good as well as to be informative. The sheet is written and designed to represent the show and hopefully present it in a good light.

All of this planning and design is done by promotion as a service to the sales department. Also, if there is something special the sales department needs, such as an overall presentation of the sales advantages of the station, the promotion department will come up with a series of slides, or a film, or a videotape, or a series of desk cards, or charts, or whatever is needed to make the particular point. Also, in television, the sales department often wants to introduce a whole season to the advertisers of the area. It's the promotion department that plans the presentation, organizes the party and the pitch, and carries the whole thing off. In a port city, the advertisers may be taken on an ocean cruise while the food and drink and new programs are brought around. In a smaller inland city, the presentation may be a buffet at the station and the showing of a videotape with information about the shows. But promotion handles it all. The sales department, then, turns to the promotion department for all kinds of sales support that can't be done by the salespeople talking to the advertiser.

## the art department

One of the sub-departments one often finds in television promotion is the art department. After all, it is promotion that uses pictures and specific typefaces and graphics of varying sorts for almost everything it does. The ID slides, the billboard designs, the schedules and program sheets used by the sales-people, the ads placed in *TV Guide* and in magazines and news-papers, and a dozen other things need the specialized touch of a graphic artist. S/he has to know the specific requirements of the media—the quality of paper, ink, and typefaces and the tricks to make something inexpensive look good—and must have the ideas to create new looks and new approaches. Appearances go stale very fast in television, and each program or season has to have something fresh about it. The art director has to have enough ideas to make these things fresh. And s/he has to have these new ideas day after day, year after year. Besides that, s/he has to design and build the sets used at the station. S/he will be responsible for how shows appear on the air. If the "Home Show" has a jumbled living room, the blame falls on the art director, just as the credit does if the news set is clean, functional, and attractive. The responsibility for the look, in sets, in logos, in print, in colors, and in overall design, is the art director's job.

## the promotion manager

That look, while created by the art department, has to be approved by the head of the promotion department, and that gives a hint of what sort of background the head of that department must have. The promotion manager needs to have a knowledge of graphic art so as to evaluate styles in ads or sets or billboard posters. S/he also needs a knowledge of advertising techniques. There's no point in creating a good-looking billboard if its message won't be effective. Furthermore, the promotion manager needs to know the production techniques of television, film, and radio. S/he will, after all, create promos in all three media. Also probably more than anyone at the station except for the news personnel, s/he needs to know English very well since s/he constantly uses words to convince people to join the station's audience.

### STATION PEOPLE—THE NEWS DIRECTOR

In radio, news is often a small concern in the overall schedule. The DJ on duty may merely read the wire copy that comes from the AP or UPI machines. S/he may go to network news on the hour, come back with a local weather forecast, and slip right back into music. Or the station may be a little more dedicated to news and have a news director and maybe even a reporter or two. They will rewrite the wire copy, but they will also go out around town to follow up on local stories. They will take a mike and tape recorder and try to get on-the-spot comments from the governor or mayor or whoever is making news that day. At demonstrations they will talk to members of the crowd as well as trying to interview the spokespeople on the speaker's stand. All this material will be hurried back to the station for those hourly newscasts. The result can be very fast reporting, probably faster than any other medium. A recorded phone interview five minutes before air time can easily go on the air, a feat difficult to match anywhere else. But still, unless the station has an all-news format, news is not a big concern at most stations.

In television, however, a local station builds its reputation more on its news department than on any other single thing it does. The programs, the specials, the contests, the personalities, and the publicity all have their impact, but viewers seem to build their impression of the sort of station it is by the people they see every night, sometimes twice a night, giving them the news. Since most Americans now get their news from television rather than from newspapers, stations are sure they reach a large portion of their audience through their news departments. Any one station, or any one news department may not reach a large audience, especially as large as a popular network show; but for day-in, day-out contact with viewers, news is vitally important.

## anchorpeople

Where does this contact start? What do you think of first when you think of the news of a particular station? Chances are you think of the people who are seen on the screen reading the stories. The anchorperson in particular is probably your first thought because you see that particular newscaster almost every time you watch and s/he seems to be the central point around which the rest of the news presentation is organized. S/he quite often introduces the sports reporter and the weather person. S/he pitches to various reporters for their special stories. But the bulk of the news and the introduction of all the special reports comes from the anchorperson. Because of this central emphasis, that job becomes one of some importance within the news department. It's also a job subject to whims and fads. Sometimes the stations in a market will all be presenting pretty boys who only read. Then perhaps the style will swing to father figures who declare the news with authority. Then, perhaps, the search goes on for a sex symbol who can also be trusted as an honest, working reporter. And so it goes. But the job remains a central one, and one the news department worries about. With the right anchorperson, the audience will appear almost as if by magic. S/he sets the tone for the reliability and hard investigating which the rest of the department does. S/he may never hit the streets following down a lead on a murder, but the viewers get that impression from the best ones and transfer a belief in the anchorperson to a belief in the rest of the news staff and thus to the rest of the station. So the primary contact with the viewers is the primary concern of the station in presenting the news.

No matter how perfect this anchorperson is, though, s/he has to have news to give or people won't watch. That's obvious. So s/he has to have help. S/he gets it from a great number of people doing a lot of hard work. These people include street reporters, film and videotape crews, film and videotape editors, an assignment editor, the producer, writers, and finally, the news director. The director is the head of the department, not the one who directs the news while it is on the air. That person is a director of the news, not the news director. But let's go on the way we started and see who's immediately behind the anchorperson.

## street reporters

First let's look at the street reporters. Their faces are also familiar to you, because they are the ones who go out to the State House to interview the governor or out to the fire to see what's happening. They show up mostly on film or videotape, as their story is done right on the scene. They have to show what's happened as well as tell about it, so they go wherever they need to for the report. Their day, then, is spent in traveling to newsworthy events and looking around and finding someone to talk to, or maybe in presenting their own analysis of the situation. Then they end up with some statement like "This is John Morris reporting from the scene of the Vendome Hotel fire." All this is on film or tape so a film-tape crew goes with him. The crew consists of generally one person, although it may be two. The film crew, or person, has the responsibility of lugging around all the heavy equipment, setting up lights if possible, putting the camera up on its tripod or on a shoulder, hooking up the mike, and checking to see everything is running properly. Then s/he cues the reporter, who faces the camera and says, "The first alarm reached fire station #28 at . . ." When the reporter and crew get back to the station, the reporter writes the introductory words to the story, and if the story was filmed, that film will now be processed. If the story was done on videotape, the reporter keeps the cassette handy until time for editing.

Let's talk about a story on film first, of a fire, for instance. Once the film is processed, the reporter will sit down with a film editor and the two of them will look at all of it and decide what parts to cut out, what to leave in, and what shots of the burning building are best. They will have been given a time allotment by the assignment editor or the producer, and they know the film cannot run longer than that. So sometimes they have a lot of cutting to do. Sometimes they have to try to talk the producer out of a bit more news time, and if the story is important, they will get it.

If the story was shot on a video cassette, the process is much the same. Again, one of those two people, the assignment editor or the producer, will have given them a time limit. So the reporter will work with a videotape engineer to pick out the best shots and figure out the best sequence for the shots. Then the engineer will dub those over from the cassette to another cassette, or perhaps to a reel of tape, for play during the news. Now what of these other two people we have just mentioned?

## the assignment editor

The assignment editor is the one who starts the whole news day rolling. S/he knows the city, the politics, and the important people. S/he senses what's important. S/he knows where to go for leads. S/he knows the layout of the town so s/he will know if s/he can send a reporter out with enough time to get back and write up the report for the newscast. S/he is, then, the one who sends others out on stories. S/he assigns what they will cover and where they will go. Without a good assignment editor, the news department will waste its time following up unimportant stories and will get only a few of the important ones. Because s/he should know how long it takes to get out, film a story, return to the station, edit the story, and write the lead-in, s/he can make the best use of the reporter's time.

## the news producer

The producer starts to take over as the assignment editor starts to ease out. Their responsibilities will overlap for a while, as they both will be dealing with stories and reporters as they come in. But ultimately, it is the producer's decision as to what goes into the newscast. Needless to say, s/he takes advice from the anchorpeople, from his or her reporters, and from the news director. But s/he is the one who is responsible for pulling the pieces together for the cast. S/he decides which stories are to be read first, second, and so on. S/he decides how much time can be spent on the various stories. S/he makes sure everyone knows how much time remains until the newscast starts. S/he also supervises the writers and talks with them about what's coming in and what they're writing. It is the writers who get news from the teletype machines, which feed stories to the station from Associated Press or United Press International. These stories, of course, are generally of national or regional events, and the writers take this wire copy and rewrite it for presentation in the local newscast. The producer needs to know if important stories are coming in, or if long stories are showing up, or if the writers aren't getting enough written to fill up the time. The local stories are more important, but s/he keeps an eye on the writers for their essential contributions nonetheless. So s/he and the assignment editor are the organizers of the newscast. If they aren't good and they don't know where to send reporters and in what order to put their stories, then the news won't be very good.

## the news director

It's up to the news director to be sure s/he has good people in those two spots as well as in the anchor position. The look of the news, the believability of it, and the thoroughness with which the staff covers local stories are all up to the news director. S/he has to know news and the essentials of news gathering so s/he can judge how well the reporters are functioning, how efficient the assignment editor is, and how skilled the producer is. This job, as with that of many department heads, is not so much to oversee the day-to-day production of the department as it is to establish the overall approach. If s/he believes the station and the public would best be served by nothing but local news, s/he may eliminate all national and regional stories. If s/he thinks more filmed or taped stories and more location work would give a better coverage of events, s/he may hire more film-tape crews and street reporters. If s/he thinks a regular series of investigative documentaries are an essential part of news, s/he may create a sub-department to produce one documentary a month. S/he is responsible for thinking about the quality of news, its presentation, and its production.

## the news department

The news department occupies a unique spot within a station. The news director is responsible to the general manager and to none other. The news department should never be interfered with by production, programming, or sales. News has to be unbiased and fair, or at least as far as is humanly possible. Therefore, the news department must be rather isolated from the other departments. The content of the news is a forbidden area to everyone else in the station. A reporter must be free to talk about what s/he discovers, even if that discovery steps on important toes, so no one at the station should be able to refuse a reporter that right. So the news department must be free from production problems, sponsor complaints, and programming headaches. The news director must know how to intercept an attempt of an outside department or person to have an effect on news presentation, even if the attempt is made in all innocence. Not all stations follow this approach, and not all news directors are successful at intercepting, but this is the ideal. It's a credit to broadcast news that this ideal is reached in a vast numbers of stations. It's also a credit to news directors that they manage to uphold this ideal in so many difficult and varying situations.

STATION PEOPLE—THE EDITORIAL BOARD

More and more, stations are developing an editorial board as part of the station organization. It doesn't have quite the status of a department, and the members of the board generally cut across other department lines, having their primary responsibility in another area. But an editorial board serves as useful a function for the station as does an editorial writer for a newspaper. The FCC believes editorials to be a good thing, helping to serve the public interest, convenience, and necessity for that area. So with that sort of prompting from the agency which reviews and renews their licenses, many stations have created editorial boards.

First of all, the stations select people from within the station. Second, they sometimes select people from outside the station to act as advisors. Let's take a look at the first situation.

Obviously, the general manager will be the head of the editorial board. Because the editorials will express station policy, they will often be given by the general manager on the air. Of course, not everyone at the station will agree with the editorials, but officially the station will take the stand expressed in the editorials. Since this is the case, the general manager, as the chief official of the station, presents them. It's entirely possible s/he doesn't agree with the editorial, but is expressing the view of the majority of the editorial board. Realistically, that seldom happens. If the general manager doesn't like the editorial, s/he doesn't give it.

The next member of the board is the program director. As the second most important person at the station, s/he has to be included. Also included will be the news director and the public affairs director. These four will quite often be joined by another member of the station, for instance the production manager or the promotion manager, so as to make five, an odd number, and thus avoid tie votes. These people will submit topics for editorials, and generally the public affairs director will write up a draft editorial. It also happens quite often that the one who suggested the topic will write the draft. At larger stations, quite often a particular person will be hired to write the editorials. This person becomes a member of the board and functions exactly as the others do.

Once a topic has been chosen, the board will discuss the point of view. They will decide what they want to say about the topic and what stand they want to take. They will decide how best to approach their point. Then a draft will be written. The board will meet again to look over this draft, make corrections or changes, and approve it for presentation. Then the general manager, or sometimes another member of the board, will tape a presentation of the editorial. It will then be scheduled in whatever way the station has decided is appropriate. Some stations bury their editorials after the late-night news or in mid-morning. Some run them only one day. Some run the same one all week. Some include them in the early evening news. All, however, invite response from people opposed to their stand, and all will give free air time to a statement in opposition.

Now, let's discuss the stations that include people from outside the station. The basic board within the station remains the same sort of thing we have been talking about. But the station, generally through the public affairs director, will invite various representatives of various groups in the area to become associates of the editorial board. Where the station board may include only four or five members, the associates may number twenty-five, thirty, or more. Obviously, they are not all consulted at all times. But when the station is contemplating a stand on a topic in which one of their associates is an expert, that person obviously gets called in. S/he then becomes part of the discussion process leading up to the recording of the editorial. For instance, say the station wants to tackle the corruption in City Hall. And say one of its associates has been a reform candidate for the office of mayor. S/he would be called in to give advice on what should be said. It even happens, in less explosive circumstances than that, that the expert will be the one to read the editorial on the air. And it's obvious, I'm sure, that these associates can contribute ideas for editorials even though the station has not specifically asked them to. This expanding of the editorial board will relate the station to the community in a number of ways, but it can also embroil the station in battling factions. It's a calculated risk many stations don't take.

Editorials in general are a risk. More and more stations, though, find the risk worth taking. Whether or not people agree with the stands taken, they at least feel the station is involved in what's going on in the community. And that sense of involvement goes a long way toward satisfying the requirement to serve in the "public interest, convenience, or necessity" which the FCC demands when it passes out licenses.

## STATION PEOPLE—ENGINEERING

Broadcasting is a matter of machines. Of course, what gets done with those machines is far more important than the machines themselves, but you can't deny the value and place of machines. Without a functioning microphone, camera, switching console, or transmitter, the greatest ideas in the world won't get out of the producer's head. So no matter how creative and innovative the station's staff is, it must turn to the engineering department for essential help.

The chief engineer should know electronics both in practice and in theory. S/he's the one you go to when you want to know how to accomplish a special trick or to get the equipment to do a bit more than it's supposed to. S/he responds to technological challenges, and if s/he's good enough, s/he'll take a paper clip, some chewing gum, and a screw driver and convert the wastebasket into two color cameras, a double re-entry switcher, and an editec videotape machine. In other words, s/he knows the system backward and forward, can design electrical systems, can see how to improve the gear you have, and can figure ways to make it do things the original designers never dreamed of. S/he knows more than just repair, s/he knows how to pick engineers who can do more for you than just the routine turning of screws and checking of dials. And s/he's a good enough administrator to keep them all happy working together.

That's the ideal. Sometimes you're lucky if the chief engineer can walk through a door and chew gum at the same time. Sometimes you'll feel that way about the general manager too. And the production manager. And the program director. And . . . So there will be problems. But remember your bad days when you can't sign your own name without misspelling it. So somewhere short of this ideal is the person you actually have to work with. S/he knows far more about the resistors and wires and circuit boards than you ever will, and s/he can do things with them you didn't think possible. S/he can help you in a dozen ways when you are faced with problems. If you are doing interviews at a roller derby, or taking the cameras outside, or trying to get a shot from above the action, or if you want a special arrangement for the election coverage, s/he's the person to talk to. Sometimes s/he will flatly tell you it's impossible. The path of wisdom is to believe that and find another way to do it. But always show a great regard for the care of the machines, and you will win any engineer's heart. The machines, after all, come right after his or her mother in an engineer's affections.

Most of the engineering staff will be concerned with working on the machines to keep them in running order. No matter how new or how perfected a machine may be, it has gremlins and crotchets which cause it to slip into a rest just at the moment you need it. The engineers have to be able to slide a transistor in its side and get it functioning again. So much of their time is spent probing and correcting and rebuilding. Then too, they try to prevent breakdowns from happening, so they continually go over equipment to see if they can spot a weak unit, or to make sure the entire thing is running up to its expected level of output. Cameras, if left alone, will slip from a clear flesh tone into bilious greens or outraged purples. Audiotape machines collect junk on their heads and stop recording every third word or so. Monitors drift from showing perfect circles to showing eggs instead. The engineers have a routine inspection path to see if these sorts of things are happening, and if they are, they start to work to correct them. So it's the engineering department we depend on to keep things working right, to fix the things which stop working, and to help us get the things to work better than anyone thought they would.

All of that falls under the general heading of maintenance. But your daily contact with the engineering staff is more likely to be in the area of production. If, in television, you are directing at a station which is staffed by union engineers, your audio person, your technical director, your camerapeople, your lighting crew, your videotape operator, and your projectionist will most likely be engineers. Of course, the people who shade the cameras and operate the transmitter will be engineers. Even at a non-union station, you still will work with engineers on videotape machines, projectors, and shading. In radio, the board may be staffed by engineers. The ones who do the actual cutting and splicing of audiotape, even if you are determining where the cuts come, may be engineers. And certainly the ones who record onto tape in the first place are engineers. The chief engineer will make rotating schedules so you won't have the same crew working for you all the time. Every month, or two months, or three months, or however often s/he chooses, s/he will move everyone to a different job. This is both good and bad for the production staff. First the good part. It moves the complete dunce out of that key job where s/he's been giving you so much grief for so long. Now the bad part. S/he moves into another key job. But generally, the engineers know the equipment so well they can do a great deal with it. Your problem is not how to get them to do something, but how to explain your ideas so they can do it for you. Because they are so intimate with the equipment, you can spend your time worrying about the concept of the show, knowing they know what to do to give you that concept.

## STATION PEOPLE—ACCOUNTING

The accounting staff is generally only of great concern to you on paydays, because they sign and give you your check. But as with all businesses, they are essential every day. Of course, they keep track of how much you should be paid, how much vacation time you get, how much sick pay you are entitled to, and all those related matters, but they have to have something to put in the bank as well.

So that's where the daily part comes in. The sales department will send them copies of the contracts signed with sponsors. It's then up to the accounting department to figure out exactly how much to bill each month and to determine if the spots really did run. This department, therefore, is generally where the official logs go, as they prove whether or not a spot was aired. If sales has sold a flight of spots to the local department store which runs for the next three months, accounting will determine what one-third of the contract price is, check to see if all the spots run the first month, then send out the first bill. Needless to say, they keep records on payment so they will know, when the second bill goes out, if the store paid for the first bill.

As money comes in, they make sure it gets into the account at the bank. Because, like any other business, the station gets bills too. The standard expenses of insurance, heating and lighting, and especially electricity have to be paid. Occasionally there are unusual expenses like the rental of lines from the telephone company for the carrying of a special program. If the station did a remote of some sort, it may have had to rent telephone lines to carry the signal back to the station. And that's an extra expense. Accounting keeps records of all this too.

One other source of revenue which accounting keeps track of is that sent by the network. Accounting will make sure the network sends the right amount. Again, they have to check the official logs to see what network commercials were carried so they will know what amount of money the station is entitled to.

In accounting it is very apparent that what the station sells is air time. Other departments tend to think of spots as a roll of videotape or audiotape, or as a certain production problem, or as a pitch saying a particular thing, but in accounting, the official log and the listing of how much time was used are all that matters. And that's what the money charge is based on.

So the accounting department in broadcasting is much like it is in other businesses. They are concerned with the money flow, both into and out of the station. And the official log is their bible and chief guide.

## STATION PEOPLE—ON-AIR TALENT

The people on the air at a station are in a funny position. They are both the central point of the station and the most dispensable. They are the daily contact with the audience, and yet they can be replaced easily in most situations. A C&W jock in Louisville sounds very like one in Little Rock, so a station could afford to fire one and hire the other, and very few in the audience would care, or even notice. But with no jock at all, the station is in bad shape. Occasionally, a personality emerges and holds a spot for a long time. John Gambling in New York City is an example, having taken over the spot from his father before him.

But because they are dispensable, most air talent end up low on the totem pole. The production manager is generally the one ordering their lives at the station, although there may have been some contact with the program director when they were first hired. And if the ratings slip, the word comes rapidly to stop showing up for work. Or it may happen that the program director wants to try a different approach and the style doesn't fit the talent now on the air. They all go. New people stream in. If the ratings show a large and loyal following for one particular person, that one may stay while the others go—but not always.

And yet, if a person does succeed in establishing a strong niche and a loyal following, and the ratings stay up, that person can end up earning more money than anyone else at the station. A successful anchor newsperson on a major television station in a major market can be earning $125,000, while the general manager gets "only" $50,000. What puts one person in such a strong position while another gets bounced? Partly it's skill in knowing how to do the job well. Partly it's determination to stick in the business, sometimes even after being fired a few times. And partly it's just plain luck. If you're in the right place at the right time, that can overcome years of trying to hit the right spot. So many people think broadcasting is glamourous that they are constantly trying to get in. That means the competition for any one spot on the air is tremendous. So landing the job depends on skill, determination, and "a little bit o' luck." But being "on" is an ego boost like few others. Maybe it's all worth it.

# 6

## STATION
## Affiliation
## ANd
## REGULATION

What does a broadcasting station, whether radio or television, have as its raw material? Time. General Motors can turn out a car—a solid, tangible item which exists even after General Motors is all through with it and has sold it. But a broadcasting station has time, and can fill it with a variety of things which exist only for a short while and then are gone forever. While there's a lot of time available to be used, it can only be used once. There's no way to reprocess yesterday's noontime. So the stations are in a perpetual scramble to fill that vanishing, yet plentiful, time with comedies and news and music and drama and movies and . . . All of these programs have to come from somewhere, and because there is so much time, there are a lot of "somewheres" providing programs. Since radio and television take very different sorts of programs, we can't say the same program sources work for each. So let's take them one at a time.

TELEVISION: NETWORK AFFILIATES

First television. Let's look at the NBC station in Two Whistle, West Virginia. At 6:45 every morning, they come on the air with a farm and market report, done by a sleepy reporter from their studio. At 7:00 they pick up the "Today" show, which is sent to them over a telephone line from a bigger West Virginia city. That city got it from a telephone line from Philadelphia, which got it from a telephone line from New York City, where the program originated in a studio much like, but somewhat larger than, the one Two Whistle's farm and market report comes from. The telephone line, too, is like, but somewhat larger than, the telephone line you're used to at home.

So from 7:00 till about noon, with only a few breaks for station breaks and commercials, this local station receives and broadcasts programs provided by NBC. Some originate in New York City, some in Los Angeles, some are live, some are on film, and some are on videotape. But for Two Whistle, NBC starts them on the telephone line out of New York City all morning long. The noontime break is for news, generally, which is done by the local station. Also, some other half-hour program is run by the local station. This may be old shows of "I Love Lucy" or "F Troop." Then NBC starts in again with the afternoon soaps and game shows. In the late afternoon, NBC stops and Two Whistle picks up again, once more providing shows like "Mike Douglas" or "Gilligan's Island," or maybe a movie with the starlet Narda Onyx. In the early evening, the station does a news show, then goes to NBC evening news. Once more the network shuts off, and the local station provides the evening edition of "The Price Is Right" or "What's My Line." After that, it's back to NBC for the prime-time shows. In the late evening, the network stops so local stations can do a half hour of late news. Then comes the "Tonight" show. After that, Two Whistle goes off the air because they figure all the farmers in the area are long since asleep and there's no point in showing anything. So the station is off the air from 1:00 A.M. till 6:45, when the farm and market report comes on again. Out of a broadcast day of about eighteen hours, NBC provides Two Whistle with thirteen hours of programs. The local station has to come up with the remaining five hours each weekday. As we have seen, some of that time is filled with news done live from their studios, some is filled with films of old programs or old movie films, and some with videotaped shows like "Mike Douglas." The film or tape shows are sold by various groups which contact the station, so that's a matter of selecting what the station can afford and what seems likely to please a large audience. The news, of course, is a local product, done by reporters and newspeople hired by the station.

This is a basic station arrangement, filling its time in basic, standard ways. This station is referred to as an affiliate of NBC because they run the programs provided by NBC. But they don't run them for free. The station has to pay its reporters, directors, and secretaries, so almost everything it does is an attempt to turn a buck. You know they collect money from G.E. every time they run a commercial for one of the refrigerators. That's where the bulk of the money comes from, of course. Those spots, plus the ones for Brown's Hardware downtown, bring in most of the station's revenue. But they don't give away air time for free, not even to the network. Suppose NBC provides a half-hour program at night and has three commercials in it. Two Whistle's rate for a commercial run at that time is $100 each. For three, that's $300. But because getting the programs is such a good deal for the station, they have agreed with NBC not to charge the full rate. They will take the program and the three commercials within it and only charge $30. If the station didn't take the program, it would have to buy one from somewhere else, and even though it could then get the full $300 for commercials, it would probably have to pay almost that much for the show itself. So taking the NBC show is a good deal. The network is content too, because it can tell the sponsors of those three commercials that the audience for the spots is nationwide, even including Two Whistle, West Virginia. And the more people who watch, no matter where they live, the happier the sponsor is and the more he is willing to pay NBC. So NBC may charge $40,000 for one of those commercials, or $120,000 total, and then split it up among all its affiliates, including the $30 to Two Whistle. Needless to say, there is some left over for the network itself to keep and play with.

## network owned and operated

Affiliation has been such a good deal that lots of stations around the country have made similar deals with NBC, CBS, or ABC. These stations are all affiliates of one network or the other and carry the programs of their particular network choice. The networks, as we have seen, make money out of this by keeping part of what they charge the sponsors. But they also saw that the stations were making money, so they decided they could make a bit more by outright ownership of some of the stations. The government stepped in here and ruled they could own no more than seven stations apiece, and of the seven no more than five could be VHF (that is, channels 2 through 13). But that's better than nothing, so the networks bought stations in major cities. These stations are referred to as the network O & O stations, which stands for owned and operated. Just like the station in Two Whistle, they carry the network offerings whenever the network sends them down the phone lines. And just like Two Whistle, they fill in the other times with material of their own choosing. Because they are in bigger cities and can make more money, the shows they choose tend to be newer and better. Also, they will produce a few shows of their own. That's an expensive proposition because you have to pay writers, actors, directors, scene designers, and a whole host of other people. A little station can't afford that sort of thing, but a big one can. So the network O & O's will slip in some shows of their own. They also run bigger, more expensive, and more elaborate news operations. They do several news shows each day and try to do news specials with some regularity. Again, smaller stations don't have the money for this, but a big station does. Also, even though these O & O stations are run as separate parts of the network, they do keep the network's interests in mind. They will provide the network with news coverage of events in that particular city which the network can then use for its nationwide news shows. They will look for new talent to hire, train, and then pass on to the network news operation. And they will keep their facilities up to date so the network will have good equipment to work with if it needs it.

So the network O & O's are just like the other affiliates, only more so. All the affiliates do the same sort of thing—take programs from the network, fill in the other time with shows of their own choosing, and get money by selling commercial time and by collecting from the network. The O & O's just have the advantage of being a little closer to the big money.

## group owned

If it's an advantage for a network to own a few stations, it ought to be some sort of advantage for anyone to own a few stations. And it is. If one station makes money, two stations ought to make about twice as much. And so on. This elementary arithmetic has caused some people to start buying up stations. They run into that same governmental rule about no more than seven stations, but that can still be seven times as much income as owning one station. So around the country there are companies owning several stations and running all of them in similar ways. These stations are referred to as *group owned*, since a group of them are owned by one company. Westinghouse, Corinthian, and Metromedia are some of the names of group owners. And like the networks, they try to get stations in the bigger cities. There's more money to be had there. Let's create a typical group situation, Rectangle Broadcasting, and see what the set-up is.

Rectangle owns a station in Boston, one in Pittsburgh, another in Philadelphia, and the last in Washington, D.C. In Boston, the station is the CBS affiliate; in Pittsburgh, NBC; in Philadelphia, ABC; and in Washington, it has no affiliation. So the four stations have a wide variety of programs during the network hours. Since each is a separate station, even though they are owned by the same company, there is no need for them to all go with the same network. Probably, when the company was buying stations, they had no choice because it was only the CBS affiliate up for sale in one town and only the ABC one in another. So Rectangle bought what it could and now has a great variety of programming. But what of the times when the networks don't provide anything, and what about that one station with no network affiliation at all?

As you might expect, each station does some news shows. Each station also buys some old shows like "Flipper" and some old movies. But for a lot of those blank periods, Rectangle has the advantage of being able to deal from a central position. That is, the company can buy "Bonanza" and show it on all four of its stations. Rectangle pays more for it than if it were buying for just one station, but less than if four individual stations were buying it. So the four stations get a good deal on a good show. Also, the station in, say, Washington may produce a pretty good game show. That station videotapes the show and sends the tape around to the other three stations. They can run it essentially for free. The station in Boston may do a talk show that the other three can carry. So by getting together, the stations can provide each other with shows and can buy on a mass basis and so cut their costs. Lower costs mean more of the income is profit. So the Rectangle group makes more money than four individually owned stations in the towns. Their affiliations can be with anybody, but their hearts belong to Rectangle.

## independents

Let's take a closer look at that Washington station, though. A lot of stations around the country aren't affiliated with any network. How do they fill up all their time? It's not easy. If, like Two Whistle, they are on the air eighteen hours a day, they don't get the thirteen-hour break a network provides. That also means they don't get the money from a network for carrying the national commercials. The programs a network affiliate gets paid to carry, the independent has to pay for. Of course the independent can charge the full rate for a commercial in any of its shows, but the full rate is probably a lot less than that of the network station. That's because fewer people are likely to be watching the independent, and you can't charge more money for a smaller crowd. So the independent faces a double bind of having to buy all of its programs and of not being able to charge advertisers as much money.

The programs the independents buy are like the programs affiliates buy—"F Troop," "I Love Lucy," and the rest. But here again the money problem comes up. The network affiliates also need to buy a certain number of shows like this, and they can afford to pay more money. So the selection left to the independent is often the really old or the really bad shows. The movies they buy may be just barely beyond the silents. The series may be one that died in 1962. And that adds to the money problem. If the shows are that old, or that bad, the audience may not watch. That means the crowd is getting smaller, and that means the station has to charge the advertiser less and less. So there's less money to buy good shows, and so on. An independent like our Washington station, part of a group, has an advantage in that it can get in on better buys like "Bonanza" or can take videotaped shows from the other stations. But it still fights uphill on the rest of its time. That's not to say the independents invariably lose. If that were so, there would be no independents left around the country. Obviously, some of their shows do catch on, and do get big crowds. Some of them carry the hometown sports team of one sort or another. That pulls in a big audience. Some carry a good movie package and really scrimp in other areas. But the audiences for the movies justify the approach. It's just that every hour of every broadcast day has to be filled by the independent by its own hard effort. Not one of them can plug into the network, sit back, and doze till the station break.

## public television

Only one other station in town works as hard for a buck as the independent. That's the public station. They used to be called "educational," but that was not a true representation of the type of stations they were, so the title was changed. These stations, like the others, are licensed by the government but as noncommercial rather than commercial stations. Even the fighting independent can charge a sponsor for running a spot on the station, but the public stations can't raise a penny that way. They are forbidden to carry normal commercials. So they obviously can't be network affiliates either. Where, then, does the money come from?

Many of these stations are connected to educational institutions of one sort or another. They are partly financed by a school board or a university. They sometimes have to carry what really are educational programs as part of their offerings, generally something like Physics I offered at 10 A.M. on school mornings. But the late afternoon and evening programs are shows as varied as "Sesame Street" and "Masterpiece Theatre." And it's usually the viewing public that comes up with the money to keep the station on the air and showing these things. If you've spent more than fifteen minutes watching a public station, you've probably caught an appeal to "send in as much as you can to help keep us on the air." That's a commercial, of course, because it is an attempt to get people to part with some money so as to have a product—the shows aired by the public station. But it's not the sort of commercial we usually think of, nor is it the sort the FCC normally thinks of, so it is allowed. So the public station is in the same situation as the commercial station. If enough people watch and like their shows, enough money will come in. That's just like the search for ratings which the commercial stations go through. Ratings, after all, are just a measure of whether or not enough people are watching. The difference comes in the range of numbers. The public station may only need a tenth of the audience of the commercial station in order to get enough contributions. Look at it this way. One person sending in five dollars to a public station is the equivalent of a lot of people each buying a bar of soap advertised on a commercial station because the profit on that bar of soap may only be five cents, and that has to be split up with the manufacturer and the advertising agency before any of it gets to the station. That's not to say the public stations have as much money as the commercial stations. They don't, because there are an awful lot of people out there buying bars of soap. But the public stations do get a large chunk of support from the public, as well as from school boards and universities.

Some of the public stations, of course, aren't connected with any educational institution. In cases like that, a great deal of the time of high-level management is spent talking the big corporations into giving money as a good public relations idea. And that usually works too. Further, if the station has some talented people around, it can start producing shows and getting the money to finance the projects from the Corporation for Public Broadcasting. This is a government agency with money given to it by Congress for exactly this use—financing program production. Other groups, like the Ford Foundation, also give large amounts of money for this sort of thing. For stations doing the programs, that money keeps people on the payroll and helps keep the station on the air.

This corporation, referred to as the CPB, is tied to another group, also paid by the government, called the Public Broadcasting Service, or PBS. The programs which stations do with CPB money get broadcast by PBS over a network much like NBC or ABC. The public stations all over the country can broadcast the offerings of PBS just as CBS affiliates can broadcast the offerings of that network. So the various public stations get some help in filling all those hours just like a commercial affiliate does.

In spite of all the obvious similarities between commercial and noncommercial stations, anyone watching the two for any length of time will come away feeling they are totally different sorts of beasts. As indeed they are. Commercial stations are interested in mass audiences and so don't air shows appealing to small crowds. A dramatization of the trial of Galileo goes on the public station while the Super Bowl goes on a commercial channel. The commercial stations have money enough to produce very polished, complex productions, maybe starting in Paris and finishing in Hong Kong. The public stations may work out of two or three relatively simple sets in one studio. The level of professionalism is generally very much the same, but the expenses are held down a lot more on public programs. That's not to say the programs are worse. No matter how slick, the story on a commercial channel can be dull. No matter how cheap, the presentation on a public station can be fascinating. But the reverse appeal can also happen, so it's unsafe to generalize. About as far as one can safely go is to say the public stations give more attention to smaller audiences and more specialized audiences. But what a difference that can make!

## RADIO AFFILIATION

Does radio have the same sort of set-up? Not any longer. Years ago, before television, the affiliations were very similar, but there simply isn't the sort of nationwide programming for radio that once made network affiliation such a valuable thing. Now, the closest a station gets to network affiliation is with a regular news feed throughout the day. You're probably familiar with a station that plays music all day but breaks at the hour for five minutes of news from a network like ABC. The station is more of an independent than a network affiliate because most of its programming depends on what the local owner wants to put on. The news is a service only and not an irreplaceable one the way a television network's is. Even those stations owned by the networks function pretty much as independents. The emphasis in radio has gone, not to affiliation, but to formats, or the style of presentation. Some stations are owned by groups, as in television, and some by networks and some by individuals, but they all approach programming in terms of format rather than in terms of variety.

So let's talk about formats rather than affiliation. For most radio stations, affiliation, when it is any concern at all, becomes more a matter of picking a source of programming. The individual station, whether owned by NBC, Westinghouse, or by John Doe, tries to build an identifiable sound on the air. Right here, let me pause to say there are still some stations concerned with offering a variety of services to their listeners. Smaller stations and public stations tend to be the ones doing a number of different things. But it's easier to talk about the single-minded bigger stations first, and then we will consider the mixed world of other stations.

Basically, formats can be music-and-news, talk, or all news. Obviously, you can get a great deal of variety within those groupings, more variety in music-and-news and less in all news. Music can be Top 40 or Country & Western or Easy Listening or Classical or Golden Oldies or any number of other sorts.

Once a station has decided to go for a particular audience, the style of music is chosen which seems most likely to appeal to those particular listeners. Suppose a station decided the teens didn't have as much money to spend as a thirty-five- to fifty-year-old audience. The station's salespeople, in other words, wanted to go to potential sponsors and say "Our audience can spend more money with you than can the audience of Station WXXX." Rather than going for Top 40, this station would pick some MOR (middle-of-the-road) music. Considerations like the number of vocals as against the number of pure instrumentals, the inclusion of a big band sound, and the frequency of DJ interruptions would then come up. The station manager, the program director, possibly the production manager, and maybe even the music librarian would sit down and talk over this sort of thing. Perhaps they would decide to have no more than one vocal for every six instrumentals. Quite likely they would decide to have the DJs on for short times only, saying as little as possible, building no particular personality a listener would identify with a particular time period. These sorts of decisions would give the station a particular sound which, hopefully, would be different from all other stations in the area. If the decisions are right, the thirty-five to fifty age group audience will indeed find that station a pleasant one to listen to. So the station will get the audience it wants. A truly careful station will even be sure the commercials it runs match its format. Suppose a national advertiser puts out a hard rock jingle for a :30 spot. That conflicts with the sound of this station, and the management may decide to turn down the account rather than run something so far out of their line. Of course, if they need the money, they may take it anyway. But the chances aren't good the audience will respond to it. So the station loses a bit of respect, and the advertiser very likely wasted his money. Just like commercials, the presentation of news will be affected by the station's style. The older audience is more interested in news than most teens. So instead of going for two minutes of news headlines on the hour, the way a Top 40 station might, this station may go for a five-minute newscast giving a bit more detail. Even five minutes every hour isn't much, so in the early evening or late afternoon, the station may go for a longer newscast, say of fifteen minutes.

Where does affiliation fit into this picture, either with this MOR station or the Top 40 one? Probably it doesn't. The MOR station is the only one likely to go for a network affiliation for news on the hour. The Top 40 will subscribe to one of the wire services, AP or UPI, and have the DJ rip off the sheet of news and read off the headlines on the air. Hence the title "rip and read" for this sort of news. Either station, though, may be owned by a group. Lotus Broadcasting may own a string of radio stations in major cities, one of which is MOR, one Top 40, and another C & W. But maybe only one is affiliated with ABC for news.

If one of their stations is all talk or all news, then affiliation is more likely, but still uncertain. If a station goes all talk, then the individual DJs build personalities which hopefully will cause people to call the station and talk over the air about various topics. Since many of these topics center around the news of the day, the station will have to have a news show of some length and regularity. Five minutes of national network news followed by five minutes of local news and weather picked up off the AP or UPI wires would not be unusual. That's ten minutes every hour. Then it's back to the listeners. For an all-news station, the wire services become essential, plus whatever other sources can be found. In some regions, a program service distributes short features, say two or three minutes about sports, every half hour. An all news station might subscribe to that service and broadcast those features. The station's staff would constantly be hard at work recording features of their own on local politics or schools or local sports teams for play during the day. But the backbone of the operation would be the wire services and their constant flow of material. Even here, a network service might be nice, but it isn't essential. Lots of other program sources are available.

Now what of the more varied smaller stations or public stations? Generally, some sort of music is the basic material for the station. As for all stations, music is an easy to get program source. Records are, after all, pretty commonly available. But instead of sticking to a particular sound all day, these stations may vary. In the morning, a public station may have nothing but classical. In the afternoon, jazz may take over for a couple hours. That may be followed with light classical till early evening. Then the station may put on a group of public affairs programs. Public affairs programs generally deal with a specific situation or a specific segment of the audience. For example, the station may do a special about the pros and cons of an upcoming vote on a bond issue. Or the station may have a weekly program with and about the Armenian segment of the population of the city. After the public affairs programs are over, the station may go back to classical music till sign off. The small station may do much the same sort of thing, but generally far less of it. Those stations may have only two or three public affairs shows a week instead of every night. They may rely more on music throughout the day, and may fill the evening with a time for C & W or for local high school band music.

The smaller stations also don't have access to NPR, National Public Radio. This is a network providing a variety of programs for public radio stations much the way PBS does for television. NPR will provide coverage of congressional hearings which are open to the public and are of particular interest. It will provide short segments discussing particular topics, like a review of a movie or a brief discussion of a particular artist. It will provide a news program of some length, with reports from all over the world. It will provide live coverage of musical events from around the country. This sort of thing can do much to enrich the local programming of an NPR affiliated station. But even so, as distinct from television, the local station still has to fill the majority of its time itself. Other sources exist: Pacifica is a group providing a nonestablishment view of happenings, and many stations use their programs. But the bulk of the day still must be programmed and filled by the local people. Affiliation is much looser and much less time-consuming for radio.

We've run the gamut from stations totally and intimately connected to a network to those not connected to anyone else at all. Affilliation, for either radio or television, can be an enormously useful and profitable condition, but it's not the only way to run a successful station. Success depends on good management decisions, and affiliation is only one of the possible decisions managers can make.


## STATION REGULATION

All of us live with some rules and some laws, and broadcasting is no exception. We don't park in front of fire hydrants; broadcasters don't broadcast lotteries. If we are debaters, we don't use lies to win our case; broadcasters present both sides of controversial issues. The laws may seem stronger, but the rules can be just as binding. Some, as in the case of lotteries, are laws passed by the United States Congress. Others, like the balance in controversial issues, are rules adopted by the Federal Communications Commission. And it's this commission, the FCC, which regulates broadcasting because Congress has told it to do so. Their rulemaking, then, becomes just as strong as law. There is a rule-making group, though, whose rules aren't that strong but are generally followed anyway. That's the National Association of Broadcasters, a group organized by the broadcasters themselves to set up standards and policies for all stations to follow. Not all stations follow their rules, but not doing so is like picking the flowers planted in public parks—some people do, but the rest of us think that's a cheap, petty thing to do. Likewise, the stations that break the NAB rules are generally the cheaper, less respectable stations. So there are three sources of law-and-rule makers which broadcasters deal with, and these three sources cover a wide variety of situations. Let's start with the laws.

We are all subject to a lot of laws, but only a few ever really have much impact on us. We know it's illegal to rob a bank, but we are more concerned with the law that says you get a parking ticket when your meter runs out. The broadcasters are in the same position. Primarily, they are involved with only a few major laws. One is the lottery law I mentioned before. Congress has said it's illegal to broadcast a lottery, and it has defined a lottery as a game involving "prize, chance, and consideration." In other words, if you can win something, if you are chosen by luck instead of by skill, and if you had to pay something to get into the game, that's a lottery. If the game involved "the best essay" or "the most beautiful picture," that's something done with skill so it's not a lottery. If you can enter the game completely free, it's not a lottery. That's why so many contests say to send in a label *or* the company name printed on a piece of paper. You have to buy a label, but not the printing you do, so it's possible to get in for free. The game would be a lottery if you could only enter by buying a label. Think of all the contests broadcasters run—TV Bingo, bowling pals, guess the beans in a jar, guess the first day it hits freezing, and on and on. None of these depends on buying anything, except maybe a stamp to send in your name, and that's not considered as important. Generally, skill isn't a factor either, but only one of the three items—prize, chance, and consideration—needs be missing and suddenly the game isn't a lottery. Broadcasters stay out of lotteries successfully because that's so easy to do.

A harder area to handle, and hence a harder area to avoid trouble, is one generally not so trivial as lotteries. That's libel and slander. These areas are generally controlled by state laws rather than by laws of Congress. And these areas deal with the damage you do a person by virtue of what you say or write about that person. If you injure a reputation or make a laughingstock of, or cause people to stay away from the business of a person by virtue of what you say or write, then you have caused injury just as much as if you hit the person with a club. And s/he can take you to court and make you pay for the damage you have done. Suppose, for example, you have an afternoon phone-in talk show on your radio station. And suppose your DJ, in talking about the problems of air pollution caused by the car traffic, mentions a bad deal s/he got from a local car dealer and goes on to say s/he thinks the dealer is dishonest. Listeners might decide not to go there in search of a new car. That person's business has been hurt. The dealer's livelihood is reduced by the comments made on the air, and s/he can sue for damages. But what if s/he is dishonest and did cheat your DJ? In some states, that doesn't matter. The business has still been damaged and s/he can still collect money from you. In these states, the phrase "truth is no defense" explains the situation. In other states, however, if you can prove s/he is dishonest, then s/he has no chance of getting anything from you. Truth *is* a defense for you in those states.

In this example we have been dealing with *slander.* That's comments spoken about a person. If the comments had been written in a script, even though that writing was only read out loud by an announcer, that's considered *libel.* The general legal distinction is that slander is spoken and libel is printed, or written down. That distinction has a great meaning for stations, because the money awarded by courts is generally a great deal less in slander cases than in libel cases. Most stations are concerned about libel because most of what they put on the air comes from a script. But what is the situation for news? Suppose you discover a dishonest member of the state government who has been taking bribes. If you broadcast that, can s/he sue you for libel? If you're in a state where truth is a defense, and if you are absolutely sure your facts are right, you can go ahead and broadcast it. In other states, again be sure your facts are right, and then still broadcast it. You may get sued, but the chances are small if you have the facts. The person won't want the facts to come out in a court of law proving s/he has been taking bribes. Sometimes you have to go ahead even if you're pretty certain you'll end up in court. That's expensive and a time hassle, but if the story is big enough, it's worth it.

What if, back at the talk show, one of the callers says something slanderous over your air? Can the station be sued? First of all, the station probably is running the calls on a seven- or ten-second delay and so would cut any such comments. But suppose the equipment malfunctions some day and you have no choice but to go on live and some bad comments get on the air. The station is not responsible for ad lib comments it had no reason to suppose would be made and against which it took all reasonable precautions. Suppose the topic of the day is funding for a new high school. And suppose the caller starts making obscene comments about the head of the school committee. Obscenity on the air is against federal law, but you had no reason to suppose the head of the school committee would get pulled into the topic. The station is not legally liable. Of course, you would want to cut the person off as soon as the comment started and you could tell what was happening, but at least you know you won't face law suits.

Both obscenity and profanity can get you into trouble, but not always so. The situation determines a great deal of what will happen. Profanity on a late night talk show is far different from the same word, or words, in the afternoon kiddies' shows. Some swear words, if used appropriately, now show up in prime time. Obscenity, which is generally anything connected with sex, is still a problem. Most broadcasters stay far away from obscene words, although some underground or progressive radio stations have broadcast words which would close down an MOR station. The standards change constantly, so good judgment exercised in the particular situation is really the only guide.

Another area of law that broadcasters deal with quite often is that of political campaigns and candidates. Basically, the law says everyone has to be treated equally, but some of the applications get a little sticky. Here's the basic idea. A station *must* provide access to its air for candidates for federal office. And it must provide the same sort of treatment to all candidates. That is, one can't get five minutes on Sunday morning while another gets a half hour on Wednesday night. All the candidates for senator are entitled to equal treatment. So are all candidates for President. And for representative. But that doesn't mean that a station giving a half hour to a candidate for President has to give a half hour to a candidate for senator. Fifteen minutes may be enough, but all candidates for senator must then get fifteen minutes. The equality has to come within any one race, not within the campaign as a whole. Now for candidates for offices less than federal, like governor or sheriff, the station doesn't have to provide any time at all. The station can use its own good judgment about what races are really important and offer time only to those few. If the race for sheriff seems unimportant, then the station can legitimately decide not to have any of the candidates for sheriff on the air. But if even one is allowed on, all the rest have to get an equal chance.

Do the candidates have to buy this time, or do they get it for free? That's up to the station. It can give time to candidates if it chooses, but if it gives time to one candidate for governor, all candidates for governor are entitled to equal amounts of free time. The station, though, can go on selling time to all other candidates for other offices. Further, if the station gives time to one candidate, the station has to contact the other candidates for that office and tell them about the free time. It doesn't have to say anything about selling time though. The assumption is that giving time away is so unusual that people won't expect it and will need to be told. Otherwise they would probably never think to ask for it.

There are some laws about the sale of time too. You have to sell to a candidate at the "lowest unit charge." That means that if you give a 20 percent discount for buying 300 spots or more, a candidate can come in, buy one spot, and get that 20 percent discount. The candidate is entitled, by law, to the lowest price you charge anyone for a spot in the particular time category. If your lowest-priced spot is at 4:00 A.M., that doesn't mean the candidate can use that rate for your most expensive time period, like drive time in radio or mid-evening in television. S/he has to use the rates for that time period, but at least s/he gets the lowest one for such times.

Suppose a candidate for governor buys time from you, comes in with a script a couple days beforehand, and has written some libelous comments about the opponents. What can you do? Can you be sued, since you have the time to change things? All you can do is try to talk the candidate out of making the statements, because the law forbids you to censor remarks. S/he can say anything s/he chooses, libelous or obscene or whatever. You cannot even demand to see a script, if s/he doesn't want to show it to you. But you can't be sued either. The courts have ruled that you have no control over the events and so can't be held at fault. Ethnic slurs have been made by candidates in some parts of the country, but the stations are powerless to stop them. Some candidates have gotten into really dirty mudslinging, but the stations can only stand aside and suggest they start acting like ladies and gentlemen. The audience may resent what's going on and may blame the station, but there's nothing the station can do to stop it. A disclaimer saying "The opinions expressed may not represent the opinions of the station . . ." is about as far as a station can go.

But having candidates in the studio giving a speech isn't the only way they use your air time. How about the news? During a campaign, some candidate or another is always doing something newsworthy and thus being reported on. Do you have to give equal time for all those appearances? No, news has been specifically excluded. So long as the candidate is part of a legitimate news event, you don't have to worry about equal time. But if you include a speech in a newscast that's just a pitch to vote for a particular candidate, or just a "see-what-a-nice-guy-I-am" type of thing, then the opponents are entitled to equal time. The news exclusion also applies to any documentaries you might do, so long as the documentary is not intended to promote one particular candidate. But what about coverage of the blatantly political acceptance speeches at a political convention? Those too have been ruled as legitimate news events, so there's no problem with equal time.

There are other problems though. Suppose your weathercaster becomes a candidate for mayor. Are all the other candidates for mayor entitled to as much time per day as s/he gets for the weather reports? Yes. And no station can do that, so the weathercaster ends up off the air. Suppose a candidate uses some free time to talk about things other than the campaign. Are the opponents still entitled to an equal amount of free time? Yes, because it doesn't matter what s/he talks about, it's still a use of the station's air. Suppose a spokesperson talks about a candidate. Do the other candidates get equal time? No, the law just speaks of candidates, not spokespeople. If a candidate buys spots for the campaign through an ad agency, but other candidates buy from you directly, do you have to give them the additional 15 percent discount you give ad agencies for placing spots? Yes, because the law talks of the lowest unit charge *you* get, not some outside firm, and that would thus have to include the agency discount.

So you can see that problems keep coming up in this area. The intent is to give everyone a fair deal and the lowest possible price, and as long as a station tries to do that, mistakes made probably won't cause the station any serious problems. But it pays to read and reread and reread Section 315 of the Communications Act to try to absorb all the details of political broadcasting and campaign coverage.

What of some of those rules now, as opposed to laws? An example is editorializing. Years ago the FCC said stations should not editorialize. With the passage of years and a change in members of the commission, a new ruling came down saying the stations could editorialize if they wanted to. Had this sort of thing been a law, it would have been a great deal more difficult to change from one position to the other. But now stations are encouraged to take stands. There are, however, some limits. For example, if a station says it opposes some question coming to a vote on an upcoming election, it has to offer an equal opportunity to be heard on free air time to the group or people supporting the question. That's the Fairness Doctrine. It's the same idea as Section 315 on political candidates, but this is only a ruling by the commission, not part of the law. That's not to say the ruling is any weaker in effect than the law; stations can lose their licenses for not following the Fairness Doctrine, and that's certainly as powerful a threat as many embodied in law. Because this doctrine is powerful, many people have worried about just how to apply it and whether they were, by mistake, violating its principles. Let me give you an example. Many radio stations carry a church service every Sunday morning. An atheist group has held that, under the Fairness Doctrine, they are entitled to an equal amount of time each week to present their point of view. The courts have so far ruled against them on the basis that religion is not a controversial issue. You see, the doctrine is written to apply only to controversial issues, ones about which the public holds strong, active, and varying opinions. Since no one seems too concerned about whether or not we are religious, the courts have said religion is not a controversial issue.

But what about something like air pollution? Some gasoline manufacturers have run commercials saying their product produces fewer contaminants in the air. Some ecology groups say they are misleading the public because even fewer is too many. So the groups have asked for time for "counter-commercials." By and large, the courts have held they don't have the right to such time as "puffery" in advertising is legitimate, and some overstating of a product's virtues is an acceptable advertising attribute. Further, the Federal Trade Commission is charged with handling any outright cases of fraud, so the Fairness Doctrine just doesn't apply in most cases like this. But because different courts can rule in different ways, broadcasters are not so sure of their ground as they once were.

Another area of rules which broadcasters are very much concerned about is *ascertainment*. As you know, all broadcasters have a license from the government that lets them use a particular frequency for a period of time. But at the end of that time, the license needs to be renewed. The broadcaster has first crack at getting the license again, but s/he has to prove s/he has served the "public interest, convenience, or necessity." S/he must have been operating like a good guy or the license can be taken away. Then too, if a group in the area challenges the broadcaster's statements and says they could do a better job with the license, the FCC may decide to hold hearings to see if the challenge is correct. Sometimes it is, and the license is then given to the challenging group. In such a hearing, the FCC is interested in what sort of service the broadcaster has been providing. That's where ascertainment comes in. The commission has laid down some rules on how to check up to see if you really have been serving your community. You "ascertain" the needs of your area and then see if you've met those needs. So when you apply for a license renewal, whether or not there is a challenge, you include the results of this "ascertainment" survey and a statement, generally lengthy, of how you have met the needs you found and how you will continue to meet those needs.

Some of the rules on ascertainment are fairly specific. You must continually survey your area throughout the period of your license to find what the needs are and whether or not they are changing. You have to use management-level people from your station to talk to the leaders of the various groups (like the leader of an ecology group, as well as the mayor) to get their ideas on the major problems facing the community. You can, though, use a professional survey-taking company to find out what people at large consider to be problems. You have to make a special effort to survey those groups which are seldom organized, like the poor, or some minorities. The commission has said you can list up to ten major problems you uncover, so everyone scurries around to find ten, even it it's a small community and there just aren't that many problems. But the commission doesn't get specific at all on what you do to meet the problems. That, they feel, is a programming decision best left up to each station, so they just ask to be told what you decide to do. They don't, further, expect stations to solve problems. Some will quite clearly be beyond the scope of a station to handle. But the commission expects a station to do whatever it can to contribute toward a solution, even if that's only getting everyone together to talk over the problem.

The next group of guidelines broadcasters look to have even less force than anything we have talked about so far. These are the NAB Codes, the rules set up by the National Association of Broadcasters and followed on a voluntary basis by most broadcasters. Here's an example of their approach. Broadcasters should "Observe the proprieties and customs of civilized society; Respect the rights and sensitivities of all people;

Honor the sanctity of marriage and the home; Protect and uphold the dignity and brotherhood of all mankind,"* and so on. I think Mom's apple pie is in there somewhere on down the list. Nonetheless, the codes (one for television and one for radio) outline some serious attitudes for broadcasters. For example, in talking of news coverage, the codes say that morbid, sensational, or alarming details which are not essential should be avoided. That might seem obvious, but some stations have built large audiences on ambulance chasing and films of car wrecks and interviews with victims. The language of the codes may seem trite and self-serving, but that's a problem of the words, not the ideas behind them. If a broadcaster takes the ideas on news coverage seriously, s/he will indeed have a better, more responsible newscast and won't be including the unnecessary, sensationalistic details. Sometimes the ideas break through the language, and some specifics emerge that directly affect what you see or hear. The best example, I suppose, is the time limits on commercials. Each code specifies how much time can be spent on "non-program" material, that is, commercials, billboards, promos, credits, and the like. For radio, eighteen minutes an hour is it. For television, it is nine and one half minutes an hour in prime time and sixteen minutes in non–prime time. For children's shows, other limits apply along with specific ways products cannot be pitched. For example, the host of a show can't be used as the pitchman. These sorts of things definitely influence what you see or hear. Have you ever run across an ad for hard liquor on the air? Beer and wine are OK, but the code says no for hard liquor. That's not to say you won't see or hear things the codes oppose. Stations may or may not follow what's recommended, and if they don't, the NAB really has very little it can do. The association is voluntary, after all, so code-breakers can't really be penalized. But broadcasters, just like all of us, depend at least to some extent on the good opinion of their peers. The stations that break the codes lose some of the respect of those around them, and that's generally enough to keep most stations on the side of the angels, with an unbroken code. Besides, by following the codes, stations prove they can regulate themselves, and Congress and the FCC feel less need to make up more laws or rules.

* Courtesy the National Association of Broadcasters.

The law, the rules, and the guidelines are part of a station as surely as the people behind the desks, microphones, and monitors. They provide part of the framework that contains the immense variety of stations around the country.

# PART 3

# CHANGING TIME

# 7
## NEiTHER
## STATiON
## NOR
## sTudio

The machines and devices and gadgets of broadcasting aren't confined to the radio and television stations we have been talking about. For an obvious example, records and turntables and amplifiers turn up in houses as well as in radio stations. There are other uses for the electronic toys of broadcasting, sometimes for the entertainment of a few people and sometimes for another business use. When they are used for business purposes other than broadcasting, they sometimes are involved in what has been called "narrow-casting."

## CATV

Cable television is an example of this narrow-casting. Instead of sending out a signal over a broad area, cable operations restrict their coverage to places joined together by a cable much like a phone line. The original purpose of this was to get television signals into areas where they otherwise wouldn't reach. The idea sprang up in West Virginia, a very hilly state, because towns down in the valleys were blocked by the hills from receiving the straight-line television signals. So someone thought of putting an antenna up on the hilltop, capturing the signal and sending it over cables down to the houses in the valley.

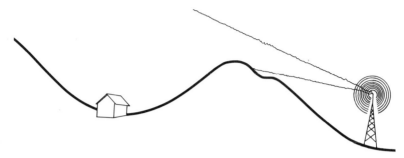

*FIGURE 7.1* Signals blocked

Thus was born the *community antenna television* (CATV) system. From that, the idea spread to little towns just beyond the reach of big cities. The television stations of the little towns were generally not as varied nor as professional looking as the big city stations. So someone thought of putting up a very high antenna to pick up the signals going over the town and sending them, again by cable, to the houses of the area.

Finally, in the big cities themselves, many people found their reception wasn't very good because the big buildings around them either blocked out the signal or bounced it around so much that all you could see was a picture with fifteen ghosts. An antenna on top of one of the tall buildings would get a clear signal which could then be sent to the houses for clear, watchable reception.

In all these examples, someone got paid money for providing the antenna, the machinery to amplify the signal, and the cables to distribute it. Each house paid a fee for the clear signal. Operators of cable systems began to see chances of big

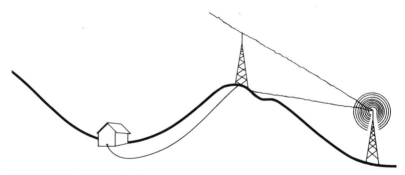

*FIGURE 7.2* Cable hook-up

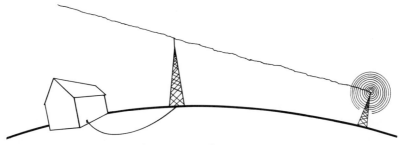

*FIGURE 7.3*   Cable for distant signals

profits. After all, they could provide dozens and dozens of channels, most of which would be available for use other than just relaying network television shows. One channel could give time and weather information, another could be used for movies run by the cable operator and sponsored by local merchants. People even began talking of using the cable connection in a two-way fashion, so a person could sit at home, turn to a channel for a particular store, select merchandise, and punch a button to indicate to the store that s/he would like to buy what was then on the screen. Some people talked of wiring a whole city together and using the cable system as a way for people to cast their votes from home. Cable operators started talking of covering the local sports events at the high school and the town council meetings. Ideas on uses flew thick and fast, and all within the reach of current technology.

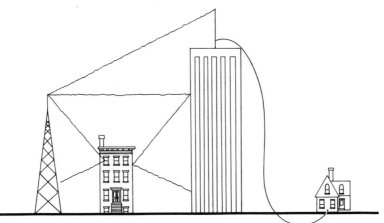

*FIGURE 7.4*   Cable in cities

So why didn't it all happen? Complaints started to be heard, first from the local stations in those little towns which now had big city stations brought into their area. They felt they would end up losing their sponsors and hence their profits and hence their ability to run at all. Here's why. Suppose a small town has an NBC affiliate as one of its local stations. The little station doesn't make as much money as a big station, so it tends to preempt some programs during the week a bit more often than the big city stations which make plenty of money running a full NBC schedule. Then too, the production on the smaller station is usually a bit sloppier. They are a bit late getting back to the net shows, so a bit of the beginnings get clipped. Also, the shows run in those preempted times and in early fringe when NBC doesn't provide anything are not as new or as good as the ones run from the city. The little station can't afford to buy as good shows. So with all these factors, the owners of the little station figure that if the big city NBC station is available in their market, people will watch it instead of the local station. Then the advertisers in the local area won't be as interested in running spots on the local station, because the audience isn't there any more. So they will switch to newspapers or radio or billboards or whatever. So the little station can afford to pay even less for syndicated shows for those preempted spots, and even less for people to run the station breaks. For less money, the people are less competent generally, and the breaks get even sloppier and more clipping happens. So a cycle is set up that really hurts the local station.

The networks, too, weren't too happy about the situation because they could see their number of affiliates decreasing if little local stations started folding. Sure, their audience size might stay up, and they could sell as much to an advertiser, but they would face a couple problems. NBC has at least a little leverage with that small, local station. The net is the major source of programming and can thus insist, successfully, that affiliates do some things for the net. Wholesale, constant preemptions just don't happen, for example, because the net does not want that. But with a cable system, picking material up from dozens of sources, the threat of losing material from any one doesn't amount to much of a threat at all. So a cable operator might end up preempting NBC shows whenever s/he wanted for the sake of profit, but much to the detriment of the network.

Also, the little station is bound by contract to take commercials the network runs. But what is to stop a cable operator from running the shows, but covering every commercial on net with one by a local advertiser? The cable operator could offer prime time spots for a very low price to local people, and NBC could do nothing. National sponsors wouldn't get the coverage they paid NBC for, and so would demand lower rates. That, of course, was something NBC didn't want to consider.

Further, there were a lot of people who felt that taking shows off the air the way cable does and rebroadcasting them is much like stealing the material from a copyrighted book. It's living off the author's brains for free, and that's not fair. Likewise, stealing a show isn't fair. A producer of a show gets paid by the network for the use of the show. If cable uses the show, producers felt they should get paid by cable operators.

Cable operators answered this way. The little station might face stiff competition from a cable operation, but all our businesses are based on competition, and if they can't measure up, then they ought to go out of business. As for the networks and producers, they had provided their material for free to the public for years, and could not now say the material had to be paid for. The shows are quite literally in the air for anyone to grab, a system the networks had agreed to and supported for years. They therefore had no say in what happened when the signals did get grabbed.

The networks and the stations appealed to the FCC, as that agency sets up rules for their operation and hence seemed the logical place to go for help. But the cable people maintained that the law said the FCC could handle broadcast matter which went out over the people's airwaves. It could not control material which is put on privately owned cables. The FCC said that since cable operations were dependent on material under the control of the FCC, the use of that material could be controlled to a limited degree by the rules of the commission. Courts agreed, so cable operations came under some control of the commission, although not totally. For example, one ruling said that small stations could demand that cable operations within their coverage area rebroadcast their programs instead of the duplicates from big cities. That still left the cable operations free to broadcast the shows which the little stations preempt, but for the majority of the time, the little station and its commercials were protected. This single rule also stopped a lot of the worry about cable operators playing around with commercial time.

Here's why. Suppose a cable operation has a thousand houses wired in. The cable owner can offer a sponsor a spot within a network show for $1000, or a dollar a house. But the local station, now carried by the cable operation, reaches those thousand houses, plus all the others that get the signal off the air. The station can offer a spot at the station break, almost as good as within the show, for the same $1000 but guarantee reaching, say, 20,000 houses. That's a nickel a house. That's such a better deal that cable now can't compete. So it's no longer worth their while to maintain the staff necessary to cut in and out of network shows. The problem vanished.

The problem of stealing material was never resolved because the courts seemed to feel that both the networks and the producers were, after all, making money on their efforts, and to try to right the wrong might break up the whole system of over-the-air broadcasting. In other words, the damage being done was not so great as the damage that might be done in trying to fix things.

The FCC went further and said cable operations with a certain number of subscribers had to start originating their own programming. If they were to be connected with a system intended to serve the public, as broadcasting is, then they would have to provide service by originating programs. That's where the town council meetings and high school football games come in. In most instances, though, the ruling became a moot point because the cable systems simply didn't grow very large. People were unwilling to spend five or ten or fifteen dollars a month to get clear pictures when for free they could watch a picture generally only a little bit less clear. Cable became a big operation only in those areas where almost no one got a decent picture. And without a large number of subscribers, the other possibilities of two-way communication and voting at home and so on simply became too expensive to start. The potential of cable remains as large, but the actual development has slowed a great deal. People are unwilling to pay for what they can get for free. Until cable offers a product which can't be had for free elsewhere, that development will stay slow.

## INDUSTRIAL AND EDUCATIONAL

There's another form of wired-in television that uses the machines and techniques of broadcasting and is familiar to us all. That's the closed-circuit systems of stores or schools or big companies. Stores use it for a check against shoplifters and other thieves. Schools use the closed-circuit system for teaching purposes. Big companies use it to train employees or to exchange information among widely separated branch offices. All three consider videotape recording to be an essential partner to the cameras themselves.

Stores, and this includes banks, probably have the simplest systems. They simply mount cameras, small viewfinderless ones, in high spots which overlook areas of the store. Then the signals are fed to some central room where the scenes are often continuously recorded on tape. That way, if anything happens, the store has a picture of it for identification purposes. Of course, a security guard watching the monitors can spot any shady activity and call people on the floor and tell them where to go to check out the suspicious person. That's a simple system, but a useful one.

Schools and companies get into more complex situations. They are interested in presenting a complete unit, or show. The show may be one lesson in a series on botany, or it may be an explanation of a new product which the company's salespeople will have to explain and sell to others. In either case, the show will most likely end up looking like what we watch at night. A title, a music theme, maybe an announcer, and an opening cover shot generally start the presentation. Then it's covers, close-ups, cuts to illustrations, and so on. The ending of the show may even have credits! The uses for the shows are different, very definitely narrow-casting, but the techniques are those of the more familiar broadcasting. And the use of videotape becomes a great deal more important here.

The point of putting a school lesson on television is to enable the instructor to use a great many more materials than would be possible for every class. Films, slides, graphics, and so on get incorporated in the presentation. Likewise, for the company the point is to better illustrate what's important. That may include having the inventor in as a guest, using an animated film, or actually taking the product apart so as to see how it works. For both groups, repeating the same thing over and over for different classes or different groups of salespeople is ridiculous. Videotape one good presentation, and you can play it back for numerous groups and occasions.

That's where some of the variations of equipment come in. The show may be put on a reel of tape, just like at a station. Or it may be put on a cassette. The more narrow widths of tape, like one-half inch, lend themselves particularly well to being fitted into a cassette. That gives you a convenient package to mail or carry around or otherwise distribute. And playback machines for smaller sizes of tape can be smaller, and hence more portable. Some quality is lost in going to smaller sizes and lighter equipment, but for non-broadcasting purposes, the loss is unimportant.


## HOME, AND THE DAY
## AFTER TOMORROW


Once you start talking about smaller and lighter equipment, you start getting close to an area of further use of broadcast equipment, and that's home use. No one in his right mind is going to buy a two-inch Ampex tape recorder for the living room. It would leave all of about two square feet to get around in. But once the machines start getting down to portable sizes, they start being reasonable additions for the home. That sort of thing has long since happened with audio equipment. Records, tape decks, turntables, cassette machines, and amplifiers are commonplace. The most recent addition on that list, cassettes, illustrates the point of what happens as things get smaller and lighter. Originally, no one thought you could get more than one track on a one-quarter inch piece of audio tape. Now we have eight tracks and cassette players that are very accurate, very sophisticated pieces of machinery in small, light boxes. When the equipment was big and bulky and the tape with one track took up a lot of space, not many people at home bothered with tape recordings. But eight-track cassettes, lighter and smaller than the original gear, are no surprise in anyone's den or living room.

As television gear gets smaller and lighter, and as variations like video discs become more easily produced, more people will start adding video gear to the audio gear they already have. At first, the quality will be below what's broadcast, but as technology improves, the quality will come up. I think we can make a reasonable guess about what will develop for home use.

The trend in technology is to miniaturization. Tape playback units and the sets themselves will end up with very small sections devoted to the electronics. By far the biggest part will be the screen. Television broadcasting right now is locked in to a 525 line standard for the picture. A clearer picture can be had at 625 or 819 or 1003 or whatever. For prerecorded shows for home playback on a giant screen that's six feet high and fifteen feet wide, a line standard of several thousand should be reasonable. Now imagine a disc, much like a 33 record, that slips into a box. On the disc, recorded probably with the use of laser technology, is a two-hour play. No interruptions, no commercials. The price of the disc to you is comparable to a three or four disc set of phonograph records. And the picture you get is superbly clear, full color of course, and in full stereo sound. That should be possible by the mid 1980s. A fully three-dimensional projection out into your living room should be possible by the turn of the century. It will be so completely three dimensional that you will be able to walk around the actors and see them from all sides.

What will this do to the network shows we now enjoy? Will individual stations be much competition for this sort of thing? Look at what's happened with radio. Record sales haven't hurt radio. You still get greater variety off the air than you can get from the comparatively few records you own. As a matter of fact, the records you buy are often ones you hear first on the radio. So too, television will go on providing the tremendous variety of shows it now gives. Some of the things seen on television stations may be available on discs, although I would expect most material on disc to be done for disc alone. A collection of discs of plays or operas or Broadway musicals, while interesting, would not be as fresh and new as the offerings of the familiar networks. Then one could expect the television networks to figure out a way to broadcast to those large, multiline, clear-image screens. It would be rather a television counter-part to FM broadcasting. So the big screens could be used for both the free stuff broadcast over the air and for the discs you buy. And suddenly we have another broadcast form to consider. But that's a topic for another day.

-0-

# Bibliography

Ashley, Paul. *Say It Safely: Legal Limits in Publishing, Radio, and Television.* 4th ed. Seattle: University of Washington Press, 1969.

Bretz, Rudy. *Techniques of Television Production.* New York: McGraw-Hill, Inc., 1953.

Hilliard, Robert L. *Writing for Television and Radio.* New York: Hastings House, 1968.

Laughton, Roy. *TV Graphics.* Reinhold Publishing Corp., 1966.

Lewis, Colby. *The TV Director/Interpretor.* New York: Hastings House, 1968.

Millerson, Gerald. *The Technique of Television Production.* 9th rev. ed. New York: Hastings House, 1972.

Nisbett, Alec. *The Technique of the Sound Studio.* 3d rev. ed. New York: Hastings House, 1972.

Oringel, Robert S. *Audio Control Handbook.* 4th ed. New York: Hastings House, 1972.

Quaal, Ward L., and Martin, Leo A. *Broadcast Management.* New York: Hastings House, 1968.

Roe, Yale, ed. *Television Station Management.* New York: Hastings House, 1964.

Stasheff, Edward, and Bretz, Rudy. *The Television Program, Its Direction and Production.* 4th ed. New York: Hill & Wang, 1968.

Zettl, Herbert. *Television Production Handbook.* 2d ed. Belmont, Calif.: Wadsworth Publishing Co., Inc., 1968.

# Glossary

**Adjacency**   Announcements next to programs. Commercials in station breaks fill adjacencies.

**Aerial**   The wire that is attached to a home radio receiver or television receiver and picks up the broadcast signal.

**Amplifier**   An electronic unit which is used to enlarge electronic signals, whether audio or video.

**Antenna**   A transmitting radiator to send out radio or television signals.

**Attenuator**   A pot or slider.

**Availability**   Time open or available for sale on a station.

**Blast-in**   Sound volume that is too high and out of proportion to the sound that immediately preceded it.

**Blocking**   Planning out the movements of all actors and cameras.

**Boom**   A moving microphone stand, generally tall enough to hold a microphone above the heads of the actors.

**Bridge**   A musical transition between scenes.

**BTA**   Best time available. Same as run of station, but with a more positive sound to it.

**Bulk**   To erase all of a tape at once.

**Call letters**   The identifying letters assigned to a station by the FCC. In this country the first letter is K or W, in Canada C, etc.

**Campaign**   Planned advertising drive.

**Cans**   Earphones.

**Cartridge**   A plastic box containing an endless loop of tape. The tape will run continuously unless electronic cues are put on it to indicate starting and stopping points.

**Cassette**   A plastic box containing a length of tape which runs between two hubs within the box. The tape runs from one hub to the other, but does not run continuously.

**Channel, mixing**   On a radio board, a key, a pot or a slider, and the pre-amplifier for that channel.

**Channel, output**   The program amplifier or amplifiers for the entire radio board. The output channel of a stereo board will have two amplifiers.

**Clearance**   Permission obtained from authors or publishers to use their material on a broadcast.

**Clip**   To cut off sharply, usually cutting off part of a word or sound. Also called up-cut.

**Commercial protection**   A specific amount of time allowed by a station or demanded by an advertiser between competitive commercials.

**Continuity**   Written script material, also called copy.

**Control console**   The radio board.

**Copy**   The material read on the air, also called continuity.

**Cross talk**   A spillover of sound from one line to another. The print-through of sound from one layer of tape to another.

**Crawl**   Credits that move slowly up the screen, can include the device used to hold and turn the credits.

**Cue**   The signal to start.

**Cueing**   Setting a record or tape at the beginning so as to be ready to start.

**Cumulative audience, Cume**   Total audience which listens to a given station or program over an extended period of time, rather than at any one time.

**Dead**   Highly absorbent of sound. Inactive, not working. A "dead" mike.

**Feed**   The transfer of program material from one location to another. A remote feed from, say, the State House to the studio.

**Filter**   A device to eliminate unwanted frequencies.

**Fixed position**   Usually refers to commercial announcements where the station promises an advertiser that his announcements will be given at a specific time.

**Flight**   The period of time during which an advertiser runs his campaign.

**Floating announcement**   One that can run any time between specified hours.

**Frequency**   In sound, the tone or pitch.

**Frequency discount**   A lower rate charged advertisers as they buy more and more time on the station. As the frequency of their spots goes up, their cost per spot goes down.

**Frequency response**   The range which equipment will handle without distortion.

**Gain**  Amplification of sound. **Riding gain** is constantly watching the volume level.

**Gen lock**  Locking the synchronizing generators of different sources together, such as a remote and the studio, so as to prevent the pictures from rolling.

**Head**  The start, or beginning, of a recording. That portion of the machine which touches the tape and is involved in the recording process.

**Homes using radio (HUR) Homes using TV (HUT)**  A figure used in audience surveys indicating the number of homes whose radio or TV sets are in use at a given time.

**Hot**  Instruments turned on, as in a hot mike.

**Input**  That part of electronic equipment into which signals are fed.

**Jack**  A socket or plug receptacle.

**Kill**  To eliminate, to cut out, to remove, to stop, i.e., "kill the mike."

**Level**  The degree of sound volume.

**Limbo**  An area of the set having a plain, light, nondescript background.

**Limiter**  An electronic device which eliminates sudden high level sounds which might damage equipment.

**Line**  Wires which carry programs.

**Live**  Equipment which is turned on, a live mike. Programs done at that moment, not presented from recordings.

**Monitor**  Television receivers used in studios or control rooms. Loudspeakers used for program sound. To listen to or watch a program going out on the air for the purpose of making technical adjustments should they be necessary.

**Multiplexing**  Mixing the two separate stereo channels to one signal to be carried by the radio station's carrier wave.

**Multi-spot plan**  A special plan or package rate for announcements.

**Music bed**  Music used as background only.

**National representative**  A firm representing several radio or television stations and selling time on those stations to advertising firms or national advertisers.

**Nemo**  Remote broadcast.

**Non-directional**  A microphone pick-up pattern that is the same as omnidirectional.

**Off mike**  Not in the pick-up pattern of the mike.

**On mike**  In the pick-up pattern of the mike.

**Output**    The terminal point on electrical equipment from which sound or picture or both can be taken.

**Package**    A particular combination of announcements that is put together to earn a special rate.

**Participating program**    A program containing commercials for various advertisers as opposed to a program sponsored totally by one advertiser.

**Receiver**    An electronic device used to receive sounds or pictures or both.

**Reel**    A metal or plastic wheel used to hold tape.

**Relay**    An electrically operated switch.

**Rep**    Same as national representative.

**Ride gain**    *See* **Gain.**

**Riser**    A small platform.

**Run of station**    Announcements purchased on a run-of-station basis give a station the right to place the announcements wherever they please in a given broadcast day. Generally abbreviated R.O.S.

**Sets in use**    The same as **Homes using radio** or **Homes using TV.**

**Share of audience**    In audience surveys, the percentage of the audience watching or listening to a particular station at a particular time. This is a relative figure, as the total audience size changes with different times.

**Spillover**    A loud sound volume causing the VU meter needle to go above the 100 mark. The leakage of sound from one line to another or from one level of tape to another.

**Strike**    To clear a studio, restoring everything to its original, stored, neutral position.

**Strip**    A program which runs every weekday (sometimes every day) at the same time.

**Tag**    Announcement added to the end of a commercial.

**Talent**    Anyone other than the announcer who appears on a broadcast.

**Talkback**    Conversation between the studio and control room which does not go on the air.

**Telco**    The telephone company.

**T.F.N.**    Till further notice. Advertising whose air schedule has no termination date and so runs "till further notice." Some stations also use "T.F." for Till forbid.

**Transcription**    A record made strictly for broadcast purposes.

**VTR**    Abbreviation for videotape recording or videotape recorder.

**Wow**    The low, growling sound of a record starting slow and coming up to speed.

# Index

Academy leader, 72
Add 1, Add 2, 86
All news radio, 206
American Broadcasting Company (ABC), 201
American Research Bureau (ARB), 211
Amplitude, 179
Amplitude modulation, 177
Anchorpeople, 238
Arc, 13
Art cards, 33, 83
Art department, 236
Ascertainment, 269
Assembly editing (videotape), 78
Assignment editor, 240
Audience flow, 229
Audio tape, 154
Audition (position of switch), 114

Backlight, 21
Bank, 46
Barn doors, 26
Bars and tone, 76
Beautiful music, 206
Bidirectional mike, 138
Blanking, 173
Book, 99
Boom, 28
Boom mike, 63
Booth tag, 101
Broad, 22
Bulk, 150

Cable, 8
Cameo, 27
Camera card, 83
Camera mount
    pedestal, 5
    tripod, 5
Capstan, 147

Cardiod pick-up pattern, 138
Carrier signal, 176
Carrier wave, 178
Cart, Cartridge machine, Cart machine, 123, 150
Cassette player-recorder, 153
CBS color system, 202
Chroma-key, 58, 88
Classical radio format, 206
Color television, 204
Columbia Broadcasting System (CBS), 198
Commands
    action, 104, 108
    ready, 104, 106, 108
Community Antenna Television (CATV), 276
Composition, 14
Condenser microphone, 136–37
Control track, 78
Corporation for Public Broadcasting (CPB), 258
Country & Western radio format (C&W), 206
Cover shot, 83
CPM, 213, 228
Cross-plugging, 233
Crystal microphones, 136
CU, 85
Cue
    position of switch, 123
    a record, 143
    tape, 150
Cut
    talent cue, 41
    video change, 46
Cyclorama, cyc, 29

Degauss, 151
Demographics, 206, 212
Desk mike, 65

Diary, 212
Dimmer, 25
Directional lights, 22
Discrepancy report, 165
Dissolve, 49
Dolly, 11, 14
Double re-entry switcher, 60
Dumont, Allen B., 200
Dynamic microphones, 136

ECU, 85
Edit (videotape)
  assembly, 78
  insert, 78, 79
8MK—WWJ, 197
Electrical transcription, 161
Electromagnetic waves, 135
Ellipsoidal spot, 24
Erase head, 148
Ethnic radio format, 206
External key, 56

Fade, 51
Fader bar, 46
Fairness Doctrine, 269
Federal Communication Commission
  (FCC), 199, 263
Federal Radio Act, 199
Federal Radio Commission
  (FRC), 199
Feed reel (tape), 147
Feedback, 116, 119
Field, 172
Fill light, 20
Film director, 224
Film island, 67
Fishhook, 12
Flat brace, leg, 32
Flat, 30
Flip card, 33, 83
Floor stand, 28
Focus control, 8
Frame, 172
Freeze (of broadcasting
  applications), 202–3
Frequency, 176, 180
Frequency discount, 231
Frequency modulation, 177, 182
Fresnel, 23
Front-silvered mirrors, 70
Full track recording, 154

Gain, 114
Ghosts, 176
Graphic, 33–34

Graphic card, 83
Green pick-up tube, 7
Ground waves, 185
Group owned, 254
Gun, 7

Half-track recording, 154
Hand mike, 65
Head
  mount, 3
  recording, 147
Headset, 8–9
Headset jack, 126
Headspace, 17
Herrold, Dr. Charles David, 196
Hertz, Heinrich, 196
Hooper, 211
Hue, 54

Iconoscope, 197
Idler arm, 148
Independents, 256
Input jack, 158
Insert editing (videotape), 78–79
Intensity, 54
Internal key, 56
Ives, H. E., 200

Jenkins, Chester, 200

KDKA, 196
Key, 54, 115
Key light, 19
Key sense, 54
Keystoning, 18
Kinescope, 204

Lash cleats, 32
Lavalier mike, 63–64
"Leading" the face, 109
Lens cap, 9
Level (microphone), 66
Libel, 264–65
Lights, lighting instruments
  broad, 22
  ellipsoidal, 24
  fresnel, 23
  quartz-halogen, 22
  scoop, 23
  spot, 22
  tungsten, 23
Lines (scan lines), 170
Live On, 87
Locks, 4, 9
Log, 162, 223
Lottery, 263

Lowest unit charge, 267
LS, 85

Make-good, 164, 232
Marconi, Guglielmo, 196
Master gain, 113
Matrix, 191
Matt, 54
Maxwell, James Clerk, 196
Medium shot, 15
Meter ratings, 212
Microphone
  bidirectional, 138
  cardiod, 138
  condenser, 136–37
  crystal, 136
  dynamic, 136
  lavalier, 63–64
  omnidirectional, 64, 138
  ribbon, 136
  shotgun, 139
  unidirectional, 138
Mike placement, 63
Minnow, Newton, 207
Monitor (television)
  air, 49
  auxiliary, 49
  film, 49
  line, 49
  net, 49
  preview, 49
  slide, 49
  VTR, 49
Monitor (radio), 114
Monitor gain, 114
Mount (camera), 5
MOR, middle-of-the-road, 206
Movie package, 218
MS, 85
Music bed, 101
Music librarian, 224
Mutual Broadcasting System, 198

NAB codes, 270
Narrow-casting, 275
National Association of
        Broadcasters (NAB), 263
National Broadcasting Company
        (NBC), 198
National Public Radio (NPR), 262
NBC Blue, 199
NBC Red, 198
Network O&O (owned & operated),
        253–54
News producer, 241
Nielsen, 211

Off mike, 140
Omnidirectional mike, 64, 138
Organizational chart, 216–17
Output (switch), 114
Output jack, 158

Packages, 228
Pan, 10
Pan handle, 8
Patch cord, 157
Patch panel, 157
Pedestal (on waveform), 175
Pedestal mount, 5
Phone coincidental, 212
Phone recall, 212
Phosphors, 170
Pick-up pattern, 138
Pick-up tube, 9, 170
Playback head, 148
Pot, potentiometer, 114, 117
Preview monitor, 60
Primary coverage pattern, 186
Prime time access rule, 208
Print-through, 156
Production charges, 231
Production manager, 226
Program (position of switch), 114
Progressive rock radio format, 206
Projector (film), 69
Public affairs director, 225
Public Broadcasting Act of 1967, 207
Public Broadcasting Service (PBS),
        258
Public interest, convenience, or
        necessity, 269
Public television, 257
Pulse, 211

Quadraphonic sound, 191
Quartz-halogen lights, 22

Radio Corporation of America (RCA),
        198
Rate card, 223
Ratings, 211
Rating period, 218
Real time, 101
Record head, 148
Research director, 228
Ribbon microphone, 136
Rip and read, 261
Roller (tape deck), 147

Safe area (graphic), 35
Sarnoff, David, 200

Saturation, 54
Scan lines, 173
Scene dock, 33
Scoop, 23
Section 315, 268
Secondary coverage pattern, 187
Segue, 120
Share, 212
Shotgun mike, 139
SIL, 85
Silhouette lighting, 27
16-mm film, 69
$64,000 Question, 205
Sky waves, 185
Slander, 264–65
Slate, 77
Slider, 114
Slip cue, 144
SOF, 85
Soft light, 22
Sound head, 71
Sound-on-sound, 149
Sound track, 71
Spotlight, 22
Sprocket holes, 71
Static, 181
Station ownership limitation, 254
Station revenue, 229
Steering ring, 6
Stereo, 205
Stereo-mono key, 128
Stiles, 32
Stingers, 156
Stops, 150
Street reporters, 239
Strike the studio, 10, 42
Strip programming, 221
Stylus, 142
Super, 50
Super card, 38
Super T. C., 87
Switcher, 44
Synchronizing, sync pulse, 173
Syndicated show, 220

Take-up reel (tape), 147
Talk radio, 206
Tally light, 3
Tape cartridge machine, 121
Tape transport, 146
Tension knobs, 4
35-mm slides, 67
Thirty seconds (time cue), 41
Three-point lighting, 21
Three-second roll, 101
Tilt, 10
Title card, 33, 82
Top 40, 206
Top 40 radio, 203
Traffic department, 223
Transduction, 136
Tripod mount, 5
Truck, 11

UHF stations, 207
Unidirectional microphone, 138

Vectorscope, 176
Video cassettes, 74
Videotape, 205
Viewfinder, 7
Volume (*see also* Gain), 114
VU meter, 117

Waveform monitor, 174
WBZ, 197
Wide shot, 15
Wipes, 52
Wire copy, 237
Wow, 144
"Wrap them up" (talent cue), 41
WWJ–8MK, 197

XCU, 85

Zoom, 14
Zoom focus, 14
Zoom lens, 3
Zworykin, Vladimir, 197

MA

I